TRAEGER Smoker Grill

Cookbook for Beginners

2000-Day Gorgeous Traeger Grill & Smoker Recipes for All Users Makes It Easy to Grill in Your Backyard

Nanci Kelley

© Copyright 2023 - All rights reserved

This document is geared towards providing exact and reliable information with regards to the topic and issue covered. The publication is sold with the idea that the publisher is not required to render accounting, officially permitted, or otherwise, qualified services. If advice is necessary, legal, or professional, a practiced individual in the profession should be ordered. - From a Declaration of Principles which was accepted and approved equally by a Committee of the American Bar Association and a Committee of Publishers and Associations. In no way is it legal to reproduce, duplicate, or transmit any part of this document in either electronic means or in printed format. Recording of this publication is strictly prohibited and any storage of this document is not allowed unless with written permission from the publisher.

All rights reserved. The information provided herein is stated to be truthful and consistent, in that any liability, in terms of inattention or otherwise, by any usage or abuse of any policies, processes, or directions contained within is the solitary and utter responsibility of the recipient reader.

Under no circumstances will any legal responsibility or blame be held against the publisher for any reparation, damages, or monetary loss due to the information herein, either directly or indirectly. Respective authors own all copyrights not held by the publisher.

The information herein is offered for informational purposes solely, and is universal as

so. The presentation of the information is without contract or any type of guarantee assurance. The trademarks that are used are without any consent, and the publication of the trademark is without permission or backing by the trademark owner.

All trademarks and brands within this book are for clarifying purposes only and are the owned by the owners themselves, not affiliated with this document

Table of Contents

- **1** Introduction
- **2** Getting Started with Your Traeger Grill & Smoker
- **11** 4-Week Diet Plan
- **13** Chapter 1 Poultry Recipes
- **31** Chapter 2 Fish and Seafood Recipes
- **42** Chapter 3 Pork Recipes
- **56** Chapter 4 Beef, Lamb, and Venison Recipes
- **70** Chapter 5 Appetizer and Sides Recipes
- **77** Chapter 6 Snack and Dessert Recipes
- **82** Chapter 7 Rubs, Marinades, and More
- **90** Conclusion
- **91** Appendix 1 Measurement Conversion Chart
- **92** Appendix 2 Recipes Index

Introduction

TRAEGER WOOD PELLET GRILL & SMOKER is an outdoor grill with modern technology and perfectly cooks vegetables, chicken, beef, seafood/fish, and other food items. It provides a safe and relaxed environment. It comes in different flavors. Adjust the cooking temperature easily with a dial and, once the grill reaches desired temperature, place food onto the grill grate. One of the advantages of this grill & smoker is how easy it is to start!

If you are new to grilling and didn't know how to use it, it can feel overwhelming at first, but no worries. I will be with you every step of the way, and it can change your lifestyle. Traeger is so simple and very user-friendly appliance. Soon, you'll be able to cook different recipes onto the grill grate and impress your friends and family. Try my recipes and read all guidance about this appliance.

Happy grilling

Getting Started with Your Traeger Grill & Smoker

We will discuss the basics of getting your Traeger grill & smoker up and running and the flavor of wood pellets. Once you understand the basics of starting it up and shutting down, you can grill food without any fear.

What Is Traeger Grill & Smoker?

TRAEGER GRILL & SMOKER is mainly a pellet-fired grill; it not only can be used for smoking, grilling and barbecuing, but also it can be used for roasting, braising and baking. It use hardwood pellets instead of charcoal or gas.

The wood provides an extra level of flavor, which makes the dish more delicious. A Traeger uses hardwood pellets that come in different flavors, such as Alder, Hickory, Oak, Apple, Maple, Cherry, Mesquite, and Pecan!

Alder
Alder is a versatile wood pellet because of its mild flavor and aroma, and it gives off ample smoke without overwhelming and provides a delicate taste.

Hickory
Hickory is the most widely used pellet in BBQ because it releases a strong flavor and gives a delicious aroma

to your foods.

Oak
Oak is stronger than cherry or apple pellets, and it is lighter than Hickory. It is mostly used to cook broth, fish, beef, etc.

Maple
Maple is a mild and sweet pellet, and it is mostly used for cooking veggies and pork.

Apple
Apple is mostly used for cooking pork and poultry because it offers sweet smoke that helps enhance the flavor of meats.

Mesquite
Mesquite is a favorite of Texas of BBQ, and it infuses your meat with a robust smoke flavor.

Cherry
Cherry is a flavorful pellet and if you want to add a hearty flavor to your food, use cherry wood pellet.

Pecan
It is delicious, nutty, and a little spicy wood pellet. It is used for cooking beef, pork, veggies, poultry, and even baked goods.

Wood Pellet Chart

Wood	Flavor Profile	Use with
Pecan	Nutty, a little spicy	pork, beef, poultry, veggies, breads
Oak	Stronger than apple and cherry but lighter than hickory	fish, beef, or broth

Getting Started with Your Traeger Grill & Smoker | 3

Hickory	Releasing a strong flavor and complement most meats	barbecue, beef, chicken, pork, veggies
Apple	Offering a lightly sweet smoke	poultry, pork, breads, veggies
Maple	Mild, a hint of sweetness	red meats, pork, breads, veggies
Cherry	Very flavorful pellet, release a hearty smoke flavor	beef, poultry, pork, breads
Mesquite	A favorite of Texas BBQ	read meats, poultry, fish and seafood
Alder	Mild flavor and aroma	almost all types of food

How It Works?

A Traeger grill & smoker uses hardwood pellets that come in a different flavor. To get started, you will fill the hopper with the pellet flavor of your choice Alder, Hickory, Oak, Apple, Maple, Cherry, Mesquite, and Pecan, etc. Once the pellets are ignited by the ignition rod in the firepot, the smoke starts rolling. The smoke created by the pellets gives your food that delicious and unique smoky flavor. You can adjust the temperature according to the recipe instructions. The Traeger grill & smoker is simple and quite easy to control the cooking temperature.

Adjust the temperature with a dial and once the grill reaches the desired temperature, place your food onto the grill grate. The drip pan under the grill grate provides a few functions. It is positioned at an angle to catch any juices or grease that may drip from the meals as it cooks.

Benefits & Main Components of Traeger Grill & Smoker

We will cover the advantages and main components of using Traeger grill & smoker cooking appliance. Take advantage of this appliance and serve delicious food!

Benefits of Using Traeger Grill & Smoker

Versatile
This grill is not used only for grilling, but also you can use it for different processes of cooking as well. You can bake, roast, smoke, barbeque, and braise your different meals. It is a multi-functional cooking appliance.

Safe & User-friendly
The Traeger grill & smoker is a safe and well-designed cooking appliance. All parts of this grill are safe and user-friendly. Drip pan catches the grease or liquid drip from the food.

Better Flavor
The Traeger grill & smoker uses all-natural woods and gives your food a spicy, nutty, mild, delicious, sweet, and smoky flavor. It is better than gas or charcoal.

Main Components of Traeger Grill & Smoker

The Traeger grill & smoker comes with an elegant design with each of its parts. There are some main components of it.

Pellet Hopper
You put different wood into the hopper. The flavor happens here as the wood ignites and cooks the food. This grill has 100% wood, and there is no gas or charcoal here to cook the food.

Controller
On the controller, you can adjust the grill temperature and food temperature of your choice and regulate it during the cooking process.

Auger (Pellet Hopper Interior)
The auger is a screw that picks and puts the wood pellets into the firepot to begin the ignition process.

Heat Baffle
The heat baffle is a surface that catches the heat from the firebox and transfer it to the grill grate.

Two Meat Probes
There are two meat probes provided for you to check the internal temperature of the meats during grilling or smoking,

which can help you to get the most wonderful flavor.

Cooking Tools

There are smokestack, extra grill rack, and porcelain-coated grill grate for this grill, you can grill or smoke with them according to the types of the food.

User Guidance

In this chapter, you will see step-by-step guidance on using this grill and how many cooking functions offer this grill. It is the main part of this book. After reading this chapter, you will be able to use your grill easily.

How to Use Traeger Grill & Smoker?

The Traeger grill & smoker is a user-friendly cooking appliance. When using it the first time, you need to do an initial firing.

a. Firstly, you need to remove the porcelain-coated grill grates, grease drip pan, and heat baffle from the inside of the grill. Plug the power cord into a safe grounded electrical outlet with the switch in the OFF position.
b. In order to ensure proper operation, you must allow the auger tube to be charged with pellets, and make sure there are no other objects in the auger, and then turn the temperature dial to HIGH.
c. When the pellets begin to fall into the firepot, turn the temperature dial to SHUT DOWN CYCLE to rest the hot rod and then turn it back to SMOKE with the pellets still in the firepot.
d. Again, rotate the temperature knob to Shut Down Cycle and switch to OFF when flames begin to emerge from the firepot. Allow the grill to cool.
e. Place the heat baffle, grease drain pan, and porcelain-coated grill grate back to the grill & smoker.

Using Meat Probes

Step: 1

There are two probes present on the grill. Insert 1 to 2 meat probes into the plug-in holes and then thread probes through the access hole grommet present on the left side of the grill barrel.

Step: 2

Then, insert the probe tip into the thickest part of the meat.

Step: 3

After that, press the probe selector switch on the control. The display shows probe temperature "5 seconds" onto the screen. Then, revert to the temperature of the appliance.

MEAT TEMPERATURE CHARTS:

Range	Poultry	Pork	Beef	Lamb
Well	170°F	170°F	170°F	160°F
Medium	170°F	160°F	160°F	155°F
Medium rare	170°F		145°F	145°F
Rare	170°F		135°F	

Main Functions

The Traeger grill & smoker is used for grilling food and for different cooking functions: Here are the following!

Grill
Grilling outdoor is an amazing feeling. Grill your favorite food like chicken, beef, pork, lamb, seafood, veggies, and many more.

Bake
Using Traeger grill & smoker cooking appliance, you can bake cakes, muffins, cupcakes, brownies, cookies, and many more.

Roast
Roast is used for cooking veggies, beef, chicken, pork, etc. The Traeger grill & smoker offers this unique cooking function. You can use it to make different dishes on any occasion.

Smoke
Smoke is the main and advanced cooking function in this grill. Using Traeger grill & smoker, you will get delicious smoky flavored meals.

Barbeque

Make your day memorable by using the Barbeque cooking function. You can take it out and enjoy Barbeque cooking function.

Braise

Braise cooking function is used to give the dish a brown touch. Using this appliance, you can make different meats like red meat, wild game, beef, and pork.

Cleaning, Maintaining and Troubleshooting

In this chapter, you will see step-by-step cleaning and maintenance tips and tricks. If you face any problem with your appliance, I added troubleshooting for your easiness.

How to Clean & Maintenance?

It is pretty simple to clean and maintain this appliance. Here, step-by-step cleaning process!

Clean the hopper:
- Turn off the grill, and disconnect the power cord. Allow to cool the grill if it is hot.
- After that, put a plastic container/bucket under the pellet clean-out door to remove the pellet's wood residue.
- Now, unscrew the clean-out door and open it. Allowing the pellets to empty into the plastic container/bucket below it. You remove the remaining residue of the pellet from the hopper with a spoon.
- When hopper is empty, close the door. Now, you can refill the hopper with another flavor of wood pellet.

Clean the smokestack flue pipe:
- Turn off the grill and disconnect the power cord. Allow to cool the appliance if it is hot.
- Now, remove the chimney cap assembly from the top of the flue pipe.
- When removed, you can clean it with warm and soapy water.
- Scrape the creosote, and grease accumulation from the inner side of the horizontal and vertical sections of the flue pipe with the stiff tool.

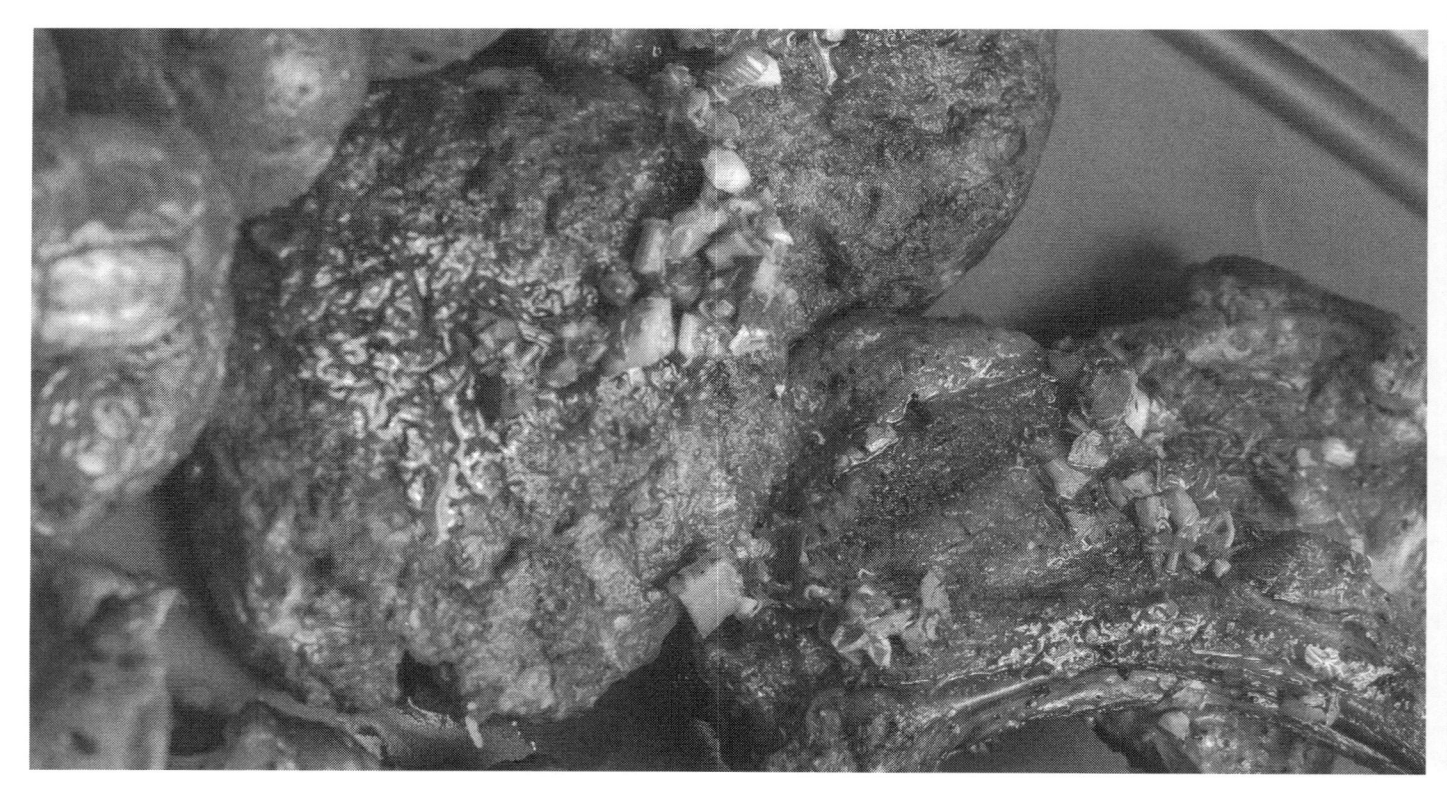

- When grease residue and creosote have loosened from the pipe lining, you can remove them with a paper towel or disposable rags.
- Remember, don't spray or other chemical liquid into the inner side of the grill. When flue pipe has been cleaned, replace the chimney cap assembly.

Clean the Grill from the Main Appliance:
- Turn off the grill and disconnect the power cord.
- Stubborn grease can be removed when the appliance is still warm – not hot. But, be careful not to burn yourself. Wear oven mitts or gloves.
- Clean the grease regularly; otherwise, too much grease takes a lot of your time.
- Remove the porcelain-coated grill grate and grease drain pan. Wipe the remaining grease residue with disposable bags or paper towels.
- You can use disposable bags or paper towels to clean the interior part of the grill.

Cleaning the Outer Surface:
- Turn off the grill, and disconnect the power cord. Allow to cool the grill if it is hot.
- You are suggested to use a disposable rag or soft cloth to clean the outer surface of the grill. Wash with warm and soapy water to remove the grease from the outer side of the grill.
- Don't use chemical liquid, oven cleaner, abrasive cleanser, or abrasive cleaning pads to clean the outer side of the grill surface.

Clean the Porcelain-coated Grill Grates:
- Cleaning the grill grate works best if it is still warm. But, be careful not to burn yourself.
- Use a long-handled cleaning brush to clean the grill grate.

Cleaning Ash from Inside and Around the Firepot:
- Turn off the grill and disconnect the power cord.
- Allow to cool the appliance before cleaning the ash.

- Excess ash in the firepot causes your fire to go out, especially when using the "Smoke" cooking function.
- Again clean the ash from the firepot.
- Remove the grill grate, grease drain pan, and heat baffle to provide access to the firepot and inner side of the grill. You can use a small metal fireplace shovel to remove the ash from the firepot.

Troubleshooting

Why won't my grill ignite?

Answer: If your grill fails to light or fire into the firepot at any time while cooking or smoking, then follow these important steps:

- If the grill failed to light or fire went out, turn off the appliance and disconnect the power cord. If the grill is hot, let it cool completely.
- Open the door and remove all food and grill grate, heat baffles, and grease drain pan when cooled.
- Remove all unburned wood pellets and ash from the inside and around the firepot.
- Power on and restart the grill.
- Place the wood pellet into the firepot, and the hot rod should start to heat, and it will turn red.
- When the flame is come out of the firepot, turn off the switch. Allow the grill to cool.
- Place the heat baffle, grease drain pan, and grill grate back into the appliance.
- Keep the door open; turn on the grill and temperature dial to SMOKE.
- Pellet will ignite within two minutes, and whitest-gray smoke will come out of the grill.
- When ignited, close the door and turn the temperature dial to any cooking function.

What dial setting is recommended for starting the grill?

Answer: Keep the door open; turn on the grill and temperature dial to Smoke. Pellet will ignite within two minutes, and the whitest-gray smoke will come out of the grill. When ignited, close the door and turn the temperature dial to any cooking function.

4-Week Diet Plan

Week 1

Day 1:
Snack: Smoked Cheese Macaroni
Dinner: Juicy Chicken Skewers with Avocado Salsa
Dessert: Cowboy Beans and Beef

Day 2:
Snack: Kidney Beans Chili
Dinner: Simple Wood-Fired Halibut
Dessert: Potato-Egg Salad

Day 3:
Snack: Sugar-Butter Carrots
Dinner: Mustard Rubbed Pork Shoulder
Dessert: Garlic Butter Cauliflower Florets

Day 4:
Snack: Homemade Smoked Guacamole
Dinner: Texas Smoked Mustard Brisket
Dessert: Cinnamon-Honey Sweet Potatoes

Day 5:
Snack: Grilled Potatoes with Onion
Dinner: Lamb Loin Chops with Mint Salsa Verde
Dessert: Smoked Mac 'N' Cheese

Day 6:
Snack: Cheesy Scalloped Potatoes
Dinner: Blackened Cajun Shrimp
Dessert: Smoked Plum Tomatoes

Day 7:
Snack: Sweet Smoked Beans & Pineapple
Dinner: Easy Smoked Dill Salmon
Dessert: Cheese Beef Stuffed Jalapeños

Week 2

Day 1:
Snack: Smoked Sweet & Sour Coleslaw
Dinner: Citrus Duck with Blue Plums
Dessert: Bacon-Wrapped Onion Meatloaf Bombs

Day 2:
Snack: Candied Bacon
Dinner: Smoked Garlic-Thyme Whole Chicken
Dessert: Delicious Cream Onion Dip

Day 3:
Snack: Tasty Smoked Onion Bombs
Dinner: Grilled Tuna Steaks
Dessert: Delicious Holiday Stuffing

Day 4:
Snack: Bacon-Wrapped Jalapeño Poppers
Dinner: Smoked Pork Chops
Dessert: Delicious Bacon Brussels Sprouts

Day 5:
Snack: Smoked Whole Cabbage
Dinner: Grilled Tri-Tip Roast
Dessert: Cheesy Hash Browns Casserole

Day 6:
Snack: Cheesy Hassel-back Russet Potatoes
Dinner: Bacon-Egg Cheeseburgers
Dessert: Grilled Chantilly Potatoes

Day 7:
Snack: Rosemary-Garlic Potato Wedges
Dinner: Ginger-Curried Lamb Chops with Yogurt Sauce
Dessert: Grilled S'mores Dip

Week 3	Week 4
Day 1: Snack: Smoked Butter Asparagus Dinner: Crusted Lemongrass Chicken with Pesto Dessert: Easy Smoked Butternut Squash **Day 2:** Snack: Lemony Artichokes Dinner: Smoked Dijon Turkey Breast Dessert: Grilled Cheese Corn Pudding **Day 3:** Snack: Spicy Bacon-Wrapped Onion Rings Dinner: Grilled Tuna Steaks Dessert: Caramel Apple Crisp **Day 4:** Snack: Hassel-back Sweet Potatoes with Pecans Dinner: Lemon Buttered King Crab Legs Dessert: Sweet Candied Pineapple **Day 5:** Snack: Smoked Deviled Eggs with Olives Dinner: BBQ Pork Belly Bites Dessert: Smoked Mac 'N' Cheese **Day 6:** Snack: Smoked Bacon-Cheddar Potato Skins Dinner: Lemon Buttered Oysters in the Shell Dessert: Cinnamon Chocolate Sauce **Day 7:** Snack: Smoked Corn on the Cob Dinner: Mustard Beef Roast Dessert: Garlic Butter Cauliflower Florets	**Day 1:** Snack: Smoked Spaghetti Squash Dinner: Smoked New York Steaks Dessert: Cinnamon-Honey Sweet Potatoes **Day 2:** Snack: Cheesy Corn with Chipotle Butter Dinner: Blackened Tilapia Tacos Dessert: Cowboy Beans and Beef **Day 3:** Snack: Smoked Garlic Cauliflower Steaks Dinner: Herb-Garlic Leg of Lamb with Zucchini Salad Dessert: Smoked Plum Tomatoes **Day 4:** Snack: Carrot Hot Dogs with Jalapeño Relish Dinner: Honey-Lemon Glazed Chicken Thighs Dessert: Potato-Egg Salad **Day 5:** Snack: Crispy Sweet Potato Chips Dinner: Juicy Lime Snapper Dessert: Bacon-Wrapped Onion Meatloaf Bombs **Day 6:** Snack: BBQ Beans with Bacon Dinner: Cumin Duck Breasts with Orange Sauce Dessert: Delicious Cream Onion Dip **Day 7:** Snack: Spaghetti Squash with Garlic-Wine Butter Sauce Dinner: Grilled Lobster Tail Dessert: Cheese Beef Stuffed Jalapeños

Chapter 1 Poultry Recipes

14	Juicy Chicken Skewers with Avocado Salsa	22	Lager-Brined Turkey with Beer Gravy
14	Flavorful Chicken Tacos	23	Turkey Cheeseburgers
14	Crusted Lemongrass Chicken with Pesto	23	Garlicky Buttermilk-Brined Chicken
14	Ranch Smoked Quail	23	Cumin Duck Breasts with Orange Sauce
15	Butter Grilled Chicken Thighs	23	Delicious Turkey Tacos
15	Grilled Chicken Breasts on Swiss Chard	24	Duck Breast and Greens Salad
15	Vinaigrette Glazed Chicken with Green Olive	24	Spiced Orange Chicken
15	Flavorful Garlic-Herb Turkey Legs	24	Delicious Barbecue Chicken
16	Moroccan Chicken Kabobs with Yogurt-Mint Sauce	24	Smoked Dijon Turkey Breast
16	Beer Smoked Whole Chicken	24	Classic Jamaican Jerk Chicken
16	Zesty Whole Smoked Jerk Chicken	25	Cinnamon Smoked Chicken
16	Feta Chicken Salad	25	Smoky Turkey and Apples
17	Sweet & Spicy Chicken Wings	25	Hot Caramel Chicken Breasts
17	Chicken Breast, Wheat Berries & Pecan Salad	25	Plum Chicken Drumsticks
17	Grilled Drumsticks & Peaches	25	Hearty Smoked Chicken Cacciatore
17	Beer-Brined Chicken Drumsticks	26	Sweet Lemon-Thyme Chicken
18	Buffalo Cheese Chicken Balls	26	Smoked Chicken Gumbo with Rice
18	Savory Chicken Romaine Salad	26	Best Smoked Chicken Marbella
18	Juicy Chicken Avocado Salad	26	Smoked Garlic-Thyme Whole Chicken
18	Garlic Chicken Lollipops	27	Citrus Duck with Blue Plums
19	Smoked Turkey with Poblano Poppers	27	Smoked Turkey-Veggie Soup with Bulgur Wheat
19	Spicy Pulled Chicken Sliders	27	Smoked Rosemary Duck Breast with Cherry Sauce
19	Chicken Broccoli Stir-Fry with Peanuts	27	Herb-Smoked Brick Chicken
19	Lemon Herb-Roasted Chicken	28	Sourdough-Sausage Stuffed Turkey
20	Cheese Chicken Enchilada Pie	28	Chipotle-Lime Chicken Skewers
20	Creole Chicken with Tomato-Peas Salad	28	Lemon Curried Chicken Breasts
20	Maple-Bacon Wrapped Chicken Breasts	28	Spiced Grilling Chicken
20	Honey Beer-Brined Chicken Wings	29	Smoky Turkey Tenders with Honey Dip
21	Lime Tequila-Marinated Chicken with Rice	29	Smoked Chicken Sandwiches
21	Honey-Lemon Glazed Chicken Thighs	29	Smoked Honey Chicken with Grapes
21	Juicy Spiced Chicken	29	Garlic Sage-Rubbed Turkey Breast
21	Turkey Cutlets with Cranberry Relish	29	Herbed Turkey Burgers
22	Spicy Chicken with Barbecue Sauce	30	Barbecue Chicken
22	Homemade Smoked Beer Chicken		

Juicy Chicken Skewers with Avocado Salsa

Prep time: 15 minutes | Cook time: 10 minutes | Serves: 4

½ teaspoon grated lime zest	thick, separated into rings, cut into
½ teaspoon ground cumin	1-inch pieces
Kosher salt	½ cup mayonnaise
Freshly ground black pepper	2 teaspoons lime juice
4 boneless chicken breast halves, skinless, (6 ounces each), cut into 1-inch cubes	2 teaspoons minced canned chipotle chili pepper in adobo sauce
1 slice yellow onion, about 1-inch-	
For Salsa	
2 or 3 small Hass avocados, chopped	1 tablespoon minced cilantro leaves
2 medium plum tomatoes, seeded and chopped	¼ teaspoon hot pepper sauce Extra-virgin olive oil
3 scallions, minced	8 flour tortillas (8 inches)
2 tablespoons lime juice	

1. If you choose bamboo skewers, please soak them in water for at least 30 minutes. 2. Mix the lime zest, ¼ teaspoon of the cumin, ½ teaspoon of salt, and ¼ teaspoon of pepper in a bowl, then add the chicken cubes and the onion pieces, mix them well; thread the chicken and the onion alternately onto skewers. 3. Prepare the Traeger grill for direct cooking over 350 degrees F/ 175 degrees C. 4. Mix the mayonnaise, lime juice, chipotle chili, and the remaining cumin in a separate bowl; add water, one splash at a time, and stir until the prepared mixture reaches a thick drizzling consistency. 5. Mix all the salsa ingredients and ½ teaspoon of salt in the third bowl. 6. Rub the skewers with oil, and season them with black pepper and salt. 7. Grill the skewers for 8 minutes with the hood closed, until the meat is tender, flipping them once or twice during grilling. 8. Remove the skewers from the hot grill and let rest for 2 to 3 minutes. 9. Warm the tortillas for 1 to 2 minutes with the hood open, turning once. 10. Push the chicken and onion off the wooden skewers onto tortillas, and serve with chipotle mayo and salsa.
Per Serving: Calories 285, Total Fat 9.8g, Sodium 639mg, Total Carbs 11.1g, Fiber 1.2g, Sugars 5.1g, Protein 27.8g

Flavorful Chicken Tacos

Prep time: 15 minutes | Cook time: 20 minutes | Serves: 6

1½ pounds chicken thighs, boneless and skinless	12 corn or flour tortillas (6 inches)
2 tablespoons extra-virgin olive oil	4 cups loosely packed shredded lettuce
For Salsa	
¼ medium white onion, cut through the root end and peeled	2 garlic cloves, chopped
8 tomatillos (1 pound)	½ jalapeño chili pepper, seeded and chopped
Extra-virgin olive oil	Kosher salt
⅓ cup cilantro leaves	
For Rub	
2 teaspoons pure ancho chili powder	½ teaspoon ground cumin
1 teaspoon salt	½ teaspoon garlic powder

1. Prepare the Traeger grill for direct cooking over medium heat (350 degrees F/ 175 degrees C to 450 degrees F/ 230 degrees C). 2. Coat the onion and the tomatillos with oil. 3. Close the lid, grill the onion (cut-side down) and the tomatillos until the onion is charred and the tomatillos are softened and beginning to collapse. The onion will take 4 to 6 minutes, and the tomatillos will take 6 to 8 minutes. 4. Remove them from the hot grill as they are done. 5. Chop the onion and the tomatillos, and add them to a food processor with the cilantro, garlic, and jalapeño. Puree them until smooth, and season with salt. 6. Mix all of the rub ingredients. Lightly brush the chicken thighs with the oil on both sides and season evenly with the spice rub. 7. Grill the prepared chicken for 10 minutes with the hood closed until the meat is tender and the juices run clear, flipping once or twice during grilling. 8. Remove the chicken from the hot grill and let rest for 5 minutes. Cut the chicken into slices. 9. Grill the tortillas for 30 seconds with the hood open, turning once. 10. Remove the tortillas from the hot grill and gently fold in half. Fill each tortilla with some chicken, lettuce, and salsa. Serve immediately.
Per Serving: Calories 272, Total Fat 19g, Sodium 389mg, Total Carbs 10.4g, Fiber 0.7g, Sugars 1.1g, Protein 15.6g

Crusted Lemongrass Chicken with Pesto

Prep time: 20 minutes | Cook time: 30 minutes | Serves: 4

Kosher salt	2 tablespoons all-purpose flour
Freshly ground black pepper	1 teaspoon crushed red pepper flakes
4 boneless chicken breast, (6 ounces each)	Olive oil cooking spray
½ cup panko bread crumbs	
For Marinade	
2 stalks lemongrass	2 tablespoons chopped fresh cilantro leaves
¼ cup cider vinegar	
¼ cup peanut oil	1 tablespoon peeled, minced fresh ginger
2 scallions, ends trimmed and chopped	1 teaspoon minced garlic
For Pesto	
2 cups chopped fresh cilantro leaves	1 tablespoon fresh ginger, peeled chopped
¾ cup loosely packed parsley leaves	1 garlic clove, chopped
¼ cup 1 tablespoon olive oil	⅛ teaspoon ground cayenne pepper

1. Peel away the dry outer layers of the lemongrass stalks, trim the ends, and mince the tender parts; you should have about ¼ cup. 2. Mix the lemongrass with the remaining marinade ingredients in a nonreactive bowl, including ¾ teaspoon of salt and ½ teaspoon of pepper. 3. Coat the prepared chicken with the prepared marinade, then let the chicken stay in the marinade, cover the bowl and refrigerate them for 1 to 6 hours, turning the chicken occasionally. 4. Mix the pesto ingredients in a food processor, including ½ teaspoon of salt and ¼ teaspoon of pepper, then process them until fairly smooth. 5. Prepare the Traeger grill for direct cooking over 350 degrees F/ 175 degrees C. 6. Remove the chicken from the marinade. 7. Blot the chicken mostly dry, leaving some of the solid bits clinging to the chicken. 8. In a shallow dish, stir the panko with the flour, red pepper flakes, and ¼ teaspoon of salt. 9. Coat the chicken with the prepared mixture, pressing so that the prepared mixture adheres. spray the chicken with oil. 10. With the lid closed, grill the prepared chicken for 12 minutes with the smooth (skin) side down first, until the meat is firm to touch and opaque all the way to the center, turning once halfway through. 11. Remove the chicken from the hot grill, and let rest for 5 minutes. 12. Serve the chicken warm with the pesto.
Per Serving: Calories 249; Total fat 13g; Sodium 556mg; Total Carbs 10g; Sugar 1.1g; Fiber 0.7g; Protein 31g

Ranch Smoked Quail

Prep time: 15 minutes | Cook time: 1 hour | Serves: 8

4 to 6 quail	1 package dry Ranch Dressing Mix
2 tablespoons olive oil	
Salt	½ cup (1 stick) butter, melted
Black pepper	

1. Close the hood, and preheat your Traeger smoker at 225 degrees F/ 105 degrees C with the hickory wood. 2. Season the quails with olive oil, black pepper and salt. Set the quail in the smoker and smoke for 1 hour. 3. In a suitable bowl, stir together the ranch-dressing mix and melted butter. 4. After 30 minutes of cooking time, rub the quail with the ranch-butter sauce and repeat at the end of the cook time. The quail are done when the internal temperature reaches 145 degrees F/ 60 degrees C. 5. Serve warm.
Per Serving: Calories 334; Total fat 14.9g; Sodium 227mg; Total Carbs 14g; Fiber 1g; Sugars 1.4g; Protein 25.7g

Butter Grilled Chicken Thighs

Prep time: 15 minutes | Cook time: 25 minutes | Serves: 4

8 chicken thighs, each 5-6 ounces and skin	1-ounce prosciutto, chopped
½ teaspoon kosher salt	1 medium shallot, minced
¼ teaspoon freshly ground black pepper	1 tablespoon chopped basil leaves
Butter	1 tablespoon grated Parmigiano-Reggiano cheese
¼ cup unsalted butter, softened	¼ teaspoon salt
	¼ teaspoon black pepper

1. Mix all the butter ingredients, then divide the seasoned butter into eight equal portions. 2. Prepare the Traeger grill for indirect and direct cooking over medium-high heat (400 degrees F/ 200 degrees C to 500 degrees F/ 260 degrees C). 3. Pat dry the chicken thighs with paper towels, then loosen the skin of the thighs, being careful not to completely separate the skin from the meat. 4. Place some of the butter underneath the skin by lifting it up. 5. Gently massage the skin to spread the butter over the surface of the meat in a uniform layer. The black pepper and salt should be applied of the thighs. 6. Close the lid, grill the thighs for 20 minutes with the skin side up first, until they are sizzling, just firm enough to hold their shape and marked on the bottom. 7. When the skin is blistered and crisp, and the meat is no longer pink at the bone, 2 to 4 minutes later, flip the thighs over and cook them over direct medium-high heat with the hood closed. 8. Remove from the hot grill and let rest for 5 minutes. 9. Serve warm.
Per Serving: Calories 336, Total Fat 17.3g, Sodium 281mg, Total Carbs 8.1g, Fiber 5.3g, Sugars 17.7g, Protein 32.3g

Grilled Chicken Breasts on Swiss Chard

Prep time: 45 minutes | Cook time: 30 minutes | Serves: 4

1-pound red Swiss chard	4 slices apple wood smoked bacon, cut crosswise into ⅓-inch strips
4 boneless chicken breast halves, skinless (6 ounces each)	
Extra-virgin olive oil	3 tablespoons sherry vinegar
2½ tablespoons chopped thyme leaves	½ cup low-sodium chicken broth
Salt, to taste	1 tablespoon Dijon mustard
Black pepper, to taste	3 shallots, sliced
	3 garlic cloves, sliced

1. Cut the thick center ribs from the chard and chop them, and chop the leaves and set them aside separately. 2. Prepare the Traeger grill for direct cooking over 350 degrees F/ 175 degrees C. 3. Brush the chicken breasts with 1 tablespoon of oil on both sides, and evenly season them with 1½ tablespoons of thyme, 1 teaspoon of salt, and ¾ teaspoon of pepper. 4. Cook the bacon in the skillet over medium-high heat for 10 minutes until crisp, stirring occasionally. 5. Drain the cooked bacon with paper towels. 6. Still in the skillet, add 1 tablespoon oil to the bacon drippings, and heat over medium heat. 7. Carefully add 2 tablespoons of the vinegar, the remaining 1 tablespoon thyme, ¼ teaspoon salt, and ¼ teaspoon pepper, and cook for 30 seconds, stirring constantly. Remove the set skillet from the heat. 8. Cover the hood, and grill the prepared chicken for 12 minutes with skin-side down first, until the meat is done; flip once or twice during grilling. 9. Mix the chicken broth, the remaining vinegar, and the mustard in a bowl. 10. Heat 2 tablespoons of oil in a deep skillet over medium-high heat; add the shallots and sauté for 3 to 4 minutes until tender and golden; add the minced garlic and chard center ribs, and sauté for 2 minutes. 11. Increase the heat to high, add the chard leaves, and toss them for 2 minutes until just wilted. Add the broth-mustard mixture, and toss for 2 to 4 minutes more until the liquid is almost evaporated but the chard is still bright green. Season the mixture with black pepper and salt. 12. Remove the cooked chicken from the grill and let rest for 5 minutes. 13. Divide the chard among four plates and top each with a chicken breast. 14. Return the skillet with the prepared dressing over medium heat, add the bacon and warm for 1 minute through. 15. Spoon the prepared dressing over the chicken, and serve warm.
Per Serving: Calories 345; Total fat 14.9g; Sodium 227mg; Total Carbs 14g; Fiber 1g; Sugars 1.4g; Protein 25.7g

Vinaigrette Glazed Chicken with Green Olive

Prep time: 15 minutes | Cook time: 15 minutes | Serves: 4

Vinaigrette

3 tablespoons red wine vinegar	1 garlic clove, chopped
1 tablespoon chopped shallot	¼ teaspoon crushed red pepper flakes
2 teaspoons chopped rosemary leaves	⅔ cup olive oil
1 teaspoon salt	

Chicken

4 boneless chicken breast halves, skinless, (6 ounces each)	2 tablespoons capers, rinsed and drained
⅓ cup chopped green olives	

1. Mix the red wine vinegar, shallot, rosemary leaves, salt, garlic, and red pepper flakes in a bowl. Add the oil, mixing constantly to emulsify. 2. Pour half of the vinaigrette into a suitable glass baking dish, and reserve the remaining vinaigrette at room temperature for serving. 3. Coat the chicken breasts with the vinaigrette in the baking dish, then cover the dish and refrigerate the chicken breasts for at least 1 hour or up to 2 hours. 4. Prepare the Traeger grill for direct cooking over 350 degrees F/ 175 degrees C to 450 degrees F/ 230 degrees C. 5. Remove the chicken from the dish, letting any excess vinaigrette drip back into the dish, and discard the vinaigrette. 6. Cover the hood, and grill the prepared chicken for 12 minutes with skin-side down first, until the meat is tender, flipping once or twice during grilling. 7. Remove the chicken from the hot grill and let rest for 5 minutes. 8. Stir the olives and the capers into the reserved vinaigrette. 9. Serve each chicken breast with vinaigrette on top.
Per Serving: Calories 272, Total Fat 19g, Sodium 389mg, Total Carbs 10.4g, Fiber 0.7g, Sugars 1.1g, Protein 15.6g

Flavorful Garlic-Herb Turkey Legs

Prep time: 30 minutes | Cook time: 4 to 6 hours | Serves: 8

For Spice Rub

3 tablespoons onion powder	1 teaspoon ground cumin
2 tablespoons paprika	½ teaspoon dried rubbed sage
1 tablespoon garlic powder	3 tablespoons vegetable oil
1 teaspoon black pepper	

For Brine

1 gallon water	1 tablespoon paprika
1 cup salt	1 tablespoon black pepper
½ cup sugar	1 tablespoon dried rubbed sage
2 tablespoons onion powder	1 teaspoon ground cumin
1 tablespoon garlic powder	8 turkey legs
1 tablespoon chili powder	

1. In a suitable bowl, stir together the onion powder, paprika, garlic powder, pepper, cumin, sage, and vegetable oil. Set aside. 2. Mix the water with the salt, sugar, onion powder, garlic powder, chili powder, paprika, pepper, sage, and cumin in a container enough to hold the brine and the turkey legs until dissolved. 3. Set the turkey legs into the brine, cover, and let it refrigerate for a minimum of 4 hours. 4. Close the lid, and preheat your Traeger smoker at 225 degrees F/ 105 degrees C with the apple wood. 5. Remove the legs, rinse them well, and discard the brine. Dry the drumsticks well with paper towels. 6. Coat the legs with the spice rub and cook them in the smoker for 4 to 6 hours until they have an internal temperature of 165 degrees F/ 75 degrees C. 7. Let them rest for 15 minutes before serving.
Per Serving: Calories 336, Total Fat 17.3g, Sodium 281mg, Total Carbs 8.1g, Fiber 5.3g, Sugars 17.7g, Protein 32.3g

Moroccan Chicken Kabobs with Yogurt-Mint Sauce

Prep time: 30 minutes | Cook time: 10 minutes | Serves: 4

4 boneless chicken breast halves, skinless, (6 ounces each), cut into 1 ½-inch piece
2 bell peppers, cut into 1 ½-inch square
1 small red onion, cut into wedges

For Marinade
¼ cup olive oil
¼ cup chopped cilantro leaves
¼ cup chopped mint leaves
2 tablespoons lemon juice
2 teaspoons honey
1½ teaspoons salt
1 teaspoon paprika
1 teaspoon ground cumin
2 garlic cloves, minced
½ teaspoon ground coriander
½ teaspoon ground cinnamon
¼ teaspoon ground cayenne pepper

For Sauce
2 cups whole-milk Greek yogurt
1 teaspoon grated lemon zest
½ cup lemon juice
¼ cup chopped mint leaves
2 garlic cloves, minced
1 teaspoon salt

1. If you choose bamboo skewers, please soak them in water for at least 30 minutes. 2. Mix the all marinade ingredients in a container. Pour ¼ cup of the prepared marinade into a medium nonreactive bowl and reserve for the vegetables. 3. Place the chicken pieces in a resealable plastic bag, and pour in the prepared marinade. 4. Shake the bag to distribute the prepared marinade, place in a suitable bowl, and let it refrigerate for 4 hours, turning occasionally. 5. Mix all the sauce ingredients in a bowl, then cover the bowl, and let the sauce refrigerate until ready to serve. 6. Prepare the Traeger grill for direct cooking over medium heat (350 degrees F/ 175 degrees C to 450 degrees F/ 230 degrees C). 7. Coat the onion and bell peppers with the reserved marinade in the bowl. 8. Thread the chicken, peppers, and onion alternately onto skewers. 9. Grill the prepared kabobs for 10 minutes with the hood closed, until the meat is tender, flipping once or twice during grilling. 10. Remove the kabobs from the hot grill and let rest for 2 to 3 minutes. Serve warm with the sauce.

Per Serving: Calories 361; Total fat 10g; Sodium 218mg; Total Carbs 16g; Sugar 1.2g; Fiber 0.7g; Protein 24g

Beer Smoked Whole Chicken

Prep time: 15 minutes | Cook time: 4 hours | Serves: 4

For Seasoning
½ cup (1 stick) melted butter
½ cup apple cider vinegar
¼ cup Cajun seasoning
1 teaspoon garlic powder
1 teaspoon onion powder
1 (3- to 4-pound) whole chicken

For Spice Rub
Olive oil
¾ cup Cajun seasoning
1 (12-ounce) can of beer

For Glaze
1 cup apple cider
½ cup olive oil

1. In a suitable bowl, mix the butter, vinegar, Cajun seasoning, garlic powder, and onion powder. 2. Inject the liquid into various locations throughout the chicken with a meat-injecting syringe. About half of the prepared mixture should be injected into the chicken breasts, with the remaining half going throughout the rest of the bird. 3. Coat the chicken all over with olive oil and generous layer of Cajun seasoning. 4. Drink or discard half the beer, and set the beer can on a stable surface. Set the bird's cavity on top of the can and position the chicken. 5. Preheat the Traeger smoker to 250 degrees F/ 120 degrees C with the apple, cherry, oak, or pecan wood. 6. In a 12-ounce or larger spray bottle, mix the cider and olive oil. Cover and shake before each use. 7. Put the chicken in the smoker and spray it with the mop every 30 minutes to keep it moist. 8. Smoke the chicken for 4 hours, or until the internal temperature of the thickest meat reaches 165 degrees F/ 75 degrees C.

Per Serving: Calories 285, Total Fat 9.8g, Sodium 639mg, Total Carbs 11.1g, Fiber 1.2g, Sugars 5.1g, Protein 27.8g

Zesty Whole Smoked Jerk Chicken

Prep time: 30 minutes | Cook time: 3 hours | Serves: 4-6

Jerk Spice Rub
2 tablespoons dark brown sugar
2 tablespoons ground allspice
1 tablespoon garlic powder
1 tablespoon onion powder
1 tablespoon ground cinnamon
1 tablespoon fine sea salt
1 teaspoon ground cayenne pepper
1 teaspoon ground cloves
1 teaspoon ground nutmeg
1 teaspoon freshly ground black pepper

Chicken
2 chickens, whole, rinsed, drained, then patted dry
Flaked sea salt
Freshly ground black pepper
1 garlic bulb, halved
8 thyme sprigs
8 rosemary sprigs
2 navel oranges, quartered and seeded
Olive oil, for coating
½ cup wildflower honey

1. Mix the sugar, allspice, garlic powder, onion powder, cinnamon, salt, cayenne, cloves, nutmeg, and black pepper in a bowl, then transfer to an airtight container for storage. 2. Preheat the Traeger smoker to 275 degrees F/ 135 degrees C. Ensure the drip tray is clean and in place. Seal the door. 3. Set the wood chips in the smoking tray or firebox, get a good smoke rolling, and seal the door. 4. Season the chicken cavities with black pepper and salt. Stuff each chicken with ½ head of garlic, 4 thyme sprigs, 4 rosemary sprigs, and 4 orange pieces. 5. Coat the chickens with olive oil and jerk spice, and season the outside of the chickens with black pepper and salt. Snugly truss the chickens for uniform smoking and to keep the ingredients in the cavity. 6. Arrange the chickens on smoking trays, leaving space between them. Drizzle the chickens with ¼ cup of honey. Smoke them for 2 to 3 hours until they have an internal temperature of 165 degrees F/ 75 degrees C. 7. Remove the chickens from the smoker. Remove the trussing and loosely tent the chickens with aluminum foil. Let them rest for 10 minutes. 8. Drizzle with the remaining honey and enjoy.

Per Serving: Calories 544; Total fat 14.9g; Sodium 227mg; Total Carbs 14g; Fiber 1g; Sugars 1.4g; Protein 25.7g

Feta Chicken Salad

Prep time: 45 minutes | Cook time: 12 minutes | Serves: 4

4 boneless chicken breast halves, skinless, (6 ounces each)
4 ounces crumbled feta cheese

For Marinade
2 tablespoons olive oil
2 tablespoons lemon juice
2 teaspoons paprika
3 garlic cloves, minced
1 teaspoon kosher salt
½ teaspoon freshly ground black pepper

For Salad
3 (1 pound) tomatoes, seeded and chopped
1 English cucumber, about 12 ounces, chopped
1 green bell pepper, chopped
4 scallions, chopped
¼ cup lemon juice
¼ cup olive oil
¼ cup chopped parsley leaves
2 tablespoons chopped mint leaves
1 teaspoon salt
½ teaspoon black pepper

1. Mix all of the marinade ingredients in a nonreactive bowl, then coat the chicken with the marinade in the bowl; cover the bowl and refrigerate them for 1 to 1½ hours. 2. Prepare the Traeger grill for direct cooking over medium heat (350 degrees F/ 175 degrees C to 450 degrees F/ 230 degrees C). 3. Mix all of the salad ingredients in a serving bowl. 4. Remove the chicken from the marinade. 5. Close the lid, and grill the prepared chicken for 12 minutes with skin-side down first, until the meat is tender, flipping once or twice during grilling. 6. Remove the chicken from the hot grill and let rest for 5 minutes. Cut the chicken into ¼-inch cubes, add them to the salad, and toss well to mix. 7. Top the dish with feta and serve immediately.

Per Serving: Calories 249; Total fat 13g; Sodium 556mg; Total Carbs 10g; Sugar 1.1g; Fiber 0.7g; Protein 31g

Sweet & Spicy Chicken Wings

Prep time: 15 minutes | Cook time: 2 hours | Serves: 40 to 50 wings

2 tablespoons packed light-brown sugar	1 tablespoon dry mustard
1½ tablespoons chipotle peppers	1 tablespoon ground cumin
1 tablespoon Hungarian smoked paprika	1½ teaspoons salt
	5½ pounds chicken wings

1. In a suitable bowl, mix together the brown sugar, chipotles, paprika, mustard, cumin, and salt. 2. Place the chicken wings in a suitable resealable freezer bag, and pour in the seasoning mix. Seal and shake the contents to coat the chicken generously. Refrigerate the wings for a minimum of 1 hour. 3. Close the hood, preheat your Traeger Smoker to 250 degrees F/ 120 degrees C with oak wood. 4. Set the chicken wings directly on the smoker rack. Smoke for 1½ to 2 hours until they are crisp and have an internal temperature of 165 degrees F/ 75 degrees C. 5. Serve hot.

Per Serving: Calories 351; Total fat 22g; Sodium 502mg; Total Carbs 15.2g; Sugar 1.1g; Fiber 0.7g; Protein 26.4g

Chicken Breast, Wheat Berries & Pecan Salad

Prep time: 20 minutes | Cook time: 12 minutes | Serves: 2

2 boneless chicken breast halves, skinless, (6 ounces each)	½ cup mayonnaise
1 cup sweet pickle brine (from the jar of sweet gherkins)	¼ cup cider vinegar
	1 tablespoon chopped dill
⅔ cup wheat berries	1 teaspoon black pepper
1 cup chopped celery	½ teaspoon salt
⅔ cup chopped sweet gherkins	¼ teaspoon celery seed
½ cup chopped pecans	2 tomatoes, cut crosswise into thick slices

1. Place the chicken breasts in a small baking dish and pour the pickle brine on top, then cover the dish and let it refrigerate for 2 hours, turning once or twice. 2. Add the wheat berries to a saucepan and fill about two-thirds full of water, bring to a boil over high heat. 3. Reduce the heat to low, partially cover the saucepan, and cook them for 1 hour until tender. 4. Drain and rinse with cool water to bring the wheat berries to room temperature. Drain again. 5. Prepare the Traeger grill for direct cooking over medium heat (350 degrees F/ 175 degrees C to 450 degrees F/ 230 degrees C). 6. Remove the chicken from the dish, and discard the brine. 7. Close the grill lid, and grill the chicken for 12 minutes with skin-side down first, until the meat is firm to touch and opaque all the way to the center, flipping once or twice. 8. Remove the chicken from the hot grill and let rest for 3 to 5 minutes, then cut the chicken into ½-inch pieces. 9. Transfer the chicken and wheat berries to a serving bowl, and add all of the remaining ingredients except the tomatoes. Stir until well mixed. 10. Serve warm or at room temperature over the sliced tomatoes.

Per Serving: Calories 236, Total Fat 13.9g, Sodium 451mg, Total Carbs 13.2g, Fiber 1.2gSugars 1.4g, Protein 14.3g

Grilled Drumsticks & Peaches

Prep time: 15 minutes | Cook time: 30 minutes | Serves: 6

Kosher salt	pounds total
Freshly ground black pepper	4 firm but ripe peaches, halved
12 chicken drumsticks, 2¾-3	2 teaspoons canola oil
Glaze	
1 cup peach preserves	1 teaspoon grated lime zest
½ cup peach nectar	2 tablespoons lime juice
4 teaspoons prepared chili powder	½ cup chopped cilantro leaves

1. Add the preserves, nectar, and chili powder to a saucepan, and bring to a simmer over medium-high heat, mixing until the prepared mixture is well blended and almost smooth. 2. Turn off the heat, and mix in the lime zest and juice. Let cool to lukewarm, then mix in the cilantro, salt, and black pepper. 3. Apportion the glaze between two small bowls: one for brushing on the chicken while grilling and the other for serving. 4. Prepare the Traeger grill for direct cooking over medium heat (350 degrees F/ 175 degrees C to 450 degrees F/ 230 degrees C). 5. Use paper towels to pat the drumsticks dry, and evenly season them with 1¼ teaspoons of salt and 1 teaspoon of pepper. Rub the peach halves with the oil. 6. Close the hood, and grill the drumsticks for 20 minutes until the skin is golden brown and the meat is almost firm to the touch, turning occasionally. 7. Rub the peach glaze from the first bowl evenly over the drumsticks, then continue grilling them for 10 minutes more with the hood closed, until the juices run clear and the meat is no longer pink at the bone, flipping once cooked halfway through and brushing occasionally with more of the glaze. 8. Grill the peach halves until charred and beginning to soften (check after 3 minutes). 9. Remove the drumsticks and the peaches from the grill, and let the drumsticks rest for 5 minutes. 10. Serve the drumsticks and the peaches warm with the reserved glaze.

Per Serving: Calories 602; Total fat 23.9g; **Sodium 345mg**; Total Carbs 46.5g; Sugar 2.9g; Protein 11.3g

Beer-Brined Chicken Drumsticks

Prep time: 45 minutes | Cook time: 2 hours | Serves: 8 to 12 legs

For Spice Rub

¼ cup light-brown sugar	½ teaspoon garlic powder
2 tablespoons paprika	½ teaspoon onion powder
1¼ teaspoons salt	¼ teaspoon freshly ground black pepper
1 teaspoon cayenne pepper	

For Beer Barbecue Sauce

2 cups ketchup	mustard
1 cup beer	1 tablespoon molasses
⅓ cup chopped onion	1 tablespoon brown sugar
2 tablespoons minced garlic	½ teaspoon salt
2 tablespoons Worcestershire sauce	½ teaspoon black pepper
2 tablespoons honey Dijon	⅓ teaspoon hot sauce

For Brine

1-quart water	Olive oil, for basting
2 (12-ounce) bottles of beer	2 tablespoons chopped fresh parsley leaves
½ cup salt	
½ cup brown sugar	2 tablespoons chopped fresh chives
8 to 12 chicken legs	

1. In a suitable bowl, mix together the brown sugar, paprika, salt, cayenne, garlic powder, onion powder, and pepper. Set aside. 2. Add the ketchup, beer, onion, garlic, Worcestershire sauce, mustard, molasses, brown sugar, salt, pepper, and hot sauce to a saucepan, and then boil them over medium-high heat. 3. Mix the chicken legs with water and beer in a large container; add the salt and sugar, and stir until dissolved. 4. Place the chicken legs in the container, making sure they are covered with brine. Cover and let it refrigerate for 3 hours. 5. Close the lid, and preheat your Traeger Smoker at 250 degrees F/ 120 degrees C with the pecan wood for indirect heat. 6. Discard the brine and rinse the chicken. Pat the chicken dry with paper towels. 7. Baste the chicken all sides with olive oil. 8. Season the chicken generously with the spice rub and sprinkle with the parsley and chives. Set the chicken legs directly on the smoker rack and smoke for 1½ to 2 hours. 9. After about 45 minutes, use an instant-read thermometer to check the temperature. When the drumsticks reach 160 degrees F/ 70 degrees C, spoon some beer-barbecue sauce onto them. The chicken is done at 165 degrees F/ 75 degrees C. 10. Serve hot.

Per Serving: Calories 254; Total fat 28g; Sodium 346mg; Total Carbs 12.3g; Sugar 1g; Fiber 0.7g; Protein 24.3g

Buffalo Cheese Chicken Balls

Prep time: 30 minutes | Cook time: 1 hour 30 minutes | Serves: 20 balls

For Chicken balls
1-pound ground chicken
2 cups dry Bisquick mix
2 cups grated Cheddar cheese
¼ cup water
For Buffalo Sauce
½ cup (1 stick) butter, melted
1 cup Frank's Red-hot sauce
2 teaspoons cayenne pepper
1 teaspoon chicken bouillon powder
1 (8-ounce) block of blue cheese, cut into 20 cubes
1 teaspoon chopped parsley leaves
Ranch dressing, for dipping

1. Preheat the Traeger smoker to 275 degrees F/ 135 degrees C with the apple wood. 2. In a suitable bowl, mix together the chicken, Bisquick mix, Cheddar cheese, water, and bouillon powder. 3. Take a cube of blue cheese, and form about 2 tablespoons (just enough to cover the cube) of the chicken mixture around the cube. Roll it into a ball. Do the same with the remaining cheese cubes and chicken mixture. 4. Place the balls on the smoker rack, and smoke for 1 to 1½ hours until they are firm and have an internal temperature of 160 degrees F/ 70 degrees C. 5. While the balls are smoking, stir together the butter, hot sauce, and cayenne in a separate bowl. 6. Dredge the cooked chicken balls in the hot sauce and sprinkle with the parsley before serving with ranch dressing.
Per Serving: Calories 307; Total fat 11g; Sodium 477mg; Total Carbs 12g; Fiber 1.2g; Sugars 1g; Protein 27g

Savory Chicken Romaine Salad

Prep time: 20 minutes | Cook time: 14 minutes | Serves: 4

For Dressing
1 cup mayonnaise
⅔ cup buttermilk
¼ cup grated yellow onion
1 tablespoon cider vinegar
Chicken
4 boneless chicken breast halves, skinless, (6 ounces each)
2 hearts of romaine, about 12 ounces total, each cut lengthwise in half, trimmed
olive oil
½ teaspoon celery seed
½ teaspoon celery salt
1 garlic clove, chopped
¼ teaspoon black pepper

1 pint small cherry tomatoes, each cut in half
2 tablespoons chopped parsley leaves
Kosher salt
Freshly ground black pepper

1. Combine all of the dressing ingredients. 2. Place the chicken and 1 cup of the prepared dressing in a resealable plastic bag, then seal this bag tightly after squeezing out the air. 3. Place the bag in a bowl, turn to distribute the dressing, and then chill them for 4 to 6 hours, turning regularly. Cover and refrigerate the remaining dressing. 4. Prepare the Traeger grill for direct cooking over medium heat (350 degrees F/ 175 degrees C to 450 degrees F/ 230 degrees C). 5. Remove the marinated chicken from the bag, shaking off the excess dressing. 6. Close the lid, and grill the prepared chicken for 12 minutes with skin-side down first, until the meat is tender, flipping the chicken halfway through. 7. Take the cooked food off the grill and let rest for 5 minutes, then cut the chicken into pieces. 8. Lightly brush the romaine halves with oil on both sides. 9. Grill the romaine halves over for 2 minutes with the hood closed, flipping once, until just beginning to wilt. 10. Serve the romaine with the chicken, dressing, tomatoes, parsley, and season the dish with the salt and pepper.
Per Serving: Calories 285, Total Fat 9.8g, Sodium 639mg, Total Carbs 11.1g, Fiber 1.2g, Sugars 5.1g, Protein 27.8g

Juicy Chicken Avocado Salad

Prep time: 25 minutes | Cook time: 12 minutes | Serves: 4

½ cup sliced red onion
3 tangerines
2 tablespoons olive oil
½ teaspoon salt
¼ teaspoon black pepper
3 small bunches of watercress, thick stems trimmed
3 Hass avocados, cut into thick slices
3 boneless chicken breast halves, skinless, (6 ounces each)
Vinaigrette
¼ cup plus 2 tablespoons olive oil
2 tablespoons sherry vinegar
1 tablespoon Dijon mustard
1 teaspoon ground black pepper
¼ teaspoon salt

1. Soak the onion in a bowl of ice water for 30 to 45 minutes until it is crisp and the flavor is mellowed. 2. Grate enough zest from the tangerines to make 1 teaspoon. 3. Remove the peel and pith from the tangerines. 4. Cut between the flesh and the white membranes separating the individual segments, working over a strainer set over a suitable bowl so you can catch the tangerine juice for the prepared dressing. You'll need 2 tablespoons of juice. 5. Set aside the tangerine zest, segments, and juice. 6. Prepare the Traeger grill for direct cooking over medium heat (350 degrees F/ 175 degrees C to 450 degrees F/ 230 degrees C). 7. Brush the chicken breasts with the oil on both sides, and evenly season them with black pepper, and salt. 8. Mix the vinaigrette ingredients until smooth and emulsified, including the reserved 1 teaspoon of tangerine zest and the reserved 2 tablespoons tangerine juice. 9. Close the lid, and grill the prepared chicken for 12 minutes with the skin-side down first, until the meat is tender, flipping once or twice during grilling. 10. Remove the chicken from the hot grill and let rest for 5 minutes. 11. Drain the onions then pat them dry with paper towels; mix the onions, tangerine segments, and watercress. 12. Drizzle with just enough vinaigrette to coat the ingredients and toss gently. Cut the chicken breasts crosswise into slices. 13. Divide the salad, chicken, and avocado among four plates, and serve with the remaining vinaigrette.
Per Serving: Calories 336, Total Fat 17.3g, Sodium 281mg, Total Carbs 8.1g, Fiber 5.3g, Sugars 17.7g, Protein 32.3g

Garlic Chicken Lollipops

Prep time: 30 minutes | Cook time: 2 hours | Serves: 4

2 pounds chicken drumsticks
8 garlic cloves, peeled
3 tablespoons sliced peeled ginger
3 tablespoons cilantro leaves more for garnish
1 jalapeño pepper, trimmed, halved, and seeded
¼ cup rice wine vinegar
2 tablespoons fish sauce
2 tablespoons soy sauce
2 tablespoons ground paprika
Flaked sea salt
Freshly ground black pepper
4 limes, quartered, for serving

1. Place the sharp knife about 1 inch below the knuckle bone and cut all the way around the bone, cutting through the skin and tendons. Push the meat down the bone toward the chicken drumstick and remove any excess skin or tendons. Trim the bone clean, as needed. Repeat with all the drumsticks. 2. Add the minced garlic, ginger, cilantro, jalapeño, vinegar, fish sauce, soy sauce, and paprika to a food processor, and then process until smooth. Transfer to a suitable food-grade plastic bag. 3. Add the chicken, remove as much of the air as possible from the bag, and seal it. Refrigerate for 24 hours to marinate, turning 2 or 3 times. 4. Preheat the Traeger smoker to 250 degrees F/ 120 degrees C. Ensure the drip tray is clean and in place. Seal the door. 5. Set the wood chips in the smoking tray or firebox, get a good smoke rolling, and seal the door. 6. Remove the drumsticks from the prepared marinade, reserving the prepared marinade in the refrigerator. Season the chicken with black pepper and salt. Arrange the drumsticks on smoking trays, leaving space between each piece. 7. Smoke them for 1 hour until they have an internal temperature of 165 degrees F/ 75 degrees C, then baste using the reserved marinade. 8. Smoke for 30 minutes more and baste again. Repeat smoking and basting about 2 times more, or until the chicken reaches an internal temperature of 165 degrees F/ 75 degrees C. 9. Remove the chicken lollipops from the smoker, baste, loosely tent with aluminum foil, and let rest for 10 minutes before serving with a lime garnish.
Per Serving: Calories 260; Total fat 7g; Sodium 104mg; Total Carbs 24.4g; Fiber 2.7g; Sugars 14.3g; Protein 25.5g

Smoked Turkey with Poblano Poppers
Prep time: 40 minutes | Cook time: 5 hours | Serves: 8

For Savory Rice
- 1 tablespoon unsalted butter
- 1 tablespoon olive oil
- 1 cup chopped yellow onion
- Flaked sea salt
- Freshly ground black pepper
- 2 cups long-grain white or brown rice
- 1 tablespoon thyme leaves, stripped and finely hopped
- 1 bay leaf
- 4 cups chicken (or vegetable) stock

For Poppers
- 2 Andouille sausages, casings removed and sliced
- 2 Roma tomatoes, quartered lengthwise, seeded, and diced
- 2 scallions, trimmed and sliced on an angle
- 2 cups shredded Monterey Jack cheese
- 8 poblano peppers, halved lengthwise, ribbed, and seeded
- 2 (4-pound) bone-in skin-on turkey breasts
- Flaked sea salt, to taste
- Freshly ground black pepper, to taste
- 4 limes, halved
- chopped cilantro leaves, for garnish
- Sour cream, for garnish

1. Add the butter, olive oil, onion, black pepper and salt to a saucepan, and sauté them over medium-high heat for 10 minutes until golden brown. 2. Add the rice, thyme, and bay leaf, stirring to coat the rice in the butter and oil. 3. Gently stir in the chicken/vegetable stock, and reduce the heat to low. Cook for 45 to 60 minutes, until the liquid is absorbed. Remove and discard the bay leaf. 4. Preheat the Traeger smoker to 275 degrees F/ 135 degrees C with the door closed. Ensure the drip tray is clean and in place. 5. Set the wood chips in the firebox, get a good smoke rolling, and seal the door. 6. Fold the sausage, tomatoes, scallions, 4 cups of savory rice, and Monterey Jack cheese in a bowl. Spoon the prepared mixture into the pepper halves, mounding and gently pressing to fill the cavity. 7. Arrange the stuffed peppers on the smoking racks. 8. Season the turkey breasts with black pepper and salt. Set the turkey breasts on the smoking racks, spaced evenly without touching. 9. Smoke the turkey breasts for 4 hours until they have an internal temperature of 165 degrees F/ 75 degrees C. 10. Let the turkey cool slightly. Gently remove the bones and slice across the breast at an angle. 11. Top the stuffed peppers with turkey slices. Serve the dish with lime halves, cilantro, and sour cream.

Per Serving: Calories 305; Total fat 15g; Sodium 548mg; Total Carbs 12g; Sugar 1.2g; Fiber 0.7g; Protein 29g

Spicy Pulled Chicken Sliders
Prep time: 15 minutes | Cook time: 30 minutes | Serves: 8

- 1½ pounds of boneless chicken thighs
- Extra-virgin olive oil

For Sauce
- 1 tablespoon olive oil
- ½ cup chopped yellow onion
- ⅔ cup ketchup
- ½ cup root beer
- 2 tablespoons unsulfured molasses

For Rub
- 2 teaspoons smoked paprika
- 1 teaspoon ground cumin
- 8 small, soft hamburger buns
- Store-bought coleslaw
- 2 tablespoons lemon juice
- 1 teaspoon prepared chili powder
- ½ teaspoon garlic powder
- ⅛ teaspoon ground cayenne pepper
- 1 teaspoon garlic powder
- 1 teaspoon salt

1. Heat the oil in a saucepan over medium heat; add the onion and cook for 5 minutes until softened. 2. Add all the remaining sauce ingredients, increase the heat to medium-high, and bring to a boil; reduce the heat to medium; cook the sauce on a simmer for 15 minutes until thickened, stirring occasionally. 3. Prepare the Traeger grill for direct cooking over medium heat (350 degrees F/ 175 degrees C to 450 degrees F/ 230 degrees C). 4. Mix all the rub ingredients, brush the chicken with oil on both sides and season evenly with the rub. 5. Grill the prepared chicken over direct medium heat, with the hood closed until the meat is tender and the juices run clear for 10 minutes, flipping once or twice during grilling. 6. Remove the chicken from the hot grill, and let rest for 5 minutes until just cool enough to handle. 7. Shred the cooked chicken, add to the sauce, and heat them over medium heat, stirring occasionally. 8. Fill the buns with the chicken mixture, and then serve with coleslaw (optional).

Per Serving: Calories 254; Total fat 28g; Sodium 346mg; Total Carbs 12.3g; Sugar 1g; Fiber 0.7g; Protein 24.3g

Chicken Broccoli Stir-Fry with Peanuts
Prep time: 15 minutes | Cook time: 30 minutes | Serves: 4

- 2 tablespoons vegetable oil
- 1 tablespoon peeled, minced ginger
- 2 teaspoons minced garlic
- 1-pound boneless chicken thighs, cut into ¾-inch pieces

For Sauce
- ⅓ cup hoisin sauce
- ¼ cup low-sodium chicken broth
- 1 tablespoon low-sodium soy sauce
- 12 ounces broccoli florets
- 1 red bell pepper, cut into ¾-inch pieces
- ⅓ cup salted peanuts
- 3 scallions, sliced
- 2 cups cooked rice
- 1 teaspoon hot chili-garlic sauce

1. Combine all the sauce ingredients in a bowl. 2. Mix the oil, ginger, and garlic in the second bowl, then add the chicken pieces and toss to coat. 3. Prepare the Traeger grill for direct cooking over high heat (450 degrees F/ 230 degrees C to 550 degrees F/ 290 degrees C). 4. Place a grill-proof wok on the cooking grate over direct high heat, close the lid, and preheat it for 10 minutes. 5. Bring the sauce, chicken mixture, broccoli, bell pepper, peanuts, and scallions out to the grill. 6. When the wok is smoking hot, stir in the chicken mixture and stir-fry for 3 minutes over direct high heat; toss the chicken frequently. 7. Add the broccoli and bell pepper, and continue to stir-fry for 2 to 3 minutes until the broccoli is bright green. Add the sauce and stir well. 8. Close the grill hood, and cook them for one minute until the sauce is bubbling. 9. Add the peanuts and the scallions, and resume cooking them for 2 minutes until the broccoli is crispy and the chicken is cooked through. 10. Remove the hot wok from the grill, and serve the stir-fry immediately over warm rice. 11. Cut all the vegetables and meat into similar-sized pieces so that they all finish cooking at the same time. 12. You can enjoy the dish over warm rice.

Per Serving: Calories 285, Total Fat 9.8g, Sodium 639mg, Total Carbs 11.1g, Fiber 1.2g, Sugars 5.1g, Protein 27.8g

Lemon Herb-Roasted Chicken
Prep time: 15 minutes | Cook time: 1 hour 30 minutes | Serves: 4

- 1 whole chicken, neck, giblets removed
- 1 lemon, cut into quarters
- 3 sprigs of thyme
- 2 garlic cloves, smashed
- Butter
- 2 tablespoons unsalted butter, softened
- 2 tablespoons thyme leaves
- 1 tablespoon chopped chives
- 1 teaspoon grated lemon zest
- 1 garlic clove, minced
- ⅛ teaspoon salt
- ⅛ teaspoon black pepper

1. Prepare the Traeger grill for indirect cooking over medium heat (350 degrees F/ 175 degrees C to 450 degrees F/ 230 degrees C). 2. Mix all the butter ingredients. 3. Take care not to break the skin as you carefully lift it from the chicken thighs and breast meat. Spread half of the butter over the skin and distribute the other half under the skin on the breast and thigh flesh. 4. Place the thyme, garlic, and lemon quarters within the cavity of the chicken. Tie the drumsticks together with butcher's twine, and fold the wings tips behind the chicken's back. 5. Grill the chicken for 1¼ to 1½ hours with the lid closed, until the juices run clear and its internal temperature reaches 160 degrees F/ 70 degrees C to 165 degrees F/ 75 degrees C. 6. Cut the chicken into serving pieces. Serve warm.

Per Serving: Calories 254; Total fat 28g; Sodium 346mg; Total Carbs 12.3g; Sugar 1g; Fiber 0.7g; Protein 24.3g

Cheese Chicken Enchilada Pie

Prep time: 20 minutes | Cook time: 60 minutes | Serves: 6-8

1½ pounds of boneless chicken thighs	1½ cups or frozen and thawed corn kernels
Extra-virgin olive oil	1 can (7 ounces) chopped fire-roasted green chilies, drained
½ teaspoon salt	
¼ teaspoon black pepper	8 ounces Mexican cheese blend, grated (2 cups)
18 corn tortillas (6 inches)	
1 medium yellow onion, chopped	Sour cream
2 garlic cloves, minced	Chopped cilantro leaves
1 can (28 ounces) enchilada sauce	Store-bought guacamole

1. Soak the wood chips in water for at least 30 minutes. 2. Coat the chicken thighs with 1 tablespoon oil on both sides, and evenly season them with salt and pepper. 3. Prepare the Traeger grill for direct and indirect cooking over medium heat (350 degrees F/ 175 degrees C to 450 degrees F/ 230 degrees C). 4. Grill the tortillas for 1 minute with the lid open, until lightly brown; turn them once during grilling. When done, arrange them in a single layer on baking sheets to cool, then tear them into quarters. 5. Add the wood chips to the charcoal with following the manufacturer's instructions, then close the lid. 6. When smoke appears, arrange the chicken thighs on the grill grate, and close the lid; grill the chicken thighs for 8 to 10 minutes until the meat is firm and the juices run clear, flipping them once or twice during grilling. 7. Let the chicken thighs cool after grilling, then shred the meat into bite-sized pieces. 8. Heat 1 tablespoon oil in the skillet over medium heat; add onion and garlic, and sauté them for 3 minutes until softened; turn off the heat. 9. Lightly oil another 12-inch cast-iron skillet, spread ½ cup of the enchilada sauce on its bottom. Top the bottom with one-third of the tortilla pieces, and cover them with 1 cup of the enchilada sauce; scatter with half of the chicken, half of the corn, half of the onion-garlic mixture, and half of the chilies; top with ⅔ cup of the cheese. 10. Repeat these layers (chicken, corn, onion-garlic mixture, and chilies), and then add the remaining tortilla pieces, sauce, and cheese. 11. Drain the remaining wood chips, and then add them to the charcoal. 12. If using the Traeger Smoker grill, top off the fuel as necessary to maintain a constant temperature. After 45 minutes, add 6 to 10 unlit briquettes to assist the briquettes light. 13. Cover the skillet with aluminum foil, and cook the enchilada pie for 20 minutes with the hood closed until the sauce starts to bubble and the cheese is melted. 14. Remove the foil and cook for 20 minutes until the center of the pie is hot. 15. Remove the skillet from the grill, and let cool for 5 minutes. 16. Serve warm with sour cream, cilantro, and guacamole.
Per Serving: Calories 307; Total fat 11g; Sodium 477mg; Total Carbs 14g; Fiber 1g; Sugars 1.4g; Protein 25.7g

Creole Chicken with Tomato-Peas Salad

Prep time: 25 minutes | Cook time: 45 minutes | Serves: 4

Kosher salt, to taste	¼ cup 2 tablespoons creole mustard
Freshly ground black pepper, to taste	1 tablespoon honey
4 chicken breast halves, each 10–12 ounces	2 teaspoons minced thyme leaves
1 tablespoon olive oil	4 cups watercress sprigs, thick stems trimmed (about 1 bunch)
2½ teaspoons Cajun seasoning	
For Dressing	
4 ½ tablespoons olive oil	1 tablespoon creole mustard
3 tablespoons cider vinegar	1 tablespoon honey
For Salad	
2 cans (15 ounces) of black-eyed peas, rinsed and drained	4 ounces smoked ham, cut into ⅓-inch cubes
10 ounces grape tomatoes, each cut in half (about 2 cups)	⅓ cup chopped celery

1. Mix the prepared dressing ingredients in a bowl; add the salad ingredients, and toss them to coat with the prepared dressing, then season them with black pepper and salt. Cover the bowl, and refrigerate the salad until ready to serve. 2. Prepare the Traeger grill for indirect cooking over medium heat (350 degrees F/ 175 degrees C to 450 degrees F/ 230 degrees C). 3. Brush the chicken breasts with oil on both sides, and evenly season them with Cajun seasoning, 1½ teaspoons salt, and 1 teaspoon pepper. 4. Combine the creole mustard and honey, place close by the grill. 5. Close the grill lid after arranging the chicken breasts on the grill grate; grill the chicken breasts for 25 to 35 minutes with bone side down, until the meat is firm; brush them all over with honey mutated mixture, and resume grilling for 5 to 10 minutes until the juices is clear and the meat is no longer pink at the bone, brushing occasionally with the remaining honey mustard mixture. 6. When grilled, remove the chicken breasts from the grill, and evenly season the skin-side with thyme. Then, allow them to stand for 3 to 5 minutes. 7. Add the watercress to the salad, and gently toss to mix. Serve the chicken warm with the salad.
Per Serving: Calories 285, Total Fat 9.8g, Sodium 639mg, Total Carbs 11.1g, Fiber 1.2g, Sugars 5.1g, Protein 27.8g

Maple-Bacon Wrapped Chicken Breasts

Prep time: 20 minutes | Cook time: 2 hours | Serves: 4

4 chicken breasts, skinless and boneless	12 bacon slices, uncooked
	1 cup maple syrup
Salt	½ cup (1 stick) butter, melted
Freshly ground black pepper	1 teaspoon liquid smoke

1. At 250 degrees F/ 120 degrees C, preheat the Traeger Smoker with mesquite wood. 2. Season the chicken breasts with black pepper and salt. 3. Wrap each breast with 3 bacon slices to cover the entire surface, and secure them with toothpicks. 4. Stir the maple syrup, butter, and liquid smoke to make maple butter. Reserve about one-third of the maple butter. 5. Submerge each breast in the maple butter to coat and place it on a grill pan. Set the pan in the smoker and smoke them for 1 to 1½ hours. 6. Rub the chicken with the reserved maple butter, then resume smoking them for 30 minutes more until they have an internal temperature of 165 degrees F/ 75 degrees C. 7. Serve and enjoy.
Per Serving: Calories 342; Total fat 14.9g; Sodium 227mg; Total Carbs 14g; Fiber 1g; Sugars 1.4g; Protein 25.7g

Honey Beer-Brined Chicken Wings

Prep time: 30 minutes | Cook time: 2 hours | Serves: 6

3 limes, sliced 3 limes, quartered lengthwise, for serving	stripped and chopped
	3 bay leaves
¼ cup coarse sea salt	3 (12-ounce) bottles pilsner beer
¼ cup wildflower honey	6 pounds bone-in skin-on chicken wings, rinsed and drained
1 jalapeño pepper, sliced more for additional heat	
	Flaked sea salt
2 tablespoons thyme leaves,	Freshly ground black pepper

1. In a suitable bowl, stir together the lime slices, coarse sea salt, honey, jalapeño, thyme, lime, bay leaves, and beer. Transfer them to a suitable food-grade plastic bag and add the wings. 2. Seal the bag, and refrigerate them for 24 hours. 3. When the time is up, drain the wings then pat them dry. 4. Preheat the Traeger smoker to 275 degrees F/ 135 degrees C with the door closed. Ensure the drip tray is clean and in place. 5. Arrange the wood chips in the firebox, get a good smoke rolling, and close the door. 6. Arrange the wings on smoking trays, leaving space between each one. Top with additional jalapeño, and season with black pepper and salt. 7. Smoke them for 2 hours until the internal temperature reaches 165 degrees F/ 75 degrees C. Serve with lime wedges on the side.
Per Serving: Calories 285, Total Fat 9.8g, Sodium 639mg, Total Carbs 11.1g, Fiber 1.2g, Sugars 5.1g, Protein 27.8g

Lime Tequila–Marinated Chicken with Rice

Prep time: 55 minutes | Cook time: 40 minutes | Serves: 4

Extra-virgin olive oil	4 boneless chicken breast halves
Kosher salt, to taste	
For Marinade	
¼ cup gold tequila	2 teaspoons ancho chili powder
¼ cup lime juice	2 garlic cloves, smashed
1 tablespoon packed golden brown sugar	1 teaspoon ground cumin
2 teaspoons Dijon mustard	1 teaspoon black pepper
For Rice	
1 tablespoon unsalted butter	pepper
¼ cup chopped yellow onion	1½ cups long-grain white rice
1 garlic clove, minced	2¼ cups low-sodium chicken broth
1 teaspoon paprika	
1 teaspoon dried oregano	¼ cup sliced scallions, ends trimmed
¼ teaspoon ground cayenne	

1. Mix all the marinade ingredients, 1 tablespoon of oil, and 1 teaspoon of salt in a bowl. 2. Place the chicken breast halves in a resealable plastic bag, and pour in the prepared marinade. 3. Flip the bag to distribute the prepared marinade, place the bag in a bowl, and refrigerate the chicken breast halves for 4 to 8 hours. 4. Prepare the Traeger grill for direct cooking over medium heat (350 degrees F/ 175 degrees C to 450 degrees F/ 230 degrees C). 5. Heat the butter and 1 tablespoon of oil in a saucepan over medium heat; add the onion and the minced garlic, and sauté them for 3 minutes until the onion softens and turns golden brown; add the paprika, oregano, cayenne pepper, and 1 teaspoon of salt, and sauté them for 30 seconds or until fragrant; add the rice, and mix for 1 minute until coated with the oil; add the broth, and then bring to a boil. 6. Cover the saucepan, and reduce the heat to low, then simmer the food for 20 to 25 minutes until all of the liquid is absorbed. 7. Remove the pan from the heat, fluff the rice with a fork, and add the scallions. Cover and keep warm. 8. Remove the chicken breast halves from the marinade. 9. Close the lid after arranging the chicken breast halves on the grill grate, and then grill them for 12 minutes with the skin side up first, until the meat is firm to touch and no longer pink in the center, turning once after 7 to 9 minutes. 10. Remove the chicken breast halves from the hot grill and let them rest for 5 minutes, then serve them warm with the rice.

Per Serving: Calories 305; Total fat 15g; Sodium 548mg; Total Carbs 12g; Sugar 1.2g; Fiber 0.7g; Protein 29g

Honey–Lemon Glazed Chicken Thighs

Prep time: 20 minutes | Cook time: 45 minutes | Serves: 4

8 chicken thighs, each 5–6 ounces,	trimmed of excess fat and skin
For Glaze	
2 teaspoons extra-virgin olive oil	3 tablespoons lemon juice
3 garlic cloves, minced	2 teaspoons cornstarch
1 tablespoon peeled, grated ginger	2 teaspoons water
½ cup honey	1 teaspoon grated lemon zest
For Rub	
1 teaspoon dried marjoram	1 teaspoon salt
1 teaspoon dried basil	¾ teaspoon black pepper
1 teaspoon garlic powder	¼ teaspoon ground cinnamon

1. Prepare the Traeger grill for direct and indirect cooking over medium heat (350 degrees F/ 175 degrees C to 450 degrees F/ 230 degrees C). 2. Heat the oil in a saucepan over medium-high heat; add the minced garlic and the ginger, and sauté them for 2 minutes until they just start to brown; add the honey, and bring to a boil, then cook them for 2 minutes; add the lemon juice and cook for 1 minute; stir in cornstarch mixture, bring to a boil, and then cook for 1 minute until thickened; add the lemon zest. 3. The glaze will continue to thicken as it cools. 4. Mix all the rub ingredients, then evenly season the chicken thighs with the rub. 5. Cover the lid, and grill the chicken thighs for 10 minutes with the skin side down first, turning occasionally. 6. Move the chicken over indirect medium heat, rub with some of the glazes, and cook for 30 minutes more, flipping once halfway through and occasionally brushing with the remaining glaze. 7. Remove the chicken from the hot grill, and let rest for 5 minutes. Serve warm.

Per Serving: Calories 351; Total fat 22g; Sodium 502mg; Total Carbs 15.2g; Sugar 1.1g; Fiber 0.7g; Protein 26.4g

Juicy Spiced Chicken

Prep time: 30 minutes | Cook time: 60 minutes | Serves: 4

4 whole chicken legs, each 10-12 ounces, excess skin and fat	removed
	Extra-virgin olive oil
For Rub	
1½ teaspoons salt	1 teaspoon dried thyme
1 teaspoon black pepper	¼ teaspoon ground allspice
1 teaspoon granulated garlic	
For Sauce	
½ cup minced yellow onion	1 tablespoon packed golden brown sugar
2 garlic cloves, minced	
1 cup orange juice	1 tablespoon cider vinegar
1 cup ketchup	1 teaspoon Worcestershire sauce
2 canned chipotle chili peppers, minced	¼ teaspoon ground allspice

1. Prepare the Traeger grill for indirect and direct cooking over medium heat (350 degrees F/ 175 degrees C to 450 degrees F/ 230 degrees C). 2. Mix all the rub ingredients in a bowl. 3. Brush the chicken legs with oil on both sides, and evenly season them with the rub. 4. Heat 2 tablespoons of oil in a saucepan over medium heat; add the chopped onion and the minced garlic, and sauté them for 5 minutes until the onion is tender but not browned; add the remaining sauce ingredients and mix until smooth; cook on a simmer over medium heat for 7 minutes, occasionally stirring. Remove from the heat. 5. Arrange the chicken legs on the grill grate, and close the grill lid; grill the chicken legs with skin side up for 40 minutes, brushing once with the sauce after 30 minutes. 6. Rub the chicken legs with the sauce again and then move the chicken over direct medium heat, then resume cooking them for 10 minutes with the hood open, until the skin is well browned, flipping once cooked halfway through. 7. Remove the chicken legs from the hot grill and let rest for 3 to 5 minutes. 8. Serve the chicken warm with the remaining sauce.

Per Serving: Calories 354; Total fat 14.9g; Sodium 227mg; Total Carbs 14g; Fiber 1g; Sugars 1.4g; Protein 25.7g

Turkey Cutlets with Cranberry Relish

Prep time: 15 minutes | Cook time: 10 minutes | Serves: 4-6

8 turkey cutlets, each about 4	ounces and ¾ inch thick
For Marinade	
¼ cup extra-virgin olive oil	3 garlic cloves, chopped
1 tablespoon Dijon mustard	1 teaspoon kosher salt
1 tablespoon chopped rosemary leaves	¼ teaspoon freshly ground black pepper
For Relish	
2 cups or frozen cranberries	⅓ cup packed golden brown sugar
1 cup 100% cranberry juice (no sugar added)	¼ cup dried tart cherries, chopped
	¼ teaspoon kosher salt

1. Mix all the marinade ingredients in a bowl, then add the cutlets to this bowl and turn to coat. Cover the bowl and let it refrigerate for 1 to 4 hours. 2. Prepare the Traeger grill for direct cooking over 350 degrees F/ 175 degrees C. 3. In a suitable saucepan over high heat, Add the relish ingredients to a saucepan, and boil them over high heat. 4. Lower the heat to a simmer and cook for 4 to 6 minutes until the cranberries are soft, stirring and crushing the cranberries against the side of the saucepan often. 5. Remove this saucepan from the heat, then transfer the relish to a suitable bowl, and let cool to room temperature. 6. Grill the cutlets over direct medium heat, with the hood closed for 5 to 7 minutes, turning once after 3 to 4 minutes. Remove from the hot grill and serve warm with the relish.

Per Serving: Calories 312; Total fat 15g; Sodium 548mg; Total Carbs 12g; Sugar 1.2g; Fiber 0.7g; Protein 29g

Chapter 1 Poultry Recipes | 21

Spicy Chicken with Barbecue Sauce

Prep time: 20 minutes | Cook time: 50 minutes | Serves: 4

1 whole chicken, 4–5 pounds, spatch-cocked	2 tablespoons olive oil
For Sauce	
1¼ cups mayonnaise	1 teaspoon lemon juice
¼ cup cider vinegar	1 teaspoon black pepper
2 teaspoons prepared horseradish	¾ teaspoon kosher salt
2 teaspoons Dijon mustard	¼ teaspoon hot pepper sauce
2 teaspoons granulated sugar	
For Rub	
1 teaspoon prepared chili powder	1 teaspoon kosher salt
1 teaspoon garlic powder	¼ teaspoon ground cayenne pepper
1 teaspoon ground cumin	

1. Prepare the Traeger grill for indirect cooking over high heat (450 degrees F/ 230 degrees C to 550 degrees F/ 290 degrees C). 2. Mix all of the sauce ingredients in a bowl, then cover the bowl and let the sauce refrigerate until ready to serve. 3. Mix all the rub ingredients in another bowl. 4. Brush the chicken with oil on both sides, and evenly season it with the rub. 5. Place the chicken on the grill grate with skin side down, and put two foil-wrapped bricks on top of the chicken; close the grill lid, and grill the chicken for 20 to 25 minutes until golden around the edges. 6. Remove the bricks, and carefully turn the chicken over, then replace the bricks on it and resume grilling it for 20 to 25 minutes until the juices run clear and it has an internal temperature of 160 degrees F/ 70 degrees C. 7. When grilled, let the chicken stand for 10 to 15 minutes. 8. Slice the chicken and serve warm with the sauce.

Per Serving: Calories 272, Total Fat 19g, Sodium 389mg, Total Carbs 10.4g, Fiber 0.7g, Sugars 1.1g, Protein 15.6g

Homemade Smoked Beer Chicken

Prep time: 15 minutes | Cook time: 1 hour 30 minutes | Serves: 4

1 whole chicken, neck, giblets removed	1 tablespoon extra-virgin olive oil
2 tablespoons kosher salt	1 can (12 ounces) of beer
For Rub	
2 teaspoons granulated onion	sugar
2 teaspoons paprika	½ teaspoon black pepper
1 teaspoon packed golden brown	

1. Soak the wood chips in the water for at least 30 minutes. 2. On the chicken's meaty sections and into the cavity, liberally sprinkle salt (but not on the back). Then, cover it with plastic wrap and refrigerate it for 2 hours. 3. When the time is up, rinse the chicken with cold water to remove the salt, and pat it dry with paper towels; brush it with oil, and season it all over with the rub, including inside. Fold the wing tips behind its back. 4. Mix all the rub ingredients in a bowl. 5. Pour about ⅔ beer, and then make two more holes in the top of the beer can; place the can on a solid surface, and lower the chicken cavity over the can. 6. Drain and add two handfuls of wood chips to the charcoal, and close the lid. 7. When the smoke appears, place the chicken-on-a-can on the grill grate, balancing it on its two legs and the can like a tripod. 8. Grill the chicken for 1¼ to 1½ hours until the juices run clear and the thickest part reaches an internal temperature of 160 degrees F/ 70 degrees C to 165 degrees F/ 75 degrees C; after 15 minutes of grilling time, drain and add the remaining wood chips to the charcoal. 9. Let the chicken stand for 10 to 15 minutes after grilling, then lift it from the beer can and carve it into serving pieces. Serve warm.

Per Serving: Calories 285, Total Fat 9.8g, Sodium 639mg, Total Carbs 11.1g, Fiber 1.2g, Sugars 5.1g, Protein 27.8g

Lager-Brined Turkey with Beer Gravy

Prep time: 25 minutes | Cook time: 3 hours | Serves: 4

1 whole turkey, 12-14 pounds, thawed if frozen	4 sprigs of thyme
4 yellow onions, about 1¾ pounds total, chopped	3 tablespoons unsalted butter, melted
	1-quart low-sodium chicken broth
For Brine	
4 bottles (12 ounces) lager	black peppercorns
1 cup packed golden brown sugar	1 tablespoon granulated garlic
¾ cup kosher salt	1 tablespoon granulated onion
3 tablespoons smoked paprika	½ teaspoon ground cayenne pepper
1½ tablespoons dried thyme	
1 tablespoon coarsely cracked	3 quarts of ice water
For Gravy	
Low-sodium chicken broth, as needed	½ cup lager
Melted and unsalted butter, as needed	1 teaspoon chopped fresh thyme leaves
	Kosher salt
½ cup all-purpose flour	Freshly ground black pepper

To make the turkey: 1. Mix all of the brine recipe ingredients except the ice water in a bowl, until the salt and sugar are dissolved. Add the ice water. 2. Remove the neck, giblets, and lumps of fat from the turkey, and set aside (discard the liver) in a bowl; cover the bowl and refrigerate them until ready to grill. 3. Place the turkey in a sturdy plastic bag, and put the bag in a 10-quart or larger stockpot; pour the brine to the bag to cover the turkey as much as possible when the bag is closed and tightly tied, discard any extra brine. 4. Seal the bag and refrigerate the turkey for at least 12 hours or up to 14 hours. When refrigerated, rinse the turkey under cold water and pat it dry with paper towels, including inside. 5. Add ⅓ of the chopped onions and all of the thyme sprigs to the turkey cavity; tuck the wing tips behind the back, and loosely tie the drumsticks together, then brush it all over with the melted butter. 6. Arrange one large disposable foil pan on a suitable roasting pan to create a single pan of double thickness; add the remaining onions and place the turkey on the top of the onions with the breast side down. Let the turkey stand at room temperature for 1 hour. 7. Soak the wood chips in water for at least 30 minutes. 8. Prepare the grill for indirect cooking over 350 degrees F/ 175 degrees C. 9. Place the reserved neck, giblets, and lumps of fat in the pan, and pour in the chicken broth. 10. Drain and add two handfuls of wood chips to the charcoal, and close the lid. When the wood begins to smoke, place the pan on the grill grate, and close the lid. 11. Grill the food for 1 hour; when the time is up, turn the turkey over so that the breast faces up; drain and add two handfuls of wood chips to the charcoal, then grill the turkey for 45 minutes more; drain and add two handfuls of wood chips to the charcoal and resume grilling for 45 minutes until the thickest part of the thigh reaches an internal temperature of 170 degrees F/ 75 degrees C. 12. After grilling, remove the pan from the grill; tilt the turkey so the juices run out of it cavity and into the pan. Transfer the turkey to a cutting board and let stand for 20 to 30 minutes. Save the pan juices to make the gravy.

To make the gravy: 1. Strain the pan juices into gravy separator, and let stand for 3 minutes until fat rises to surface. 2. Pour the pan juices into a 1-quart measuring cup, reserving the fat. Add the chicken broth to the 1-quart measuring cup so that you have 1 quart of liquid if necessary. 3. Measure the reserved fat, you can add melted butter to make ½ cup if necessary. Heat the fat (and butter) in a medium saucepan over medium heat; whisk in the flour, and let it bubble for 1 minute, stirring constantly; whisk in the pan juices and lager, then bring the gravy to a simmer, whisking frequently. 4. Reduce the heat to medium-low, stir in the thyme, and simmer the gravy for 3 to 5 minutes until slightly thickened. 5. Turn off the heat, and season with the salt and pepper if necessary. 6. Carve the turkey and serve the meat with the warm gravy.

Per Serving: Calories 336, Total Fat 17.3g, Sodium 281mg, Total Carbs 8.1g, Fiber 5.3g, Sugars 17.7g, Protein 32.3g

Turkey Cheeseburgers
Prep time: 15 minutes | Cook time: 12 minutes | Serves: 4

¼ cup mayonnaise	each about ¼ inch thick (about 4 ounces)
2 teaspoons grated lemon zest	4 ciabatta rolls, split
Extra-virgin olive oil	1 cup baby arugula
4 slices of mozzarella cheese,	
For Patties	
10 sun-dried tomato halves packed in oil, drained	meat
10 basil leaves	¾ teaspoon salt
1 ½ pounds of ground turkey thigh	½ teaspoon dried oregano
	¼ teaspoon black pepper

1. Prepare the Traeger grill for direct cooking over medium heat (350 degrees F/ 175 degrees C to 450 degrees F/ 230 degrees C). 2. Chop the sun-dried tomatoes and basil together as possible to make a paste (you should have about ¾ cup). Gently mix the remaining patty ingredients with the paste. Form four evenly sized, patties that are each about ¾-inch thick using damp hands. The prepared patties won't be tender if the meat is overly compacted. 3. Make a small indentation at the center of each patty that is about 1 inch broad with your thumb. 4. Mix the mayonnaise and the lemon zest, and set aside. 5. Oil the prepared patties just a little bit on each side. The prepared patties should be grilled for 10 minutes with the lid closed, rotating once they release from the grate easily and without sticking. 6. Throughout the final 2 minutes of grilling, top each patty with a slice of cheese to melt, and toast the rolls over direct heat. Remove from the hot grill and build the burgers with arugula and lemon mayonnaise. 7. Serve warm.
Per Serving: Calories 249; Total fat 13g; Sodium 556mg; Total Carbs 10g; Sugar 1.1g; Fiber 0.7g; Protein 31g

Garlicky Buttermilk–Brined Chicken
Prep time: 20 minutes | Cook time: 2 hours | Serves: 4

1 whole chicken, 5 ½–6 pounds, neck, giblets, wing tips, and excess fat removed	2 tablespoons extra-virgin olive oil
Brine	
1½ quarts buttermilk	6 garlic cloves, minced
1 medium yellow onion, chopped	1 tablespoon ground coriander
¼ cup kosher salt	½ teaspoon ground cayenne pepper
¼ cup granulated sugar	
2 tablespoons hot pepper sauce	

1. Mix all of the brine ingredients in a suitable nonreactive pot; submerge the chicken in the brine with breast side down, and then refrigerate them for 8 to 24 hours. 2. Prepare the Traeger grill for indirect cooking over medium heat (350 degrees F/ 175 degrees C to 450 degrees F/ 230 degrees C). 3. Remove the chicken from the pot and discard the brine. Pat the soaked chicken dry with paper towels and tie the drumsticks together with butcher's twine. 4. Arrange the chicken on disposable foil pan and drizzle with the oil, then place the pan on the grill grate. 5. Close the grill lid, and grill the chicken for 1¾ to 2 hours, baste the chicken with its juices and rotate the pan occasionally. 6. Let the chicken rest for 15 minutes after grilling. 7. Cut the chicken into serving pieces. Serve warm.
Per Serving: Calories 285, Total Fat 9.8g, Sodium 639mg, Total Carbs 11.1g, Fiber 1.2g, Sugars 5.1g, Protein 27.8g

Cumin Duck Breasts with Orange Sauce
Prep time: 20 minutes | Cook time: 18 minutes | Serves: 4

4 boneless duck breast halves, (6 ounces each), skin removed,	patted dry
	Extra-virgin olive oil
For Spice Rub	
2 teaspoons ground cumin	1 teaspoon salt
1 teaspoon ground coriander	1 teaspoon black pepper
1 teaspoon ground cardamom	
For Sauce	
1 cup orange juice	1 teaspoon salt
¼ cup balsamic vinegar	½ teaspoon ground cardamom
1 tablespoon packed golden brown sugar	⅛ teaspoon black pepper
1 teaspoon ground cumin	2 teaspoons cornstarch dissolved in 1 tablespoon orange juice

1. Mix all the rub ingredients. 2. Lightly brush the duck breasts with oil on both sides, and evenly season them with the rub. 3. Prepare the Traeger grill for direct cooking over medium heat (350 degrees F/ 175 degrees C to 450 degrees F/ 230 degrees C). 4. Add the orange juice, vinegar, brown sugar, cumin, salt, cardamom, and pepper to the saucepan, bring to a boil over medium-high heat and cook for 10 minutes until the liquid is reduced by one-third, stirring regularly. 5. Reduce the heat to medium, and mix in the cornstarch mixture. Bring the sauce back to a simmer and cook on a simmer for 1 minute until the sauce thickens slightly, stirring constantly. Remove from the heat. 6. Grill the duck breasts for about 8 minutes for medium rare, turning once. Remove from the hot grill and let rest for 5 minutes. Meanwhile, rewarm the sauce over low heat. 7. Cut the duck breasts crosswise into ⅓-inch slices. Serve the duck warm with the sauce.
Per Serving: Calories 354; Total fat 14.9g; Sodium 227mg; Total Carbs 14g; Fiber 1g; Sugars 1.4g; Protein 25.7g

Delicious Turkey Tacos
Prep time: 30 minutes | Cook time: 4 hours | Serves: 4

For Turkey	
1 cup cilantro leaves, chopped more for garnish	1 tablespoon toasted sesame oil
3 garlic cloves, minced	1 teaspoon ground coriander
1 jalapeño pepper, trimmed, seeded, and diced	1 teaspoon freshly ground black pepper
¼ cup packed dark brown sugar	1 (4- to 6-pound) bone-in & skin-on turkey breast
3 tablespoons canola oil	Flaked sea salt
3 tablespoons soy sauce	Freshly ground black pepper
For Pickled Slaw	
1 red onion, sliced	1 carrot, trimmed and sliced with a vegetable peeler
1 cup apple cider vinegar	
4 cups sliced Savoy cabbage	1 cup cilantro leaves
4 scallions, trimmed and sliced on a sharp angle	Flaked sea salt
	Freshly ground black pepper
For Tacos	
12 flour tortillas	and cut into slices
2 avocados, peeled, halved, pitted,	

1. Mix the cilantro, garlic, jalapeño, sugar, canola oil, soy sauce, sesame oil, coriander, and pepper in a bowl. 2. Add the turkey breast to the prepared marinade and massage the prepared marinade into the turkey. 3. Cover this bowl with plastic sheet and refrigerate the turkey for at least 4 hours, or overnight for best results, turning the turkey occasionally. 4. Preheat the Traeger smoker to 275 degrees F/ 135 degrees C with the door closed. Ensure the drip tray is clean and in place. 5. Set the wood chips in the firebox, get a good smoke rolling, and seal the door. 6. Remove the turkey from the prepared marinade, reserving the prepared marinade in the refrigerator. Season the turkey with black pepper and salt. 7. Arrange the turkey breast on a smoking tray. Smoke the turkey for 2 hours. 8. Remove the turkey from the smoker, loosely tent it with aluminum foil, and allow it to rest for 10 minutes. 9. Slice the turkey across the grain (across the width rather than the length). 10. In a suitable saucepan, mix the red onion and vinegar. Set the pan in the smoker and then cook for 30 minutes until tender. Remove. 11. Mix the cabbage, scallions, carrot, cilantro, black pepper, and salt in a separate bowl. 12. Add the warm pickled red onion and liquid to the slaw. Toss until evenly mixed. 13. Cook the reserved marinade in the saucepan over medium heat for 15 minutes until reduced to a rich sauce. 14. Arrange the tortillas on the smoking racks, spaced evenly apart. Smoke them for 5 minutes to warm. 15. Build tacos on the warmed tortillas with layers of slaw, avocado, and turkey, topped with the prepared marinade sauce. Enjoy.
Per Serving: Calories 336, Total Fat 17.3g, Sodium 281mg, Total Carbs 8.1g, Fiber 5.3g, Sugars 17.7g, Protein 32.3g

Duck Breast and Greens Salad

Prep time: 15 minutes | Cook time: 8 minutes | Serves: 4

4 boneless duck breast halves (with skin), (6 ounces each), patted dry	4 cups mixed baby greens
1 teaspoon Chinese five spice	3 scallions, sliced
1 teaspoon salt	12 ounces of raspberries
Dressing	½ cup slivered almonds, preferably toasted
⅔ cup vegetable oil	sauce
¼ cup rice vinegar	1 tablespoon peeled, minced ginger
2 tablespoons toasted sesame oil	1 tablespoon sesame seeds
2 tablespoons water	1 garlic clove, roughly chopped
1 tablespoon 1 teaspoon hoisin	

1. Prepare the Traeger grill for direct cooking over medium heat (350 degrees F/ 175 degrees C to 450 degrees F/ 230 degrees C). 2. Each duck breast's skin should be scored diagonally in a crisscross pattern, and equally use the salt and Chinese five spice. 3. Blend the prepared dressing components in a blender until completely smooth. 4. Close the lid, and grill the duck breasts for 8 minutes (medium rare) with skin side down first, flipping once, or until the skin is browned and the flesh is cooked to your chosen doneness (if flare-ups occur, move the breasts temporarily over indirect heat). Take the food off the hot grill and give it 5 minutes to rest. 5. Slice the meat into ⅓-inch thick crosswise pieces. 6. Combine the mixed greens, scallions, raspberries, and almonds in a bowl, and toss with ½ cup of the prepared dressing. Distribute the duck and salad equally among the four dishes. 7. Serve alongside the leftover dressing.

Per Serving: Calories 336, Total Fat 17.3g, Sodium 281mg, Total Carbs 8.1g, Fiber 5.3g, Sugars 17.7g, Protein 32.3g

Spiced Orange Chicken

Prep time: 15 minutes | Cook time: 2 hours | Serves: 4

For Poultry Spice Rub	
4 teaspoons paprika	2 teaspoons salt
1 tablespoon chili powder	2 teaspoons garlic powder
2 teaspoons ground cumin	1 teaspoon black pepper
2 teaspoons dried thyme	
For Prepared Marinade	
4 chicken quarters	½ cup soy sauce
2 cups frozen orange-juice concentrate	1 tablespoon garlic powder

1. In a suitable bowl, mix together the paprika, chili powder, cumin, thyme, salt, garlic powder, and pepper. Set aside. 2. Set the chicken quarters in a dish that will accommodate the prepared marinade and chicken. 3. In a suitable bowl, mix the orange-juice concentrate (do not add water), soy sauce, garlic powder, and half the spice-rub mixture. Pour the prepared marinade over the chicken, cover the dish, and let it refrigerate for a minimum of 8 hours. 4. Preheat the Traeger smoker with the apple wood to a stabilized 275 degrees F/ 135 degrees C. 5. Discard the prepared marinade and rub all surfaces of the chicken generously with the remaining spice rub. Set the chicken quarters in the smoker for 1½ to 2 hours until they have an internal temperature of 165 degrees F/ 75 degrees C. 6. Let the dish rest for 10 minutes before serving.

Per Serving: Calories 272, Total Fat 19g, Sodium 389mg, Total Carbs 10.4g, Fiber 0.7g, Sugars 1.1g, Protein 15.6g

Delicious Barbecue Chicken

Prep time: 30 minutes | Cook time: 2 hours | Serves: 3-4

1 cup sriracha	¼ cup brown sugar
½ cup (1 stick) butter	¼ cup prepared yellow mustard
½ cup molasses	1 teaspoon salt
½ cup ketchup	1 teaspoon black pepper
1 whole chicken, cut up	leaves
½ teaspoon chopped parsley	

1. Close the lid, and preheat your Traeger Smoker at 250 degrees F/ 120 degrees C with the cherry wood. 2. Cook the sriracha, butter, molasses, ketchup, brown sugar, mustard, salt, and pepper in the saucepan over low heat until the sugar and salt dissolve. Set aside. 3. Divide the sauce into two portions. Rub the chicken with half the sauce and reserve the remaining sauce to serve with the meat. 4. Divide the sauce before basting the chicken and discard any remaining sauce used to baste the chicken, to eliminate cross-contamination. 5. Arrange the chicken on the smoker's rack and smoke for 1½ to 2 hours until it has an internal temperature of 165 degrees F/ 75 degrees C. 6. Sprinkle the chicken with parsley and serve with the reserved barbecue sauce.

Per Serving: Calories 305; Total fat 15g; Sodium 548mg; Total Carbs 12g; Sugar 1.2g; Fiber 0.7g; Protein 29g

Smoked Dijon Turkey Breast

Prep time: 20 minutes | Cook time: 4 hours | Serves: 4-5

4 tablespoons unsalted butter	1 teaspoon black pepper
8 teaspoons Dijon mustard	½ teaspoon salt
2 tablespoons chopped thyme leaves	1 (6- to 7-pound) bone-in turkey breast

1. Mix the butter, mustard, thyme, ¼ teaspoon of black pepper, and salt in a bowl, then add the turkey breast, and rub it with the butter mixture. Cover the bowl and refrigerate it overnight. 2. Close the lid, and preheat your Traeger Smoker at 250 degrees F/ 120 degrees C with the apple wood. 3. Sprinkle the turkey breast with the remaining ¾ teaspoon of pepper and place it on the smoker rack. 4. Cover the grill and cook for 4 hours (about 30 minutes per pound). 5. When a thermometer registers 165 degrees F/ 75 degrees C, remove the turkey from the smoker. 6. Let the dish cool for 10 to 15 minutes before serving.

Per Serving: Calories 336, Total Fat 17.3g, Sodium 281mg, Total Carbs 8.1g, Fiber 5.3g, Sugars 17.7g, Protein 32.3g

Classic Jamaican Jerk Chicken

Prep time: 15 minutes | Cook time: 1 hour 30 minutes | Serves: 4

4 chicken leg quarters, scored	smoking
¼ cup canola oil	2 tablespoons salt
¼ cup cane syrup	2 teaspoons freshly ground black pepper
8 whole cloves	
6 habanero peppers, sliced	2 teaspoons ground cinnamon
1 scallion, white and green parts, chopped	1 teaspoon cayenne pepper
	1 teaspoon dried thyme
2 tablespoons whole allspice (pimento) berries more for	1 teaspoon ground cumin

1. Preheat the Traeger smoker to 275 degrees F/ 135 degrees C with the mesquite wood. Throw in a handful of whole allspice (pimento) berries with the mesquite. 2. Coat the chicken leg quarters with the canola oil. 3. Add the cane syrup, cloves, habaneros, scallion, allspice, salt, pepper, cinnamon, cayenne, thyme, and cumin to the food processor, and then pulse them until smooth and sticky. 4. Reserve 2 tablespoons of the prepared mixture. Rub the chicken leg quarters with the remaining mixture, on and under the skin. 5. Smoke the chicken leg quarters for 1½ hours until they have an internal temperature of 165 degrees F/ 75 degrees C. 6. Baste the chicken leg quarters with the reserved jerk seasoning before serving.

Per Serving: Calories 249; Total fat 13g; Sodium 556mg; Total Carbs 10g; Sugar 1.1g; Fiber 0.7g; Protein 31g

24 | Chapter 1 Poultry Recipes

Cinnamon Smoked Chicken

Prep time: 15 minutes | Cook time: 1 hour 30 minutes | Serves: 4

1-quart water	1 lemon, sliced
¼ cup salt	2 cinnamon sticks, halved
¼ cup brown sugar	1 tablespoon ground cinnamon
4 chicken breasts	1 tablespoon red pepper flakes
1 onion, sliced	1 tablespoon seasoned salt

1. Stir the water, salt, and brown sugar in a bowl until dissolved; add the chicken breasts, onion, lemon, and cinnamon sticks, then cover the bowl with plastic sheet and refrigerate them for 1 hour. 2. At 250 degrees F/ 120 degrees C, preheat your Traeger Smoker with the apple or cherry wood. 3. Remove the chicken breasts from the refrigerator. 4. Sprinkle the chicken breasts with cinnamon, red pepper flakes, and seasoned salt; smoke them for 1½ hours until they have an internal temperature of 165 degrees F/ 75 degrees C. 5. Serve warm.

Per Serving: Calories 272, Total Fat 19g, Sodium 389mg, Total Carbs 10.4g, Fiber 0.7g, Sugars 1.1g, Protein 15.6g

Smoky Turkey and Apples

Prep time: 40 minutes | Cook time: 4 to 5 hours | Serves: 6-8

For Brine

2 gallons of cold water	¼ cup black pepper
1½ cups salt	2 tablespoons ground allspice
1¼ cups brown sugar	

For Turkey

1 (10-pound) whole turkey, neck, giblets, and gizzard removed and discarded	1 onion, quartered
⅓ cup vegetable oil	1 tablespoon dried thyme
1 Granny Smith apple, quartered	½ cup (1 stick) butter, melted
	3 tablespoons dried rosemary, divided

1. Mix the turkey with water, salt, brown sugar, pepper, and allspice in a large container until dissolved. 2. Fully immerse the turkey in the brine, cover the container, and refrigerate them overnight. 3. At 250 degrees F/ 120 degrees C, preheat your Traeger Smoker with the apple wood. 4. Remove the bird from the brine, drain it well. 5. Fold the wingtips behind the back of the bird and tie the legs together with kitchen wire. 6. Coat the turkey all over with the oil and stuff both the main cavity and the neck with the apple, onion, and thyme. Arrange the turkey directly on the smoker rack, and smoke for 3 hours with breast-side up. 7. Mix the melted butter and rosemary in a bowl. 8. After smoking, coat the turkey breast with the rosemary butter, then continue to smoke for 2 hours more until it has internal temperature of 165 degrees F/ 75 degrees C (try not to open the smoker any more than you have to as it adds 15 to 20 minutes of cook time etyma you do). 9. Let the turkey rest for 20 minutes before carving.

Per Serving: Calories 285, Total Fat 9.8g, Sodium 639mg, Total Carbs 11.1g, Fiber 1.2g, Sugars 5.1g, Protein 27.8g

Hot Caramel Chicken Breasts

Prep time: 15 minutes | Cook time: 2 hours 15 minutes | Serves: 4-6

1 onion, sliced	chicken breasts
2 tablespoons butter	1 (5-ounce) bottle Frank's Red-hot sauce
½ cup plus 1 tablespoon olive oil, divided	Salt
1 cup honey	Freshly ground black pepper
4 to 6 boneless and skinless	

1. Add the onion, butter, and 1 tablespoon of olive oil to a saucepan, sauté the onion over medium-low heat for 15 minutes until caramelized; add the honey and set the sauce aside. 2. At 250 degrees F/ 120 degrees C, preheat the Traeger Smoker with cherry or pecan wood. 3. Coat the chicken breasts with the remaining olive oil, and generously cover them with some hot sauce, then season them with black pepper and salt. 4. Set the chicken directly on the smoker rack. Smoke for 1 hour, baste with additional hot sauce and some caramelized onion and return the chicken to the smoker rack. 5. Total cook time is 1½ to 2 hours, depending on how often you open the smoker lid. Use an instant-read meat thermometer to check for an internal temperature of 165 degrees F/ 75 degrees C. 6. Remove the cooked chicken from the smoker and let it stand for 15 minutes. Baste the dish with the remaining caramelized onion again before serving.

Per Serving: Calories 342; Total fat 14.9g; Sodium 227mg; Total Carbs 14g; Fiber 1g; Sugars 1.4g; Protein 25.7g

Plum Chicken Drumsticks

Prep time: 35 minutes | Cook time: 2 hours | Serves: 12

12 chicken drumsticks	pepper
2 teaspoons salt	Plum Sauce
2 teaspoons freshly ground black	

1. At 250 degrees F/ 120 degrees C, preheat your Traeger Smoker with the cherry wood. 2. Stretch the skin away from the drumsticks as much as possible, and remove the tendons from each leg. 3. Sprinkle each drumstick with black pepper and salt. 4. Arrange the prepared chicken on the smoker rack, and smoke for 1½ hours. 5. Lather the pops in plum sauce and re-place them to the smoker for 30 minutes more until the internal temperature is just less than 165 degrees F/ 75 degrees C. 6. Coat the meat in additional plum sauce to serve.

Per Serving: Calories 336, Total Fat 17.3g, Sodium 281mg, Total Carbs 8.1g, Fiber 5.3g, Sugars 17.7g, Protein 32.3g

Hearty Smoked Chicken Cacciatore

Prep time: 30 minutes | Cook time: 4 hours | Serves: 4

2 chickens, whole, separated into breasts, thighs, legs, and wings	and quartered
All-purpose flour, for dusting	8 garlic cloves, sliced
Flaked sea salt	2 tablespoons tomato paste
Freshly ground black pepper	1 cup white wine
2 tablespoons olive oil	4 Roma tomatoes, quartered and diced
1 yellow onion, sliced	2 rosemary sprigs, leaves stripped and chopped
1 green bell pepper, trimmed, seeded, and sliced	2 oregano sprigs, leaves stripped and chopped
1 red bell pepper, trimmed, seeded, and sliced	1 cup chicken (or vegetable) stock
12 white mushrooms, stemmed,	

1. Preheat the Traeger smoker to 275 degrees F/ 135 degrees C with the door closed. Ensure the drip tray is clean and in place. 2. Set the wood chips in the smoking tray or firebox, get a good smoke rolling, and seal the door. 3. Dust the chickens with flour and season them with black pepper and salt. Arrange them on smoking trays, leaving space between each piece. 4. Smoke the chickens for 2 hours until they have an internal temperature of 165 degrees F/ 75 degrees C. 5. In a suitable cast iron casserole, gently stir together the olive oil, onion, green and red bell peppers, mushrooms, and garlic; season them with black pepper and salt. Add the tomato paste. Set the casserole on a smoking tray. 6. Smoke the vegetables for 1 hour, until tender. 7. Add the white wine to deglaze the casserole, scraping up any browned bits from the bottom. 8. Add the tomatoes, rosemary, oregano, and chicken stock to the casserole. Stir to mix. 9. Nestle the smoked chicken into the casserole and return it to the smoker. Smoke uncovered for 1 hour, or until tender and the sauce is reduced to a velvety consistency.

Per Serving: Calories 254; Total fat 28g; Sodium 346mg; Total Carbs 12.3g; Sugar 1g; Fiber 0.7g; Protein 24.3g

Sweet Lemon–Thyme Chicken

Prep time: 15 minutes | Cook time: 2 hours 15 minutes | Serves: 4

4 boneless & skinless chicken breasts	Juice of 2 lemons
2 tablespoons olive oil	2 lemons, halved, for serving
Flaked sea salt	4 thyme sprigs, leaves stripped and chopped more for garnish
Freshly ground black pepper	¼ cup clover honey
Grated zest of 2 lemons	

1. Preheat the Traeger smoker to 275 degrees F/ 135 degrees C. Ensure the drip tray is clean and in place. Seal the door. 2. Set the wood chips in the smoking tray or firebox, get a good smoke rolling, and seal the door. 3. Rub the chicken with olive oil. 4. Season the chicken breasts with salt, pepper, lemon zest, and thyme. Arrange the chicken on smoking trays with breast-side up, leaving space between each piece. 5. Smoke the chicken breasts for 2 hours until they have an internal temperature of 165 degrees F/ 75 degrees C. 6. Squeeze the juice of the zested lemons over the chicken breasts and drizzle with the honey. Smoke them for 15 minutes more. 7. Garnish the dish with thyme, and serve with additional lemon halves for squeezing.
Per Serving: Calories 285, Total Fat 9.8g, Sodium 639mg, Total Carbs 11.1g, Fiber 1.2g, Sugars 5.1g, Protein 27.8g

Smoked Chicken Gumbo with Rice

Prep time: 40 minutes | Cook time: 4 hours | Serves: 6-8

For Rice

1 tablespoon unsalted butter	1 tablespoon thyme leaves, stripped and chopped
1 tablespoon olive oil	1 bay leaf
1 cup chopped yellow onions	4 cups chicken (or vegetable) stock
Flaked sea salt	
Freshly ground black pepper	
2 cups long-grain white rice	

For Gumbo

½ cup canola oil	1 green bell pepper, trimmed, seeded, and diced
3 pounds bone-in skin-on chicken thighs	1-quart chicken (or vegetable) stock
Flaked sea salt	12 okras, cut into ½-inch slices
Freshly ground black pepper	6 Roma tomatoes, cored, quartered, and diced
8 ounces andouille sausage, sliced	
6 thick-cut smoked bacon slices	1 tablespoon thyme leaves
1 cup all-purpose flour	3 fresh or dried bay leaves
6 garlic cloves, chopped	Hot sauce, for serving
1 cup chopped yellow onion	
1 cup chopped celery heart	

1. Add the butter, olive oil, onion, black pepper, and salt to a saucepan, and sauté them over medium-high heat for 10 minutes until the onion is golden brown; add the rice, thyme, and bay leaf, stirring to coat the rice in the butter and oil; gently stir in the chicken stock, cover the pan, reduce the heat to low, and then cook them for 45 to 60 minutes until the liquid is absorbed. 2. Preheat the Traeger smoker to 275 degrees F/ 135 degrees C with the door closed. Ensure the drip tray is clean and in place. 3. Set the wood chips in the smoking tray or firebox, get a good smoke rolling, and seal the door. 4. Place a suitable cast iron casserole or deep roasting pan on a smoking rack to preheat and pour in the canola oil. 5. Pat the chicken thighs dry with a paper towel, and season them with salt and pepper on both sides. Arrange the chicken on smoking trays with skin-side up, leaving space between each piece. 6. Smoke the chicken thighs for 2 hours until they have an internal temperature of 165 degrees F/ 75 degrees C. 7. Add the sausage and bacon to the preheated casserole. Cook them for 45 minutes, or until browned and the fat renders, turning the casserole 2 or 3 times. 8. Add the flour, creating a roux; add the minced garlic, onion, celery, and green pepper. Cook for 20 minutes, until tender. 9. Add the chicken stock to deglaze this pan, scraping up any browned bits from the bottom. Add the okra, tomatoes, thyme, and bay leaves. Stir to incorporate. 10. When the chicken thighs are fully cooked, nestle it into the casserole on top of the other ingredients. Smoke for 1 hour more, or until the okra is tender and the liquid has reduced to your desired consistency. 11. Remove the chicken thighs from the gumbo. Debone the chicken. Remove and discard the skin. Shred the meat into bite-size pieces and flip the chicken to the gumbo. Season them with black pepper and salt. 12. Serve the dish with rice and Southern hot sauce.
Per Serving: Calories 336, Total Fat 17.3g, Sodium 281mg, Total Carbs 8.1g, Fiber 5.3g, Sugars 17.7g, Protein 32.3g

Best Smoked Chicken Marbella

Prep time: 40 minutes | Cook time: 4 hours | Serves: 6-8

½ cup red wine vinegar	separated into breasts, legs, thighs, and wings
¼ cup olive oil	Flaked sea salt
1 cup dried pitted prunes	Freshly ground black pepper
½ cup capers	2 cups sauvignon blank or Riesling
½ cup pitted green olives	
6 garlic cloves, minced	½ cup packed light brown sugar
¼ cup oregano leaves, chopped	¼ cup flat-leaf parsley leaves, freshly chopped
3 or dried bay leaves	
2 (3- to 4-pound) chickens, whole,	

1. Mix the vinegar, olive oil, prunes, capers, olives, garlic, oregano, and bay leaves in a large bowl, then add the chickens and turn to coat. 2. Cover this bowl with plastic sheet and let it refrigerate for 24 hours, turning the chickens 2 or 3 times. 3. Preheat the Traeger smoker to 275 degrees F/ 135 degrees C. Ensure the drip tray is clean and in place. Seal the door. 4. Set the wood chips in the smoking tray or firebox, get a good smoke rolling, and seal the door. 5. Place a suitable roasting pan on the smoking rack to preheat. 6. Strain the chickens and pat them dry, then season them with salt and black pepper. Reserve the prepared marinade in the refrigerator. 7. Arrange the chickens on smoking trays, skin-side up, leaving space between each piece. 8. Smoke them for 2 hours until they have an internal temperature of 165 degrees F/ 75 degrees C. 9. Arrange the prepared chicken in a single layer in the roasting pan and coat it evenly with the reserved marinade. 10. Pour in the white wine and drizzle sugar over the chickens, then smoker them for 60 to 90 minutes more, basting it occasionally, until the sauce reaches the desired consistency. 11. Top the dish with parsley, the prune and olive pan sauce, remove and discard the bay leaves. Enjoy.
Per Serving: Calories 484; Total fat 14.9g; Sodium 227mg; Total Carbs 14g; Fiber 1g; Sugars 1.4g; Protein 25.7g

Smoked Garlic–Thyme Whole Chicken

Prep time: 15 minutes | Cook time: 2 hours | Serves: 12

1-quart apple cider	1 lemon, sliced
4 garlic cloves, crushed	2 chickens, whole, spatchcocked
4 thyme sprigs	Flaked sea salt
3 or dried bay leaves	Freshly ground black pepper

1. In a food-grade plastic bag, mix the cider, garlic, thyme, bay leaves, and lemon slices. Add the chickens, turn to coat, and remove as much air as possible from the bag before sealing it. 2. Refrigerate the chickens for 12 to 24 hours, turning the chickens occasionally. 3. Preheat the Traeger smoker to 275 degrees F/ 135 degrees C with the door closed. Ensure the drip tray is clean and in place. 4. Set the wood chips in the smoking tray or firebox, get a good smoke rolling, and seal the door. 5. Strain the chickens, reserving the brine, then pat the chickens dry. Strain the brine. Using an injection needle, inject the chickens with all the brining liquid. Space your injections evenly around the chicken. 6. Season the chickens with black pepper and salt, then place them on a smoking rack with the skin-side up. 7. Smoke the chickens for 2 hours until they have an internal temperature of 165 degrees F/ 75 degrees C. 8. Transfer the chickens to a cutting board, loosely tent them with aluminum foil, and let them rest for 10 minutes. Enjoy.
Per Serving: Calories 272, Total Fat 19g, Sodium 389mg, Total Carbs 10.4g, Fiber 0.7g, Sugars 1.1g, Protein 15.6g

Citrus Duck with Blue Plums

Prep time: 30 minutes | Cook time: 4 hours | Serves: 4

2 tablespoons canola oil	8 shallots, halved
1 duck, whole	4-star anise, whole
Flaked sea salt	4 cloves, whole
Freshly ground black pepper	2 cinnamon sticks, whole
4 mandarin oranges, halved	1 (750-mL) bottle Sauvignon
8 thyme sprigs	Blanc
8 blue plums, halved and pitted	

1. Preheat the Traeger smoker to 275 degrees F/ 135 degrees C with the door closed. Ensure the drip tray is clean and in place. 2. Coat a roasting pan with canola oil. Set aside. 3. Set the wood chips in the smoking tray or firebox, get a good smoke rolling, and seal the door. 4. Season the duck all over, inside and out, with black pepper and salt. Stuff the cavity with 4 orange halves and 4 thyme sprigs. Set the duck in the prepared roasting pan, breast-side up. 5. Arrange the plums, shallots, star anise, cloves, cinnamon sticks, the remaining 4 orange halves, and the remaining 4 thyme sprigs around the duck. 6. Pour the white wine over the ingredients surrounding the duck, and season with black pepper and salt. 7. Set the roasting pan on a smoking tray. Smoke them for 2 hours, opening the smoker occasionally to spoon the rendered liquids over the entire dish. Continue to smoke for 2 hours more until the duck has an internal temperature of 165 degrees F/ 75 degrees C. 8. Remove the duck from the smoker, loosely tent it with aluminum foil, and let it rest for 20 minutes. 9. Remove and discard the thyme, star anise, and cinnamon sticks. Serve the duck with a side of plums and shallots.

Per Serving: Calories 305; Total fat 15g; Sodium 548mg; Total Carbs 12g; Sugar 1.2g; Fiber 0.7g; Protein 29g

Smoked Turkey-Veggie Soup with Bulgur Wheat

Prep time: 60 minutes | Cook time: 3 hours | Serves: 4-6

1 tablespoon canola oil	stock
1 tablespoon unsalted butter	4 Yukon gold potatoes, peeled and
2 turkey thighs	diced
1 cup chopped carrots	1 cup cored and chopped Roma
1 cup chopped celery hearts	tomatoes
1 cup chopped yellow onions	2 tablespoons flat-leaf parsley
4 garlic cloves, minced	leaves, minced
Flaked sea salt	3 or dried bay leaves
Freshly ground black pepper	1 cup bulgur wheat
2 quarts hot water	Grated Parmesan cheese, for
1 quart chicken (or vegetable)	garnish

1. Preheat the Traeger smoker to 250 degrees F/ 120 degrees C with the door closed. Ensure the drip tray is clean and in place. 2. Set the wood chips in the smoking tray or firebox, get a good smoke rolling, and seal the door. 3. Place a suitable cast iron Dutch oven on a smoking rack to preheat, then pour in the canola oil and add the butter to melt. 4. Arrange the turkey thighs on smoking trays, leaving space between them. 5. Add the carrots, celery, onions, and garlic to the Dutch oven, then season them with black pepper and salt. Smoke them for 1 hour until they have an internal temperature of 165 degrees F/ 75 degrees C. 6. Add the hot water and chicken stock to deglaze the pan, scraping up any browned bits from the bottom. 7. Add the potatoes, tomatoes, parsley, and bay leaves to the Dutch oven. Smoke for 1 hour more. 8. Add the bulgur wheat and turkey thighs to the Dutch oven. Smoke for 1 hour more, and then remove from the smoker. 9. Remove the prepared thighs from the pot and remove all the meat from the bones. Cut the meat into bite-size pieces and return it to the soup. Discard the bay leaves. 10. Finish with a sprinkle of Parmesan cheese, then enjoy.

Per Serving: Calories 299; Total fat 18.4g; Sodium 116mg; Total Carbs 21.1g; Fiber 6g; Sugars 5g; Protein 14.7g

Smoked Rosemary Duck Breast with Cherry Sauce

Prep time: 15 minutes | Cook time: 2 hours | Serves: 4

1 tablespoon canola oil	1 cup duck stock, chicken stock,
4 duck breasts	or vegetable stock
Flaked sea salt	12 cherries, halved and pitted
Freshly ground black pepper	½ cup tawny port or ruby port
4 rosemary sprigs more for	2 tablespoons unsalted butter,
garnish	chilled
2 shallots, diced	

1. Preheat the Traeger smoker to 275 degrees F/ 135 degrees C. Ensure the drip tray is clean and in place. Seal the door. 2. Set the wood chips in the smoking tray or firebox, get a good smoke rolling, and seal the door. 3. Place a medium cast iron pan on a smoking rack to preheat and pour in the canola oil. 4. Score the duck fat in a ½-inch diamond pattern without slicing into the flesh. 5. Season the breasts with black pepper and salt and arrange them on smoking trays, leaving small spaces between each piece. Add a rosemary sprig on top of each duck breast. 6. Set the cooking temperature to 135 degrees F/ 60 degrees C. 7. Add the shallots to the cast iron pan and toss gently to coat in the oil; then season with black pepper and salt. Smoke them for 30 minutes. 8. Add the duck stock to deglaze the pan, scraping up any browned bits from the bottom. Add the cherries. Smoke for 90 minutes more, or until the internal temperature reaches 135 degrees F/ 60 degrees C. 9. Remove the duck from the smoker, loosely tent it with aluminum foil, and let rest for 10 minutes. 10. Continue to cook the shallots until the liquid in the pan is almost dry, for 8 to 10 minutes. Add the port and cook until the sauce is reduced to your desired consistency. 11. To finish the sauce, add the chilled butter and swirl it in the pan to incorporate. slice the duck breast, and serve topped with the cherry sauce and garnished with rosemary.

Per Serving: Calories 283; Total fat 12.5g; Sodium 108mg; Total Carbs 38.2g; Fiber 6.5g; Sugars 20.9g; Protein 12g

Herb-Smoked Brick Chicken

Prep time: 30 minutes | Cook time: 3 hours | Serves: 4

2 chickens, whole	4 rosemary sprigs, leaves stripped
¼ cup ground ancho chili pepper	and chopped
2 tablespoons paprika	8 garlic cloves, chopped
2 tablespoons ground coriander	Olive oil, for drizzling
4 thyme sprigs, leaves stripped	Flaked sea salt
and chopped	Freshly ground black pepper

1. To prepare the chickens, place them breast-side down on a cutting board. Working one at a time, locate the spine. 2. Using poultry shears or heavy-duty kitchen shears, cut on either side of the spine, one side at a time, cutting as close to the spine as possible. Remove the spine and separate the chicken halves. 3. Preheat the Traeger smoker to 275 degrees F/ 135 degrees C with the door closed. Ensure the drip tray is clean and in place. 4. Set the wood chips in the firebox, get a good smoke rolling, and seal the door. 5. Wrap 4 clean bricks in several layers of aluminum foil. Set them on the smoking racks to preheat. 6. Mix the chili pepper, paprika, coriander, thyme, rosemary, and garlic in a bowl. Set aside. 7. Rinse the chicken in water then pat it dry with a paper towel. 8. Drizzle the prepared chicken with olive oil and season with black pepper and salt. 9. Completely coat the chicken with the spice mixture, rubbing the prepared mixture into the skin and flesh. Set the chicken on a smoking rack with skin-side down. 10. Place 1 brick on top of each chicken half. 11. Smoke the chickens for 3 hours until they have an internal temperature of 165 degrees F/ 75 degrees C. 12. Gently remove the chicken from the racks, being careful to keep the skin intact.

Per Serving: Calories 424; Total fat 14.9g; Sodium 227mg; Total Carbs 14g; Fiber 1g; Sugars 1.4g; Protein 25.7g

Sourdough-Sausage Stuffed Turkey

Prep time: 15 minutes | Cook time: 5 hours | Serves: 12

Brine and Turkey
- 2 gallons' cold water
- 2 cups coarse sea salt
- 1 cup wildflower honey
- ¼ cup peppercorns
- 12 garlic cloves, unpeeled and smashed
- 2 lemons, sliced
- 6 bay leaves
- 6 rosemary sprigs
- 6 thyme sprigs
- 6 flat-leaf parsley sprigs
- 1 (12-pounds) or frozen turkey, thawed
- Flaked sea salt
- Freshly ground black pepper

Sourdough and Sausage Stuffing
- ½ loaf sourdough bread, cut into bite-size cubes
- ½ loaf pumpernickel bread, cut into bite-size cubes
- 1-pound pork sausage, casings removed
- 1-quart chicken (or vegetable) stock
- 8 ounces (2 sticks) unsalted butter more, melted, for brushing
- 2 cups chopped celery hearts
- 2 cups chopped yellow onions
- 2 cups leeks, white parts only, quartered lengthwise and sliced
- 1 tablespoon thyme leaves
- 1 tablespoon rosemary leaves
- 1 tablespoon sliced sage leaves
- 3 or dried bay leaves
- Flaked sea salt
- Freshly ground black pepper

1. Add the cold water, salt, honey, peppercorns, garlic, lemons, bay leaves, rosemary, thyme, and parsley to the stockpot, and boil them over high heat. 2. Reduce the heat to maintain a simmer, and cook for 5 minutes. Mix to fully incorporate all the recipe ingredients, remove from the heat, and let them cool completely (to below 39 degrees F/ 5 degrees C) before using. 3. Completely submerge the turkey in the cooled brine and cover the pot. Refrigerate them for 24 hours. 4. Remove the turkey from the brine. Season the turkey cavity with black pepper and salt. 5. If possible, the day before making the stuffing, leave the sourdough and pumpernickel bread cubes uncovered on the counter to dry. Set the bread cubes in a suitable bowl and set aside. 6. Sauté the sausage in a skillet over high heat for 10 minutes until browned. Remove the sausage and set it aside. 7. Return the set skillet to the heat, and mix the chicken stock, butter, celery, onions, leeks, thyme, rosemary, sage, and bay leaves. Sauté them for 20 minutes until golden brown. Remove and discard the bay leaves. 8. Transfer the vegetables and herbs to this bowl with the bread cubes. Add the sausage and fold the prepared mixture together. Refrigerate the stuffing until fully cooled. 9. Stuff cavities of the turkey with the stuffing, tucking the skin beneath it to seal. Using a bamboo skewer, sew the front cavity closed; tie the legs together with butcher's twine. 10. Preheat the Traeger smoker to 275 degrees F/ 135 degrees C with the door closed. Ensure the drip tray is clean and in place. 11. Set the wood chips in the smoking tray or firebox, get a good smoke rolling, and seal the door. 12. Coat the turkey skin with melted butter and season with black pepper and salt. Set the turkey on a smoking rack, and smoke them for 4 hours (20 minutes per pound) until they have an internal temperature of 165 degrees F/ 75 degrees C. 13. Remove the turkey from the Traeger smoker and loosely tent it with aluminum foil. Let the turkey rest for at least 20 minutes to 1 hour before slicing and serving.

Per Serving: Calories 336, Total Fat 17.3g, Sodium 281mg, Total Carbs 8.1g, Fiber 5.3g, Sugars 17.7g, Protein 32.3g

Chipotle-Lime Chicken Skewers

Prep time: 40 minutes | Cook time: 2 hours | Serves: 4

- ½ cup extra-virgin olive oil
- 2 tablespoons mint leaves, chopped
- 2 limes, sliced
- 2 tablespoons chopped canned chipotle peppers
- 2 tablespoons tomato paste
- 1 tablespoon dark brown sugar
- 2 boneless chicken breasts, cut into bite-size pieces
- 2 boneless & skinless chicken thighs, cut into bite-size pieces
- Flaked sea salt
- Freshly ground black pepper

1. Combine the olive oil, mint, lime slices, chipotle, tomato paste, and brown sugar in a bowl. 2. Toss in the chicken and turn to coat completely. Season with black pepper and salt and then Cover this bowl with plastic sheet and let it refrigerate for 12 to 24 hours, turning the chicken 2 or 3 times. 3. Divide the chicken breast and thigh pieces into 8 portions, reserving the prepared marinade in the refrigerator. Press the chicken onto 8 (10- to 12-inch) bamboo or metal skewers, alternating breast and thigh meat. 4. Preheat the Traeger smoker to 250 degrees F/ 120 degrees C with the door closed. Ensure the drip tray is clean and in place. 5. Set the wood chips in the smoking tray or firebox, get a good smoke rolling, and seal the door. 6. Arrange the wooden skewers on smoking trays, leaving space between each skewer. 7. Smoke them for 30 minutes, then baste the chicken with the reserved marinade. 8. Smoke for another 30 minutes and baste again. The internal temperature of the chicken should reach 165 degrees F/ 75 degrees C.

Per Serving: Calories 285, Total Fat 9.8g, Sodium 639mg, Total Carbs 11.1g, Fiber 1.2g, Sugars 5.1g, Protein 27.8g

Lemon Curried Chicken Breasts

Prep time: 15 minutes | Cook time: 8 minutes | Serves: 4

- Grated zest of 1 lemon
- 2 garlic cloves, chopped
- 2 tablespoons chopped cilantro
- 1½ teaspoons curry powder
- ½ teaspoon salt
- 1 teaspoon light brown sugar
- ¼ cup olive oil
- 2 tablespoons fish sauce or soy sauce
- 4 boneless chicken breast, skinless, pounded to a ½-inch thickness

1. In a blender, mix the lemon zest, garlic, cilantro, curry powder, salt, brown sugar, olive oil, and fish sauce. Pulse to blend the ingredients. Put the chicken pieces in gallon-size resealable bag and pour the prepared marinade over them. Seal the bag, removing all the air. Refrigerate to marinate for 1 to 3 hours. 2. Prepare the grill for direct grilling and bring the temperature to medium-high heat (400 degrees F/ 200 degrees C to 450 degrees F/ 230 degrees C). Rub the cooking grates clean. 3. Oil the cooking grates, then remove the chicken breasts from the prepared marinade and set them over direct heat. 4. Discard the prepared marinade. Cook the chicken breasts for 5 minutes per side, until the chicken reaches an internal temperature of 165 degrees F/ 75 degrees C. 5. Serve the dish directly with your favorite side dish.

Per Serving: Calories 315; Total fat 12.6g; Sodium 259mg; Total Carbs 37.3g; Fiber 2.5g; Sugars 11.5g; Protein 13.1g

Spiced Grilling Chicken

Prep time: 15 minutes | Cook time: 10 minutes | Serves: 4

- 1 garlic clove, minced
- 1 tablespoon ground coriander
- 1 tablespoon ground cumin
- 2 teaspoons paprika
- 1 teaspoon salt
- ½ teaspoon cayenne pepper
- ½ teaspoon black pepper
- ¼ teaspoon ground cardamom
- 2 tablespoons lemon juice
- 3 tablespoons olive oil
- 8 to 10 boneless & skinless chicken thighs

1. Mix the minced garlic, coriander, cumin, paprika, salt, cayenne pepper, black pepper, cardamom, lemon juice, and olive oil in a bowl. 2. Place the chicken thighs in a gallon-size resealable bag and pour the prepared marinade over them. Seal the bag tightly, removing all the air, and refrigerate them for 2 hours to marinate. 3. Prepare the grill for direct grilling over medium heat (350 degrees F/ 175 degrees C to 400 degrees F/ 200 degrees C). Rub the cooking grates clean. 4. Oil the cooking grates, then remove the chicken thighs from the prepared marinade and set them over direct heat. Discard the prepared marinade. Close the hood and cook the chicken for 15 minutes until the internal temperature reaches 165 degrees F/ 75 degrees C, turning every 5 minutes. 5. Let the chicken rest for 2 to 3 minutes. Cut the chicken as desired, and serve immediately.

Per Serving: Calories 538; Total fat 33.6g; Sodium 842mg; Total Carbs 38.8g; Fiber 12.7g; Sugars 14.3g; Protein 21g

Smoky Turkey Tenders with Honey Dip
Prep time: 30 minutes | Cook time: 1 hour | Serves: 4

1 boneless skinless turkey breast	1 tablespoon black pepper more for seasoning
2 tablespoons dried mustard	2 cups all-purpose flour
2 tablespoons paprika	3 eggs, beaten
1 tablespoon ground chipotle chili pepper	4 cups panko bread crumbs
1 tablespoon salt more for seasoning	1 cup wildflower honey, for dipping

1. Slice the turkey across the grain into ½-inch strips. Set aside. 2. Mix the mustard, paprika, chili pepper, 1 tablespoon of salt, and 1 tablespoon of pepper in a bowl, then add the turkey and toss to coat. 3. Set the flour in a shallow bowl, the eggs in another shallow bowl, and the bread crumbs in a third shallow bowl. 4. Working in batches, dip each seasoned turkey strip into the flour, then dip it into the eggs, and finally into the bread crumbs. Set aside the strips on baking sheets, leaving space between each piece. Season with black pepper and salt. 5. Preheat the Traeger smoker to 275 degrees F/ 135 degrees C with the door closed. Ensure the drip tray is clean and in place. 6. Set the wood chips in the smoking tray or firebox, get a good smoke rolling, and close the door. 7. Arrange the turkey strips on smoking trays, leaving space between each piece. Smoke for 1 hour. 8. Remove the turkey strips from the smoker, loosely tent them with aluminum foil, and let them rest for 5 minutes. 9. Divide the prepared turkey into 4 equal portions, and serve with ¼ cup of wildflower honey on the side of each portion for dipping.
Per Serving: Calories 399; Total fat 22.3g; Sodium 267mg; Total Carbs 34.3g; Fiber 6.2g; Sugars 4.2g; Protein 18.4g

Smoked Chicken Sandwiches
Prep time: 30 minutes | Cook time: 1 hour | Serves: 4

4 boneless & skinless chicken breasts	Freshly ground black pepper
2 cups buttermilk	6 tablespoons olive oil
2 tablespoons white wine vinegar	2 cups sliced Savoy cabbage
1 tablespoon whole-grain mustard	1 cup sliced red onion
1 tablespoon wildflower honey	1 tablespoon flat-leaf parsley leaves, finely chopped
Flaked sea salt	4 brioche buns, halved

1. In a suitable food-grade plastic bag, mix the chicken and buttermilk. Seal it and refrigerate for 12 to 24 hours, turning the bag occasionally. 2. Drain the chicken then pat it dry with a paper towel. Discard the prepared marinade. 3. In a suitable bowl, mix the vinegar, mustard, and honey to mix. Season with black pepper and salt and mix again. While mixing, slowly drizzle in the olive oil and mix until emulsified. 4. Fold in the cabbage, red onion, and parsley. Set the slaw aside. 5. Preheat the Traeger smoker to 275 degrees F/ 135 degrees C. Ensure the drip tray is clean and in place. Seal the door. 6. Pour the wood chips in the smoking tray or firebox, get a good smoke rolling, and seal the door. 7. Arrange the chicken breasts on smoking trays, leaving space between them. Smoke for 1 hour. 8. Remove the chicken from the smoker, loosely tent it with aluminum foil, and let rest for 10 minutes. 9. Slice the chicken across the grain (the grain runs the length of the breast) at an angle. 10. Build the sandwiches with chicken on the bottom bun, topped with slaw, and seasoned with black pepper and salt. Enjoy.
Per Serving: Calories 485; Total fat 17.7g; Sodium 366mg; Total Carbs 67.5g; Fiber 14.1g; Sugars 35.6g; Protein 21g

Smoked Honey Chicken with Grapes
Prep time: 40 minutes | Cook time: 2 hours | Serves: 4

2 tablespoons canola oil	Flaked sea salt
2 tablespoons unsalted butter	Freshly ground black pepper
4 bone-in skin-on chicken breasts	4 thyme sprigs, leaves stripped and chopped more for garnish
4 bone-in skin-on chicken thighs	
1 bunch of seedless green grapes	2 cups white wine
1 bunch of seedless red grapes	1 cup chicken stock
¼ cup wildflower honey	

1. Preheat the Traeger smoker to 250 degrees F/ 120 degrees C. Ensure the drip tray is clean and in place. Seal the door. 2. Set the wood chips in the smoking tray or firebox, get a good smoke rolling, and seal the door. 3. Place a suitable cast iron skillet on a smoking rack to preheat, then pour in the canola oil and add the butter to melt. 4. Season the chicken breasts and thighs with salt, pepper, and thyme, then arrange them in a single layer in the skillet. 5. Add the grapes in small bunches. Smoke them for 1 hour until the internal temperature reaches 165 degrees F/ 75 degrees C. 6. Drizzle the chicken with honey. 7. Stir the white wine and chicken stock into the set skillet to deglaze it, scraping up any browned bits from the bottom. Return the skillet to the smoker, and cook for 30 minutes, or until the pan sauce is reduced to your desired consistency. 8. Serve the chicken with the sauce 9. Garnish it with thyme.
Per Serving: Calories 411; Total fat 16.7g; Sodium 131mg; Total Carbs 60.2g; Fiber 9.7g; Sugars 22.5g; Protein 21g

Garlic Sage–Rubbed Turkey Breast
Prep time: 15 minutes | Cook time: 6 hours | Serves: 4

1 tablespoon poultry seasoning	1 (3-pound) frozen boneless turkey breast, thawed
1 tablespoon dried sage	4 tablespoons (½ stick) butter, melted
1 tablespoon garlic powder	
1 teaspoon salt	
½ teaspoon black pepper	

1. In a suitable bowl, stir together the poultry seasoning, sage, garlic powder, salt, and pepper until mixed. 2. Rub the melted butter over the entire turkey breast. Sprinkle the seasoning mix over the entire turkey breast. 3. Cover and let sit at room temperature for 30 minutes. 4. Prepare and light the grill for indirect grilling and bring the temperature to medium heat (350 degrees F/ 175 degrees C to 400 degrees F/ 200 degrees C). Rub the cooking grates clean. 5. Oil the cooking grates, then set the turkey over indirect heat. Close the hood and cook for 1½ hours, turning every 30 minutes, until the internal temperature reaches 150 degrees F/ 65 degrees C. Move the turkey breast to the hot side and cook for 3 minutes per side for additional browning. 6. Let the turkey breast rest for 15 minutes before cutting.
Per Serving: Calories 411; Total fat 16.7g; Sodium 131mg; Total Carbs 60.2g; Fiber 9.7g; Sugars 22.5g; Protein 21g

Herbed Turkey Burgers
Prep time: 15 minutes | Cook time: 8 minutes | Serves: 4

1-pound ground turkey	1 egg
2 tablespoons chopped parsley	¼ cup bread crumbs
1 tablespoon chopped cilantro	1 teaspoon salt
2 tablespoons chopped chives	½ teaspoon black pepper
2 garlic cloves, minced	4 hamburger buns

1. Mix the ground turkey, parsley, garlic, cilantro, egg, chives, and bread crumbs in a bowl. 2. Divide the prepared turkey mixture into 4 equal portions, and press each into a patty about ½ inch thick. Evenly sprinkle black pepper and salt over both sides of each burger. Set aside while preparing the grill. 3. Prepare the grill for direct grilling over medium-high heat (400 degrees F/ 200 degrees C to 450 degrees F/ 230 degrees C). Brush the cooking grates clean. 4. Oil the cooking grates, then cook the burgers for 5 minutes per side until they have an internal temperature of 165 degrees F/ 75 degrees C and begin to brown lightly. 5. Serve warm.
Per Serving: Calories 249; Total fat 14g; Sodium 172mg; Total Carbs 16.7g; Fiber 2.7g; Sugars 3.8g; Protein 15.1g

Barbecue Chicken

Prep time: 30 minutes | Cook time: 55 minutes | Serves: 4

¼ cup paprika	1 tablespoon onion powder
2 tablespoons light brown sugar	1 (3- to 4-pound) whole chicken, cut into 8 pieces
1 tablespoon salt	½ cup Kansas City–Style Barbecue Sauce
1 tablespoon black pepper	
1 tablespoon chili powder	
1 tablespoon garlic powder	

1. Blend the paprika, brown sugar, salt, pepper, garlic powder, chili powder, and onion powder in a bowl. Season and fully coat each piece of chicken with the spice rub. Set aside for later use. 2. Set the grill to medium-low heat (300 degrees F/ 150 degrees C to 350 degrees F/ 175 degrees C). Rub the cooking grates clean. 3. Oil the cooking grates, then set the chicken on the grill opposite the hot side. Close the hood, and add wood chips; cook for 45 minutes until the internal temperature reaches 165 degrees F/ 75 degrees C, turning once halfway through, 4. Cook the chicken for 10 minutes more, turning and basting with the sauce for 2 to 3 minutes. 5. Serve with any remaining sauce.

Per Serving: Calories 253; Total fat 20.1g; Sodium 322mg; Total Carbs 4g; Fiber 1g; Sugars 2.2g; Protein 15.3g

Chapter 2 Fish and Seafood Recipes

32	Simple Wood-Fired Halibut
32	Easy Smoked Dill Salmon
32	Grilled Tuna Steaks
32	Lemon Buttered Oysters in the Shell
32	Buttered Salmon
32	Smoked Cajun Catfish
32	Grilled Shrimp Skewers
32	Blackened Cajun Shrimp
33	Lemon Buttered King Crab Legs
33	Grilled Lobster Tail
33	Grilled Mayo Salmon
33	Salmon Cheese Sandwich
33	Barbecued Dill Scallops
33	Ginger-Soy Mahi-Mahi with Bang Sauce
33	Wood-Fired Scallops
33	Grilled Salmon Fillet
34	BBQ Lemon Trout
34	Basil Shrimp Pops with Coconut Peanut Sauce
34	Smoky Sweet Salmon
34	Shrimp- Mussels Paella
34	Smoked Lemony Whole Trout
35	Grilled Crabs with Butter Sauce
35	Grilled Salmon with Vegetable Salsa
35	Lemon Buttered Baby Shrimp
35	Spicy Grilled Shrimp Skewers
35	Lemony Oysters
35	Salmon Skewers with Thai Curry–Coconut Sauce
36	Juicy Shrimp Skewers with Avocado-Chili Sauce
36	Sugar Mustard-Glazed Salmon
36	Savory Seafood Tomato Salad
36	Lemon Shrimp with Orzo
37	Cheesy Shrimp Asparagus Risotto
37	Smoked Lime Cod Fillets
37	Grilled Halibut with Pepper Vinaigrette
37	Grilled Swordfish Steaks with Mango Salsa
38	Cedar-Planked Salmon Fillet
38	Bourbon-Candied Salmon
38	Sweet & Spicy Cedar Planked Salmon
38	Smoked Salmon Candy
38	Homemade Crab Cakes with Spicy Mayo
39	Garlic-Butter Lobster Tails
39	Alder-Smoked Garlic Salmon Steaks
39	Flavorful Smoked Salmon
39	Juicy Garlic Tuna Steaks
39	Lemon Buttered Sea Bass
39	Herbed Butter Lobster Tails
40	Juicy Lime Snapper
40	Lime-Butter Shrimp
40	Wine-Flavored Oysters
40	Planked Butter Scallops
40	Herbed Catfish with Comeback Sauce
41	Spicy Grilled BBQ Shrimp
41	Cajun Garlic Butter Shrimp Pasta
41	Lemon-Herb Whole Trout
41	Blackened Tilapia Tacos
41	Sweet Smoked Salmon
41	Smoky Buttered Crab Clusters
41	Grilled Garlic-Soy Tuna Steaks

Simple Wood-Fired Halibut

Prep time: 15 minutes | Cook time: 20 minutes | Serves: 4

1-pound halibut fillet	1 batch Dill Seafood Rub

1. Fill your Traeger Smoker with wood pellets and follow the manufacturer's specific start-up procedure. Preheat the grill to 325 degrees F/ 160 degrees C with the hood closed. 2. Sprinkle the halibut fillet on all sides with the rub. 3. Set the prepared halibut directly on the grill grate, and grill until its internal temperature reaches 145 degrees F/ 60 degrees C. 4. Remove the cooked halibut from the grill and serve immediately.

Per Serving: Calories 244; Total fat 15.7g; Sodium 528mg; Total Carbs 4.7g; Fiber 0.1g; Sugars 4.4g; Protein 21.1g

Easy Smoked Dill Salmon

Prep time: 15 minutes | Cook time: 6 hours | Serves: 4

1 (2-pound) half salmon fillet	1 batch Dill Seafood Rub

1. Fill your Traeger Smoker with wood pellets and follow the manufacturer's specific start-up procedure. Preheat the grill, with the hood closed, to 180 degrees F/ 80 degrees C. 2. Season the salmon with the spice rub. 3. Set the salmon directly on the grill grate, skin-side down, and smoke until its internal temperature reaches 145 degrees F/ 60 degrees C. 4. Remove the cooked salmon from the hot grill, and serve.

Per Serving: Calories 360; Total fat 10.6g; Sodium 618mg; Total Carbs 54.3g; Fiber 3g; Sugars 5.2g; Protein 13g

Grilled Tuna Steaks

Prep time: 15 minutes | Cook time: 10 minutes | Serves: 2

| 2 (1½- to 2-inch-thick) tuna steaks | Salt |
| 2 tablespoons olive oil | Black pepper |

1. Fill your Traeger Smoker with wood pellets and follow the manufacturer's specific start-up procedure. Preheat the grill to High (500 degrees F/ 260 degrees C) with the hood closed. 2. Rub the tuna steaks with olive oil and season with black pepper and salt. 3. Set the prepared tuna steaks directly on the grill grate, and grill them for 5 minutes on each side. 4. Remove the cooked tuna steaks from the grill, and serve.

Per Serving: Calories 311; Total fat 21.7g; Sodium 212mg; Total Carbs 0.2g; Fiber 0g; Sugars 0g; Protein 26.9g

Lemon Buttered Oysters in the Shell

Prep time: 15 minutes | Cook time: 20 minutes | Serves: 4-6

8 medium oysters, rinsed and scrubbed	1 batch Lemon Butter Mop for Seafood

1. Fill your Traeger Smoker with wood pellets and follow the manufacturer's specific start-up procedure. Preheat the grill to 375 degrees F/ 190 degrees C with the hood closed. 2. Set the oysters directly on the grill grate, and grill them for 20 minutes. 3. Oysters that don't open should be thrown away. The glaze should be added after shucking the remaining oysters and placing them in a bowl. 4. Serve.

Per serving: Calories 312; Total fat 25g; Sodium 847mg; Total Carbs 3.1g; Fiber 0.3g; Sugars 0g; Protein 19.3g

Buttered Salmon

Prep time: 15 minutes | Cook time: 1 hr. 15 minutes | Serves: 4

| 1 batch dill seafood rub | 2 tablespoons butter, sliced |
| 1 (2-pound) salmon fillet, half | |

1. Fill your Traeger Smoker with wood pellets and follow the manufacturer's specific start-up procedure. Preheat the grill to 180 degrees F/ 80 degrees C with the hood closed. 2. Coat the salmon fillets with the seafood rub. 3. Place the salmon fillets on the grill grate with the skin-side down, and smoke them for 1 hour. 4. Evenly put the butter slices on the salmon, then increase the cooking temperature to 300 degrees F/ 150 degrees C, and resume cooking them until they have an internal temperature of 145 degrees F/ 60 degrees C. 5. Serve warm.

Per Serving: Calories 451; Total fat 27.9g; Sodium 1162mg; Total Carbs 34.1g; Fiber 5.8g; Sugars 8.3g; Protein 20.3g

Smoked Cajun Catfish

Prep time: 15 minutes | Cook time: 15 minutes | Serves: 2

| 2½ pounds catfish fillets | 1 batch Cajun Rub |
| 2 tablespoons olive oil | |

1. Fill your Traeger Smoker with wood pellets and follow the manufacturer's specific start-up procedure. Preheat the grill to 300 degrees F/ 150 degrees C with the hood closed. 2. Apply olive oil to the catfish fillets, and season with the spice rub. Rub the substance into the flesh with your hands. 3. Set the fillets directly on the grill grate, and smoke them until the internal temperature reaches 145 degrees F/ 60 degrees C. 4. Remove the catfish from the grill and serve immediately.

Per serving: Calories 353; Total fat 21.8g; Sodium 665mg; Total Carbs 1g; Fiber 0.1g; Sugars 0g; Protein 36.2g

Grilled Shrimp Skewers

Prep time: 15 minutes | Cook time: 10 minutes | Serves: 4

| 1 pound peeled and deveined shrimp | 2 tablespoons olive oil |
| | 1 batch Dill Seafood Rub |

1. Fill your Traeger Smoker with wood pellets and follow the manufacturer's specific start-up procedure. Preheat your grill to 375 degrees F/ 190 degrees C with the hood closed. 2. Thread 4 or 5 shrimp per skewer. 3. Coat the shrimp with olive oil, and season with shrimp skewers with the rub. 4. Set the wooden skewers directly on the grill grate, and grill the them for 5 minutes per side. 5. Remove the wooden skewers from the grill and serve immediately.

Per serving: Calories 470; Total fat 41.2g; Sodium 940mg; Total Carbs 6.1g; Fiber 0.9g; Sugars 1.7g; Protein 22.2g

Blackened Cajun Shrimp

Prep time: 15 minutes | Cook time: 20 minutes | Serves: 4

| 1 pound peeled and deveined shrimp | 8 tablespoons (1 stick) butter |
| 1 batch Cajun Rub | ¼ cup Worcestershire sauce |

1. Provide wood pellets for your Traeger Smoker and according to the manufacturer's particular startup instructions. 2. A cast-iron pan should be placed on the grill grates after preheating the grill to High setting with the hood closed. 3. Once the grill has heated up, give it a few minutes to get hot before using the set skillet. 4. Rub the shrimp with the Cajun rub in the interim. 5. When the set skillet is hot, set the butter in it to melt. Once the butter melts, add the Worcestershire sauce. Gently toss in the shrimp to coat. 6. The shrimp should be smoke-braised for 10 minutes on each side, or until opaque and thoroughly cooked. 7. Take the shrimp from the grill and serve right away.

Per serving: Calories 439; Total fat 38.8g; Sodium 813mg; Total Carbs 11.5g; Fiber 3.7g; Sugars 6g; Protein 16.8g

Lemon Buttered King Crab Legs

Prep time: 15 minutes | Cook time: 10 minutes | Serves: 4

8 cooked king crab legs	Seafood
1 batch Lemon Butter Glaze for	

1. Fill your Traeger Smoker with wood pellets and follow the manufacturer's specific start-up procedure. Preheat the grill to 325 degrees F/ 160 degrees C with the hood closed. 2. Set the crab legs directly on the grill grate, and grill them for 10 minutes, flipping once after 5 minutes. 3. Serve the crab with the glaze on the side for dipping.

Per serving: Calories 352; Total fat 18.4g; Sodium 1486mg; Total Carbs 35g; Fiber 10g; Sugars 11.1g; Protein 15.2g

Grilled Lobster Tail

Prep time: 15 minutes | Cook time: 25 minutes | Serves: 2

2 lobster tails	1 batch Lemon Butter Glaze for
Salt	Seafood
Black pepper	

1. Fill your Traeger Smoker with wood pellets and follow the manufacturer's specific start-up procedure. Preheat the grill to 375 degrees F/ 190 degrees C with the hood closed. 2. The top of the lobster shells should be cut down the middle almost to the tail using kitchen shears. Once the shell has been cut, expose as much meat as you can. 3. Season the lobster tails with black pepper and salt. 4. Set the tails directly on the grill grate, and grill them until they have an internal temperature of 145 degrees F/ 60 degrees C. Remove the lobster from the grill and serve with the glaze on the side for dipping.

Per serving: Calories 347; Total fat 11.6g; Sodium 217mg; Total Carbs 46g; Fiber 6g; Sugars 3.1g; Protein 16.3g

Grilled Mayo Salmon

Prep time: 15 minutes | Cook time: 25 minutes | Serves: 4

1 (2-pound) half salmon fillet	1 batch Dill Seafood Rub
3 tablespoons mayonnaise	

1. Fill your Traeger Smoker with wood pellets and follow the manufacturer's specific start-up procedure. Preheat the grill to 325 degrees F/ 160 degrees C with the hood closed. 2. Rub the salmon fillet with the mayonnaise and sprinkle it with the spice rub. 3. Arrange the salmon on the grill grate with skin-side down, and grill until its internal temperature reaches 145 degrees F/ 60 degrees C. 4. Serve warm.

Per Serving: Calories 249; Total fat 14g; Sodium 172mg; Total Carbs 16.7g; Fiber 2.7g; Sugars 3.8g; Protein 15.1g

Salmon Cheese Sandwich

Prep time: 15 minutes | Cook time: 5 minutes | Serves: 1

1 English muffin, split	4 ounces smoked salmon
2 tablespoons cream cheese	2 (1-ounce) slices Swiss cheese

1. Fill your Traeger Smoker with wood pellets and follow the manufacturer's specific start-up procedure. Preheat the grill to 375 degrees F/ 190 degrees C with the hood closed. 2. Directly place the muffin halves on the grill grate with cut-side down, and grill them for 2 minutes. 3. Remove the warmed muffin halves, and spread 1 tablespoon of cream cheese on each half. Top each with smoked salmon, and then Swiss cheese. 4. Set the topped muffin halves on a baking sheet, and put the sheet on the grill. Grill them for 3 minutes. 5. Serve warm.

Per serving: Calories 481; Total fat 4.1g; Sodium 1150mg; Total Carbs 70.5g; Fiber 8.7g; Sugars 3.7g; Protein 40.5g

Barbecued Dill Scallops

Prep time: 15 minutes | Cook time: 10 minutes | Serves: 4

1 pound scallops	1 batch Dill Seafood Rub
2 tablespoons olive oil	

1. Fill your Traeger Smoker with wood pellets and follow the manufacturer's specific start-up procedure. Preheat the grill to 375 degrees F/ 190 degrees C with the hood closed. 2. Sprinkle the spice rub on all sides of the scallops after coating them in olive oil. 3. Grill the scallops for 5 minutes on each side. 4. Serve warm.

Per serving: Calories 481; Total fat 28.4g; Sodium 932mg; Total Carbs 9.3g; Fiber 4.8g; Sugars 2.6g; Protein 49.5g

Ginger-Soy Mahi-Mahi with Bang Sauce

Prep time: 15 minutes | Cook time: 16 minutes | Serves: 4

4 mahi-mahi fillets	½ tablespoon garlic paste
¼ cup soy sauce	½ cup mayonnaise
1 tablespoon olive oil	½ cup sweet Thai chili sauce
1 tablespoon ginger paste	2 tablespoons sriracha

1. Place the mahi-mahi fillets in a plastic bag about one gallon. 2. Add the sauce to the bag containing the mahi-mahi after thoroughly combining the soy sauce, olive oil, ginger and garlic paste in a suitable bowl. In order to coat the fish, massage the bag. Refrigerate them for an hour to marinate. 3. Set the Traeger smoker to High (400 degrees F/ 200 degrees C). The fish should be placed on the hot grill and cooked for 6 to 8 minutes per side. 4. Mix the mayonnaise, chili sauce, and sriracha thoroughly in a bowl to make the bang sauce. 5. Along with the mahi-mahi, serve the bang sauce.

Per Serving: Calories 375; Total fat 19.8g; Sodium 2105mg; Total Carbs 29g; Fiber 0.7g; Sugars 24.8g; Protein 24.3g

Wood-Fired Scallops

Prep time: 15 minutes | Cook time: 10 minutes | Serves: 4

1 pound scallops	Superb Seafood Rub
2 tablespoons olive oil	

1. Fill your Traeger Smoker with wood pellets and follow the manufacturer's specific start-up procedure. Preheat the grill to 375 degrees F/ 190 degrees C with the hood closed. 2. Coat the scallops with the olive oil and liberally season with the seafood rub. 3. Place the scallops on the grill grate, close the lid, and grill them for 5 minutes per side. 4. Serve immediately.

Per serving: Calories 289; Total fat 14.3g; Sodium 368mg; Total Carbs 23.3g; Fiber 3.5g; Sugars 2.2g; Protein 18.6g

Grilled Salmon Fillet

Prep time: 15 minutes | Cook time: 20 minutes | Serves: 4

1 (2-pound) half salmon fillet, skin-on	Superb Seafood Rub

1. Fill your Traeger Smoker with wood pellets and follow the manufacturer's specific start-up procedure. Preheat the grill to 350 degrees F/ 175 degrees C with the hood closed. 2. Sprinkle the salmon with the spice rub to taste. 3. Place the salmon on the grill grate with the skin-side down. 4. Close the hood and grill the salmon for 20 minutes, or until the internal temperature reaches 145 degrees F/ 60 degrees C. 5. Remove the cooked salmon from the hot grill and serve immediately.

Per serving: Calories 311; Total fat 17.4g; Sodium 557mg; Total Carbs 4.8g; Fiber 0.2g; Sugars 4.4g; Protein 34.7g

BBQ Lemon Trout

Prep time: 15 minutes | Cook time: 25 minutes | Serves: 4

2 (1-pound) trout fillets, butterflied 1 lemon, sliced into rounds
Superb Seafood Rub

1. Fill your Traeger Smoker with wood pellets and follow the manufacturer's specific start-up procedure. Preheat the grill to 325 degrees F/ 160 degrees C with the hood closed. 2. Sprinkle the inside of the trout fillets with the seafood rub to taste. 3. Set the lemon slices inside the trout fillets. 4. Set the trout fillets on the grill grate, close the lid, and grill them for 25 minutes. 5. Serve immediately.

Per serving: Calories 312; Total fat 3.2g; Sodium 654mg; Total Carbs 42g; Fiber 3.4g; Sugars 1.5g; Protein 26.9g

Basil Shrimp Pops with Coconut Peanut Sauce

Prep time: 15 minutes | Cook time: 6 minutes | Serves: 4

For Sauce
1 cup coconut milk
⅓ cup well-stirred natural peanut butter
1 teaspoon grated lime zest
3 tablespoons lime juice
1 tablespoon soy sauce
1 tablespoon packed light brown sugar
1 teaspoon hot chili-garlic sauce, such as Sriracha
½ teaspoon peeled, grated ginger

For Shrimp Pops
1-pound lean ground pork
12 ounces shrimp, peeled and deveined
½ cup chopped basil leaves
¼ cup panko (Japanese-style bread crumbs)
2garlic cloves
1 tablespoon soy sauce
½ teaspoon black pepper
¼ cup vegetable oil

1. Add all the sauce ingredients in a heavy-bottomed saucepan, and heat them for 2 to 3 minutes over medium heat, stirring continuously. 2. Place over medium heat and stir continuously for 2 to 3 minutes, or just until the sauce is smooth and thickened, without simmering. 3. The components for shrimp pop, excluding the oil, are pulsed in a good food processor or blender until a thick paste is created. Rub the oil evenly over the bottom and sides of a sheet pan after pouring it there. Shape the shrimp pop mixture into quenelles (little ovals) using two tablespoons, placing them on the oiled sheet pan. To firm up the texture, refrigerate for 30 to 1 hour. 4. Prepare the Traeger grill for direct cooking over high heat (450 degrees F/ 230 degrees C to 550 degrees F/ 290 degrees C). 5. Rub the grilling grates with cooking spray. Slide a quenelle onto the end of each skewer. Grill the quenelles for 4 to 6 minutes over direct high heat, with the hood closed until opaque throughout, flipping once halfway through (cut one open with a sharp knife to test for doneness). Remove from the hot grill. 6. Serve warm with the dipping sauce.

Per serving: Calories 338; Total fat 3.6g; Sodium 470mg; Total Carbs 56.1g; Fiber 8.1g; Sugars 44.6g; Protein 22.9g

Smoky Sweet Salmon

Prep time: 15 minutes | Cook time: 50 minutes | Serves: 4

1 (2-pound) half salmon fillet, skin-on
Carne Asada Marinade
Sweet Brown Sugar Rub

1. Set the salmon and the prepared marinade in a 1-gallon sealable bag or container of your choice. Marinate this salmon in the refrigerator for at least 20 minutes, and up to 24 hours. 2. Fill your Traeger Smoker with wood pellets and follow the manufacturer's specific start-up procedure. Preheat the grill to 250 degrees F/ 120 degrees C with the hood closed. 3. Remove the salmon from the prepared marinade. Discard the prepared marinade, sprinkle generously with the spice rub. 4. Arrange the salmon on the grill grate with the skin-side down. 5. Close the hood and smoke the salmon for 50 minutes until the internal temperature reaches 145 degrees F/ 60 degrees C. 6. Serve.

Per serving: Calories 516; Total fat 23.7g; Sodium 577mg; Total Carbs 50.9g; Fiber 3.8g; Sugars 6g; Protein 26.8g

Shrimp– Mussels Paella

Prep time: 15 minutes | Cook time: 37 minutes | Serves: 6

8 ounces shrimp (2⅓0 count), peeled and deveined
olive oil, to cook
Salt and black pepper, to taste

Broth
Reserved shrimp shells
4 cups low-sodium chicken broth
¾ cup dry white wine
2 bay leaves
1½ teaspoons smoked paprika
1 teaspoon salt
½ teaspoon crushed red pepper flakes
¼ teaspoon saffron threads
4 ounces thickly sliced prosciutto, diced
1 cup chopped red onion
¾ cup chopped red bell pepper
1 tablespoon minced garlic
2 cups Arborio rice
1 cup frozen baby peas
12 live mussels, scrubbed and beards removed

1. Toss the shrimp with salt, black pepper, and 2 teaspoons of oil in a bowl. Cover the bowl and let it refrigerate until ready to grill. 2. In a saucepan, bring the broth ingredients to a simmer over high heat. Simmer for 5 minutes. Pour the broth through a fine-mesh strainer placed over a separate bowl, and discard the shells and bay leaves. Set aside. 3. Prepare the Traeger grill for direct cooking over high heat (450 degrees F/ 230 degrees C to 550 degrees F/ 290 degrees C) on one side of the grill and over 350 degrees F/ 175 degrees C on the other side. 4. Rub the grilling grates with cooking spray. Grill the prepared shrimp for 2 minutes with the hood closed until cooked halfway, turning once halfway through. Remove from the hot grill and set aside to cool. 5. Heat 3 tablespoons of oil in a deep 12-inch cast-iron skillet over direct high heat; add the prosciutto, and sauté for 3 minutes; add the chopped onion, bell pepper, and garlic, and sauté them for 5 minutes until the onion is translucent, rotating the skillet for even cooking. 6. Slide the set skillet over direct medium heat, add the rice, and cook for 2 minutes until well coated with the pan juices; add the shrimp broth and peas. Close the grill hood, and let the rice cook at a brisk simmer for 15 minutes until al dente. 7. Nestle the shrimp into the rice, then add the mussels, hinged side down. Cook them over direct medium heat for 10 minutes with the hood closed until the mussels open. 8. Remove the set skillet from the grill, cover with aluminum foil, and let leave for 5 minutes. Serve the paella hot directly.

Per serving: Calories 318; Total fat 17.3g; Sodium 310mg; Total Carbs 6.7g; Fiber 1.5g; Sugars 2.8g; Protein 33.5g

Smoked Lemony Whole Trout

Prep time: 15 minutes | Cook time: 2 hours | Serves: 4

2 quarts water
½ cup salt
½ cup brown sugar
2 whole, medium-sized trout
2 tablespoons butter
8 lemon slices

1. In a suitable bowl, mix the water, salt, and sugar and stir until completely dissolved. 2. Set the trout in a shallow dish and pour the brine over top. Cover and let it refrigerate for 6 to 12 hours. 3. Preheat the Traeger smoker or grill to a temperature between 200 degrees F/ 95 degrees C and 225 degrees F/ 105 degrees C. 4. Remove the marinated trout from the brine and rinse with cold water. Place 1 tablespoon of butter and 4 lemon slices inside each fish. 5. Set the trout on the grill or smoker. Smoke for 1½ to 2 hours. 6. Remove from the hot grill or smoker, gently open the fish, and remove the lemon slices. The bones will separate from the fish as it cooks and should be easy to remove. 7. Serve.

Per Serving: Calories 323; Total fat 17.9g; Sodium 838mg; Total Carbs 4.3g; Fiber 1.5g; Sugars 1g; Protein 35.5g

Grilled Crabs with Butter Sauce

Prep time: 15 minutes | Cook time: 10 minutes | Serves: 3

2 Dungeness crabs, cleaned	2 tablespoons dried dill weed
8 tablespoons (1 stick) butter	1 teaspoon garlic powder
Salt	

1. Fill your Traeger Smoker with wood pellets and follow the manufacturer's specific start-up procedure. Preheat the grill to 325 degrees F/ 160 degrees C with the hood closed. 2. Set the crabs on the grill grate, close the lid, and cook for 10 minutes, or until the crab shell turns a reddish pink. 3. While the crabs are cooking, melt the butter in a microwave-safe bowl in the microwave. Add the salt, dill weed, and garlic powder to the melted butter and mix well. 4. Remove the crabs from the grill, and serve with the seasoned butter.

Per serving: Calories 362; Total fat 17.6g; Sodium 515mg; Total Carbs 4.5g; Fiber 2g; Sugars 0.2g; Protein 45.8g

Grilled Salmon with Vegetable Salsa

Prep time: 15 minutes | Cook time: 24 minutes | Serves: 6

2 ears corn, husked	1 cup chopped arugula
olive oil	2 scallions, chopped
Salt	2 tablespoons lime juice
Black pepper	1 Hass avocado, chopped
¼ teaspoon prepared chili powder	6 skin-on salmon fillets, each 8 ounces
2 cups cherry tomatoes, red, yellow, or a mixture, cut into quarters	1 lime, cut into 6 wedges

1. Prepare the Traeger grill for direct cooking over high heat (450 degrees F/ 230 degrees C to 550 degrees F/ 290 degrees C). 2. Rub the corn with oil and evenly season with ¼ teaspoon of salt, ¼ teaspoon of pepper, and the chili powder. 3. Rub the grilling grates with cooking spray. Grill the corn over direct high heat, with the hood closed until browned in spots and tender, for 12 minutes, turning occasionally. Remove from the heated grill and let cool. 4. Cut the corn kernels off the cobs and transfer them to a medium serving bowl. Add the tomatoes, arugula, scallions, 2 tablespoons of oil, the lime juice, ½ teaspoon salt, and ¼ teaspoon pepper to the corn and stir gently to mix. Fold in the avocado. Set aside. 5. Coat the flesh side of the salmon with oil and season evenly with black pepper and salt. 6. Close the hood, grill the fillets over direct high heat for about 6 to 8 minutes with the flesh-side down first, until they are not sticking when you lift them. Turn the fillets over and resume cooking, you can cook for 2 to 4 minutes more for medium rare. 7. Serve the salmon warm with the salsa and lime wedges.

Per serving: Calories 203; Total fat 6.8g; Sodium 313mg; Total Carbs 8.8g; Fiber 1.8g; Sugars 3.6g; Protein 26.2g

Lemon Buttered Baby Shrimp

Prep time: 15 minutes | Cook time: 15 minutes | Serves: 4

8 tablespoons (1 stick) butter	2 tablespoons dried dill weed
Juice of 1 lemon	1 teaspoon garlic powder
Salt	1-pound baby shrimp

1. Fill your Traeger Smoker with wood pellets and follow the manufacturer's specific start-up procedure. Place a cast-iron skillet onto the grill, and at 400 degrees F/ 200 degrees C, preheat your Traeger Smoker with the hood closed. 2. When the grill has reached temperature, melt the butter in the set skillet. 3. Once the butter is melted, add the lemon juice, salt, dill weed, and garlic powder, and mix. Then add the shrimp. 4. Close the hood and braise the shrimp for 15 minutes, or until pink. 5. Serve immediately.

Per serving: Calories 425; Total fat 25g; Sodium 408mg; Total Carbs 33.3g; Fiber 10.8g; Sugars 15.1g; Protein 22.3g

Spicy Grilled Shrimp Skewers

Prep time: 15 minutes | Cook time: 10 minutes | Serves: 4

1-pound shrimp, tails on, peeled and deveined	2 tablespoons olive oil
	Spicy Rub

1. Fill your Traeger Smoker with wood pellets and follow the manufacturer's specific start-up procedure. Preheat the grill, with the hood closed, to 400 degrees F/ 200 degrees C. 2. Thread 4 to 5 shrimp per skewer. 3. Coat the shrimp with olive oil and season with the spice rub to taste. 4. Arrange the skewers on the grill grate, close the lid, and cook them for 5 minutes per side. 5. Remove the wooden skewers from the grill, and serve immediately.

Per serving: Calories 282; Total fat 12.7g; Sodium 378mg; Total Carbs 0.2g; Fiber 0.1g; Sugars 0g; Protein 39.2g

Lemony Oysters

Prep time: 15 minutes | Cook time: 20 minutes | Serves: 4

10 oysters, washed	Juice of 1 lemon
Superb seafood rub	

1. Fill your Traeger Smoker with wood pellets and follow the manufacturer's specific start-up procedure. Preheat the grill to 375 degrees F/ 190 degrees C with the hood closed. 2. Place the oysters on the grill grate, close the lid, and cook them for 10 to 20 minutes until they open. 3. Remove the prepare oysters from the grill and shuck them, disposing of the disconnected portion of the shell. Discard any oysters that didn't open. 4. Sprinkle the oysters liberally with the rub, and drizzle with the lemon juice. Enjoy.

Per serving: Calories 209; Total fat 1.8g; Sodium 187mg; Total Carbs 3.3g; Fiber 1.2g; Sugars 0.8g; Protein 43.4g

Salmon Skewers with Thai Curry–Coconut Sauce

Prep time: 15 minutes | Cook time: 6 minutes | Serves: 4

1 can (14 ounces) coconut milk, unopened	1½ teaspoons brown sugar
3½ tablespoons Thai red curry paste	1 skinless salmon fillet, about 2 pounds
1 tablespoon fish sauce	2 tablespoons vegetable oil
1 tablespoon soy sauce	2 tablespoons chopped scallion

1. Remove ¼ cup of coconut cream from the coconut milk's surface and place in a saucepan. 2. Stir the remaining can content, then remove 1 cup of the milk and reserve it for another time. Keep the leftover milk for future use. 3. Cook the contents of the pan to a boil over medium heat. Stirring continuously, add 2 tablespoons of the curry paste, and simmer for 5 minutes until aromatic. 4. While continuously stirring, gradually add the 1 cup of coconut milk to the curry paste mixture. Stir thoroughly, and then the sugar, soy sauce, and fish sauce. Bring to a boil while stirring continuously. Reduce the heat to a simmer, and cook the mixture until it reaches a thick consistency. 5. Prepare the Traeger grill for direct cooking over high heat (450 degrees F/ 230 degrees C to 550 degrees F/ 290 degrees C). 6. Cut the fillet into ¾-inch-thick slices. Thread the fish slices onto the wooden skewers lengthwise, keeping the wooden skewers inside the fish as much as possible. 7. Mix the remaining 1½ tablespoons of curry paste with the oil in a basin. Apply a generous coat of the prepared mixture to the fish. Apply cooking spray with a rub on the grilling grates. 8. The wooden skewers should be grilled for 2 to 4 minutes at direct high heat with the hood closed, or until you can pull them off the cooking grate with tongs without them sticking. For medium rare, flip the wooden skewers over and cook for an additional 2 minutes with the hood closed. 9. Pour the heated sauce into a pool on a small serving plate, and place the wooden skewers on top of the sauce, then add the scallion for decoration. Enjoy.

Per serving: Calories 564; Total fat 10.1g; Sodium 366mg; Total Carbs 64g; Fiber 16.4g; Sugars 5.8g; Protein 55.3g

Juicy Shrimp Skewers with Avocado-Chili Sauce

Prep time: 15 minutes | Cook time: 16 minutes | Serves: 4

For Sauce	
3 Anaheim chili peppers	¼ cup mayonnaise
1 Hass avocado	2 tablespoons chopped dill
1 garlic clove	½ teaspoon salt
¼ cup sour cream	¼ teaspoon black pepper
For Rub	
1 teaspoon garlic powder	¼ teaspoon black pepper
1 teaspoon paprika	2 pounds shrimp (21/30 count), peeled and deveined, tails left on
¾ teaspoon salt	
½ teaspoon ground cumin	Olive oil

1. Prepare the Traeger grill for direct cooking over 350 degrees F/ 175 degrees C. 2. Clean the cooking grates with a brush. 3. Grill chili peppers for 12 minutes with the hood closed, flipping them occasionally. 4. To contain the steam, place the chilies in a suitable bowl and wrap the container with plastic. Observe for 10 minutes. The burnt stems, seeds, and skin should be removed and discarded. 5. Blend the chilies in a blender until smooth add the other sauce ingredients and process again. Transfer the sauce to a serving bowl. 6. Mix all the rub ingredients in a bowl. Lay 5 to 7 of the shrimp on a work surface, arranging them so the single shrimp on one end lies one way and all the rest of the shrimp lie in the same way. 7. Select shrimp of the same size so that you may nestle them together without any gaps. The shrimp won't spin around as much on the skewer and won't burn on the grill by doing this. 8. Pick up and slide each shrimp onto a skewer, piercing it through the middle and pushing the shrimp together as they are added to the skewer. Do the same with the remaining shrimp and skewers. 9. Season the shrimp evenly with the spice rub after oiling both sides. 10. Turn up the grill's heat to setting (450 degrees F/ 230 degrees C to 550 degrees F/ 290 degrees C). The shrimp should be grilled for 2 to 4 minutes with the hood closed, until firm to the touch and just beginning to turn opaque in the center, flipping once halfway through. 11. Warm the dipping sauce and serve it with the shrimp.

Per serving: Calories 364; Total fat 23.8g; Sodium 534mg; Total Carbs 6.2g; Fiber 5g; Sugars 0.8g; Protein 32.2g

Sugar Mustard-Glazed Salmon

Prep time: 15 minutes | Cook time: 30 minutes | Serves: 6

1 tablespoon packed light brown sugar	1 tablespoon olive oil
2 teaspoons unsalted butter	2 teaspoons peeled, grated ginger
1 teaspoon honey	1 skin-on whole salmon fillet, about 2½ pounds and ¾ to 1-inch-thick, any pin bones removed
2 tablespoons Dijon mustard	
1 tablespoon soy sauce	

1. Prepare the Traeger grill for indirect cooking over 350 degrees F/ 175 degrees C. 2. Add the sugar, butter, and honey to the sauté pan, and heat over medium heat on the stove until melted. 3. Remove the pan from the heat, and mix in the mustard, soy sauce, oil, and ginger. Let cool to room temperature. 4. Place an appropriate piece of aluminum foil down on top of the salmon, skin side down. Trim the foil so that it has a 14 to 12 inch border all the way around the fish. Apply the brown sugar mixture to the salmon's top. 5. Brush the grilling grates with cooking spray. Over indirect medium heat, place the salmon on the foil, cover the pan, and cook the salmon for 25 to 30 minutes, or until it is opaque inside. 6. Without cutting through the skin, slice the animal in six to eight pieces crosswise. 7. Transfer the pieces to individual dishes using a spatula to separate the skin from the flesh, and then serve immediately.

Per serving: Calories 227; Total fat 4.8g; Sodium 90mg; Total Carbs 14g; Fiber 4g; Sugars 8.2g; Protein 32.4g

Savory Seafood Tomato Salad

Prep time: 15 minutes | Cook time: 5 minutes | Serves: 6

¼ cup 2 tablespoons olive oil	1-pound bay scallops
3 tablespoons red wine vinegar	5 medium tomatoes, cut into ½-inch-thick slices
½ teaspoon minced garlic	
½ teaspoon salt	½ cup pitted green olives, cut into halves or quarters
½ teaspoon dried oregano	
¼ teaspoon crushed red pepper flakes	½ cup sliced celery
	¼ cup chopped red onion
1-pound small shrimp (36/45 count), peeled and deveined	2 tablespoons chopped Italian parsley leaves

1. Mix all the dressing ingredients in a bowl. 2. Mix the shrimp and scallops in another bowl; add ¼ cup of the prepared dressing to the seafood, and mix well, then cover the bowl and refrigerate the seafood for 20 to 30 minutes. Reserve the remaining dressing. 3. Prepare the Traeger grill for direct cooking over high heat (450 degrees F/ 230 degrees C to 550 degrees F/ 290 degrees C). 4. Arrange the tomato slices on a platter. Mix the olives, celery, and onion in the third bowl. 5. Rub the grilling grates with cooking spray. Preheat a perforated grill pan over High heat. 6. Drain the seafood in a fine-mesh strainer. Spread the seafood in a single layer on the grill pan, and grill them for 5 minutes with the hood closed until firm to the touch and opaque in the center, flipping once halfway through. 7. Remove the pan from the grill, and place it on a heatproof surface. Transfer the seafood to a suitable bowl to stop the cooking. 8. Spoon the seafood over the tomatoes. Scatter the olive mixture on top. Spoon the reserved dressing over the entire salad, and garnish with the parsley. Serve at room temperature.

Per serving: Calories 295; Total fat 12.3g; Sodium 332mg; Total Carbs 11.9g; Fiber 3.2g; Sugars 6.5g; Protein 34.2g

Lemon Shrimp with Orzo

Prep time: 15 minutes | Cook time: 4 minutes | Serves: 4

16 extra-shrimp (16/20 count), peeled and deveined, tails left on	⅓ cup pitted Kalamata olives, cut into quarters
1 cup dried orzo pasta	2 tablespoons sliced scallions
⅓ cup 1 tablespoon crumbled feta cheese (about 2 ounces)	1½ tablespoons chopped oregano leaves
¾ cup chopped red bell pepper	
For the Vinaigrette:	
½ cup olive oil	1 teaspoon minced garlic
1 teaspoon grated lemon zest	½ teaspoon salt
¼ cup lemon juice	¼ teaspoon black pepper
1 tablespoon chopped dill	

1. Mix all the vinaigrette ingredients in a serving bowl. 2. Add the shrimp in another bowl, and pour ¼ cup of the vinaigrette over the shrimp, then toss them to coat the shrimp evenly. 3. Cover the bowl and marinate the seasoned shrimp in the refrigerator for 30 minutes. Set the serving bowl with the remaining vinaigrette aside. 4. Prepare the Traeger grill for direct cooking over high heat (450 degrees F/ 230 degrees C to 550 degrees F/ 290 degrees C). 5. Bring a suitable saucepan three-fourths full of salted water to a boil on the stove. 6. Add the orzo pasta and cook until soft, according to package directions. 7. Drain the cooked pasta and then transfer to the vinaigrette in the serving bowl. Add the feta, bell pepper, olives, scallions, and oregano and toss to mix. Set aside at room temperature. 8. Thread 4 shrimp onto each wooden skewer. 9. Rub the grilling grates with cooking spray. 10. Grill the marinated shrimp skewers for 2 minutes per side with the hood closed, until they are firm to the touch and just turning opaque in the center. 11. Serve with the pasta.

Per serving: Calories 361; Total fat 23.7g; Sodium 580mg; Total Carbs 10.9g; Fiber 1.8g; Sugars 7.2g; Protein 25.3g

Cheesy Shrimp Asparagus Risotto

Prep time: 15 minutes | Cook time: 8 minutes | Serves: 6

1-pound asparagus	18 extra-shrimp (16/20 count), peeled and deveined
Olive oil	
Salt	1 tablespoon lemon juice
For Risotto	
6 cups low-sodium chicken broth	Parmigiano-Reggiano cheese
3 tablespoons unsalted butter	1 tablespoon grated lemon zest
2 tablespoons olive oil	¼ cup lemon juice
½ cup chopped yellow onion	2 tablespoons chopped Italian parsley leaves
1 teaspoon salt	
2 cups Arborio rice	1 tablespoon chopped mint leaves
½ cup dry white wine	Black pepper, to taste
½ cup (2 ounces) grated	

1. Prepare the Traeger grill for direct cooking over 350 degrees F/ 175 degrees C. 2. Snap the asparagus spears and discard the tough bases. Set the asparagus on a plate, drizzle with oil, and turn to coat. Season with salt. On another plate, rub the shrimp with oil and season with salt. 3. Rub the grilling grates with cooking spray. Grill the asparagus spears for 6 to 8 minutes with the hood closed until browned in spots and crisp-tender, turning occasionally. 4. At the same time, grill the shrimp for 5 minutes, turning once. Remove the shrimp from the grill as they are ready and place in a suitable bowl. 5. Stir in the lemon juice and mix to coat evenly. When the asparagus and shrimp are cool enough to handle, cut them into 1-inch pieces. Set aside. 6. In a suitable saucepan over high heat on the stove, bring the broth to a simmer. Keep warm over the lowest heat setting. 7. In another saucepan over medium heat on the stove, melt 2 tablespoons of the butter with the oil; add the onion and ½ teaspoon of the salt, and sauté for 3 to 4 minutes until the onion is softened but not browned. 8. Stir in the rice and cook until the grains are coated with the butter mixture and turn opaque, about 2 minutes, stirring frequently. 9. Stir in the wine and cook for 3 minute until evaporated; add 1 cup of the warm broth, and cook on a simmer until the rice has absorbed nearly all of the liquid, stirring occasionally. 10. Add all the remaining broth, ½ cup at a time, stir for 25 to 30 minutes until nearly all the liquid is absorbed before adding the next addition. At this point, the risotto should be creamy and the grains should be plump and tender, yet still firm to the bite. 11. Remove the prepared risotto from the heat and add the remaining 1 tablespoon of butter, ¼ cup of the cheese, the lemon juice and zest, and the remaining ½ teaspoon of salt. Fold in the asparagus, shrimp, parsley, and mint and season with pepper. 12. Divide the risotto among individual bowls, garnish with the remaining cheese, dividing it evenly, and serve.

Per serving: Calories 525; Total fat 23.2g; Sodium 698mg; Total Carbs 6g; Fiber 2.7g; Sugars 0.9g; Protein 69.7g

Smoked Lime Cod Fillets

Prep time: 15 minutes | Cook time: 60 minutes | Serves: 6

6 (6-ounce) cod fillets	2 teaspoons ancho chili powder
¼ cup olive oil	2 teaspoons ground cumin
Juice of 2 limes	1 teaspoon onion powder
2 garlic cloves, minced	1 teaspoon sea salt
2 teaspoons honey	½ teaspoon black pepper

1. Place the cod fillets in a glass baking dish with flesh-side up. 2. In a suitable bowl, mix the olive oil, lime juice, garlic, honey, chili powder, cumin, onion powder, salt, and black pepper. Pour the prepared mixture over the fish, then cover the dish with plastic sheet and refrigerate the fillets for 1 hour. 3. Remove the fillets from the prepared marinade and gently blot away excess marinade. Set them onto a suitable plate or platter and put them back into the refrigerator uncovered for another hour. 4. At 225 degrees F/ 105 degrees C, preheat your Traeger smoker with its hood closed. Depending on your cooker type, add your choice of wood. 5. Set the fillets directly onto the grates, close the lid, and cook for 45 minutes to 1 hour or until they have an internal temperature of 145 degrees F/ 60 degrees C. 6. Gently transfer the fillets to a serving dish. Serve immediately.

Per Serving: Calories 414; Total fat 20.8g; Sodium 156mg; Total Carbs 4.5g; Fiber 0.4g; Sugars 1.6g; Protein 49.8g

Grilled Halibut with Pepper Vinaigrette

Prep time: 15 minutes | Cook time: 22 minutes | Serves: 4

4 skinless halibut fillets, (6 ounces each)	olive oil
	Salt and black pepper
Vinaigrette	
3 bell peppers	½ teaspoon minced garlic
3 tablespoons olive oil	½ teaspoon ground cumin
2 tablespoons orange juice	¼ teaspoon salt
2 tablespoons chopped Italian parsley leaves	¼ teaspoon black pepper
1 tablespoon lemon juice	¼ teaspoon hot-pepper sauce

1. Prepare the Traeger grill for direct cooking over high heat (450 degrees F/ 230 degrees C to 550 degrees F/ 290 degrees C). 2. Brush the grilling grates with cooking spray. 3. Grill the bell peppers over high direct heat for 12 minutes with the hood closed until they are browned and blistered, turning occasionally. 4. To contain the steam, place the peppers in a good basin and wrap them in plastic. Allow to sit for around 10 minutes. Each pepper should be cut lengthwise into ¼-inch-wide strips after the charred skin, stalks, and seeds have been removed and discarded. 5. Mix the remaining vinaigrette ingredients in a separate basin. The peppers should be added to the vinaigrette, mixed to uniformly coat, then covered and left for up to a day. 6. Rub a thin layer of oil of the fillets before seasoning with salt and black pepper. Grill them over direct high heat for 5 to 7 minutes with the hood closed until the meat is opaque in the center but still moist, flipping once halfway through. 7. With the vinaigrette spooned on top, serve the fish warm.

Per serving: Calories 319; Total fat 11.7g; Sodium 1026mg; Total Carbs 5.2g; Fiber 0g; Sugars 5.2g; Protein 45.7g

Grilled Swordfish Steaks with Mango Salsa

Prep time: 15 minutes | Cook time: 12 minutes | Serves: 4

For Marinade	
¼ cup olive oil	¼ teaspoon ground cloves
Juice of 4 limes	¼ teaspoon black pepper
2 tablespoons light rum	4 swordfish steaks, each 7 to 8 ounces and about 1 inch thick
2 tablespoons soy sauce	
For Salsa	
1 mango (1 pound), peeled and cut into ½-inch dice	and chopped
	1 tablespoon chopped basil leaves
2 teaspoons sliced scallions	1 teaspoon lime juice
1 jalapeño chili pepper, seeded	

1. Mix all the marinade ingredients in a wide bowl. 2. Add the swordfish steaks to this bowl and turn to coat evenly with the marinade, then cover bowl and refrigerate them for at least 30 minutes or up to 4 hours, turning the swordfish once. 3. Prepare the Traeger grill for direct cooking over 350 degrees F/ 175 degrees C. 4. In a suitable bowl Gently mix all the salsa ingredients in another bowl. Set aside. 5. Transfer the marinated steaks and the prepared marinade to a suitable saucepan, and boil over medium-high heat, then remove the saucepan from the heat. 6. Brush the grilling grates with cooking spray. 7. Grill the prepared steaks for 12 minutes with the hood closed until just opaque in the center but still juicy, turning and brushing once with the boiled marinade. 8. Serve the prepared steaks warm with the salsa spooned over the top.

Per serving: Calories 487; Total fat 13.5g; Sodium 293mg; Total Carbs 42.6g; Fiber 20.7g; Sugars 2.9g; Protein 47.4g

Cedar-Planked Salmon Fillet
Prep time: 15 minutes | Cook time: 25 minutes | Serves: 6

1 tablespoon hoisin sauce	½ teaspoon toasted sesame oil
1 tablespoon Dijon mustard	1 skin-on whole salmon fillet, 2 to 2½ pounds and about ¾ inch thick
1 tablespoon lemon juice	½ teaspoon salt
1 tablespoon unsalted butter, melted	¼ teaspoon black pepper

1. Prepare the Traeger grill for direct cooking over 350 degrees F/ 175 degrees C. 2. Thoroughly mix the hoisin sauce, Dijon mustard, lemon juice, butter, and sesame oil in a basin. 3. Place the salmon on a chopping board skin side down. Don't cut through the salmon's skin when cutting it in half lengthwise. Then, taking extra care to avoid cutting through the skin, slice the salmon crosswise into six to eight servings. 4. Rub some of the glaze in between each dish and spread it evenly over the salmon flesh. Use equal amounts of salt and black pepper to season. 5. Rub the grilling grates with cooking spray. 6. Set the soaked plank over direct medium heat and close the lid. 7. After 10 minutes, when the plank begins to smoke and char, flip the plank over. Place the salmon pieces on the plank with the skin-side down. 8. Close the hood and cook the salmon for 15 to 25 minutes, or until the outside is only barely browned and the interior is opaque but still moist. 9. Serve warm.
Per serving: Calories 409; Total fat 13.4g; Sodium 285mg; Total Carbs 3.6g; Fiber 1.3g; Sugars 2.2g; Protein 64.5g

Bourbon-Candied Salmon
Prep time: 15 minutes | Cook time: 4 hours | Serves: 4

2 pounds salmon fillets	½ cup brown sugar
1 cup bourbon	½ cup water
¼ cup salt	½ cup maple syrup

1. Salmon should be de-skinned and chopped into 1- to 2-inch chunks. 2. Combine the water, salt, brown sugar, and bourbon in an appropriate container. Before adding the salmon, stir the brown sugar and salt until they are totally dissolved. This may take a few minutes. The salmon bites should be added to this mixture, covered, and chilled for 8 to 10 hours. 3. Remove the salmon bites, pat dry, and place them on a foil. Let them air-dry for an hour. 4. Flip the Traeger smoker on and set the temperature to 180 degrees F/ 80 degrees C. 5. Place the salmon-filled baking foil on the grill grate and cook for 3 to 4 hours. Several times throughout the previous hour, brush with the maple syrup. 6. Serve warm.
Per Serving: Calories 392; Total fat 23.4g; Sodium 88mg; Total Carbs 10.4g; Fiber 1.9g; Sugars 3.7g; Protein 34.5g

Sweet & Spicy Cedar Planked Salmon
Prep time: 15 minutes | Cook time: 60 minutes | Serves: 4

4 (6-ounce) salmon fillets	½ teaspoon sesame oil
2 tablespoons reduced-sodium soy sauce	2 scallions, chopped
	2 garlic cloves, minced
2 tablespoons vegetable oil	1 teaspoon grated ginger
2 tablespoons balsamic vinegar	¼ teaspoon salt
1 tablespoon chili sauce	1 untreated cedar plank, or 2 small ones
1 tablespoon brown sugar	

1. Place the salmon fillets to a glass baking dish with the skin-side down. 2. In a suitable bowl, mix the soy sauce, vegetable oil, balsamic vinegar, chili sauce, brown sugar, sesame oil, the white parts of the scallions, garlic, ginger, and salt. Pour the sauce evenly over the salmon. 3. Cover this dish with plastic sheet and refrigerate the salmon fillets for 1 hour. At the same time, soak the cedar plank in tepid water for 1 hour. 4. At 225 degrees F/ 105 degrees C, preheat your Traeger smoker with its hood closed. Depending on your cooker type, add a small amount of wood chunks or chips to the fire. 5. Once preheated, set the presoaked plank on the grate to heat up, about 4 to 5 minutes. 6. Once it becomes aromatic, set the marinated salmon pieces on the plank with skin-side down, close the hood, and cook them for 1 hour until the internal temperature of the salmon reaches 140 degrees F/ 60 degrees C. 7. Remove the salmon from the smoker and serve immediately.
Per serving: Calories 492; Total fat 32g; Sodium 530mg; Total Carbs 16.8g; Fiber 3g; Sugars 2.9g; Protein 32.1g

Smoked Salmon Candy
Prep time: 15 minutes | Cook time: 4 hours | Serves: 8

2¼ cups brown sugar	1½-inch strips
1½ cups salt	1¼ cups real maple syrup
5 pounds skin-on salmon, cut into	

1. Mix the brown sugar and salt in a bowl. 2. Fill a suitable glass dish or resealable plastic container ¼ inch deep with the prepared mixture. Place the strips in the prepared mixture with the skin-side down. Spread them out a little. If you need to add another layer, repeat the process with ¼ inch of the curing mixture between the layers. Cover and let it refrigerate for 2 hours. 3. Remove the fish, rinse it off under cold water, and blot dry with paper towels. Set the strips in a clean dish or pan and let them dry in the refrigerator for 24 hours uncovered. 4. Preheat the Traeger grill or smoker to 165 degrees F/ 75 degrees C. Depending on your cooker type, add your choice of wood. 5. Set the salmon strips directly onto the grates, and if your cooker has space, set an aluminum drip pan underneath the fish. Gradually bring the temperature up to 200 degrees F/ 95 degrees C over the span of 1 hour. Go no higher. Smoke the fish for 3 to 4 hours total, depending on thickness and desired texture. After 90 minutes of cooking time, brush the salmon with the maple syrup. 6. Once cooked, the candied salmon will have a deep color with a shiny finish. Remove from the smoker and place onto cooling racks for 1 hour before serving or eating. 7. Store in the refrigerator or freezer in a vacuum-sealed bag.
Per serving: Calories 478; Total fat 19.2g; Sodium 591mg; Total Carbs 2.6g; Fiber 0.9g; Sugars 0.7g; Protein 69.5g

Homemade Crab Cakes with Spicy Mayo
Prep time: 15 minutes | Cook time: 20 minutes | Serves: 4

3 tablespoons olive oil	1½ tablespoons seafood seasoning
1 red bell pepper, seeded, diced	1 pound cooked jumbo lump crabmeat
1 onion, diced	
3 celery stalks, diced	2 eggs, beaten
Salt	1 cup panko bread crumbs
Black pepper	1 cup mayonnaise
Pinch red pepper flakes	A few dashes hot sauce of choice
3 garlic cloves, minced	Lemon wedges, for serving
2 tablespoons lemon juice	

1. Heat 1 tablespoon of olive oil in the skillet over medium-high heat; add a pinch of each salt, black pepper, and red pepper flakes once the bell pepper, onion, and celery have heated through. Cook them for 8 to 10 minutes with occasional stirring. 2. Cook for a further minute after adding the minced garlic, 1 tablespoon of lemon juice, and ½ tablespoon of seafood seasoning. 3. Remove the prepared sauce from the heat and leave it to cool. 4. Add the crabmeat, eggs, and bread crumbs when the prepared mixture has cooled. Form the mixture into eight patties after thoroughly combining the ingredients. They should be placed on a tray or baking sheet and chilled for an hour. 5. Place a cast-iron skillet or baking sheet on the grill grate. Then, turn on the smoker and set the temperature to High. 6. Wait another 10 minutes for the skillet to warm up when it reaches the greatest temperature. 7. Add the crab cakes to the set skillet, being careful not to crowd them, and drizzle the remaining olive oil over them. 8. Flip the crab cakes over and cook for a further 10 minutes. Combine the remaining 1 tablespoon of lemon juice, 1 tablespoon of seafood spice, spicy sauce, and mayonnaise while the crab cakes cook. 9. Serve the crab cakes with the spicy mayo and lemon wedges.
Per Serving: Calories 396; Total fat 11.4g; Sodium 448mg; Total Carbs 30.7g; Fiber 3.7g; Sugars 0.8g; Protein 40.2g

Garlic–Butter Lobster Tails

Prep time: 15 minutes | Cook time: 40 minutes | Serves: 4

1 cup butter	2 teaspoons chopped basil
2 tablespoons olive oil	⅛ teaspoon salt
1 tablespoon lemon juice	⅛ teaspoon black pepper
3 to 4 garlic cloves, minced	4 (8- to 10-ounce) lobster tails

1. Melt the butter in a saucepan over medium-high heat for 4 to 5 minutes until foam starts to collect on the surface, then reduce the heat to low, and cook for an additional 8 to 10 minutes. 2. Pour the butter through a cheesecloth-lined strainer or sieve into a suitable bowl. Cover and set aside. 3. At 250 degrees F/ 120 degrees C, preheat your Traeger smoker with its hood closed. 4. Mix the olive oil, lemon juice, garlic, basil, salt, and pepper in a suitable bowl. Set aside. 5. Cut the lobster shells on the top of the tail from the cut end to where the tail fans out. Fold open the shell carefully to expose the flesh underneath. Lift the meat portion out and set it on top of the shell. Do not remove it completely; you just want to shift its position upward. 6. Rub ¼ of the olive oil–herb mixture onto the exposed meat portion of each lobster tail. 7. Set the tails on the cooking grate. Close the hood and cook for 40 minutes, or until the internal temperature reaches between 135 degrees F/ 60 degrees C and 140 degrees F/ 60 degrees C. 8. Once the lobster tails are cooked, remove them from your cooker, and serve with the drawn butter.

Per Serving: Calories 305; Total fat 16.7g; Sodium 148mg; Total Carbs 2.5g; Fiber 1.1g; Sugars 0.1g; Protein 36.5g

Alder–Smoked Garlic Salmon Steaks

Prep time: 15 minutes | Cook time: 60 minutes | Serves: 4

2 tablespoons olive oil	2 garlic cloves, minced
2 tablespoons Dijon mustard	4 salmon steaks
2 teaspoons black pepper	1 untreated alder plank, soaked in
1 teaspoon sea salt	water for 1 hour

1. At 250 degrees F/ 120 degrees C, preheat the Traeger smoker with its hood closed. Depending on your cooker type, add a handful of alder wood to the fire. 2. Mix the olive oil, mustard, black pepper, salt, and garlic in a bowl. Spoon about 1 tablespoon of the prepared mixture onto each salmon steak. Gently work it onto both sides of the steak. 3. Remove the alder plank from the water, pat dry, and set the salmon steaks on top. 4. Set the plank into your Traeger Smoker or grill, close the lid, and cook the salmon steaks for 1 hour. 5. Serve warm.

Per serving: Calories 452; Total fat 29.3g; Sodium 3091mg; Total Carbs 3.2g; Fiber 0.8g; Sugars 1.3g; Protein 40.3g

Flavorful Smoked Salmon

Prep time: 15 minutes | Cook time: 1 hour 30 minutes | Serves: 6

4 cups ice-cold water	½ cup chopped fennel
¼ cup salt	2 tablespoons dried onion
¼ cup brown sugar	2 teaspoons granulated garlic
2 bay leaves	2 pounds salmon fillets

1. In a suitable bowl, mix the water, salt, brown sugar, bay leaves, fennel, dried onion, and granulated garlic. Mix until the sugar is dissolved. 2. Set the salmon fillets in a glass baking dish, skin-side down. Pour the brine mixture over top. Cover and let it refrigerate for 6 to 12 hours. 3. Remove the fillets from the brine, rinse them in cold water, then pat them dry with paper towels. 4. Arrange the fillets on a clean plate. Set them in the refrigerator for 5 hours, uncovered. 5. Preheat the Traeger grill or smoker to a temperature between 180 degrees F/ 80 degrees C and 200 degrees F/ 95 degrees C with indirect cooking. 6. Set the salmon fillets on the cooker. 7. Smoke for 1 to 1½ hours until they reach an internal temperature of 140 degrees F/ 60 degrees C. 8. Serve warm.

Per serving: Calories 213; Total fat 8.1g; Sodium 420mg; Total Carbs 2.8g; Fiber 0.7g; Sugars 1g; Protein 31.1g

Juicy Garlic Tuna Steaks

Prep time: 15 minutes | Cook time: 1 hour 30 minutes | Serves: 4

4 (7- to 8-ounce) ahi tuna steaks	3 garlic cloves, minced
½ cup reduced-sodium soy sauce	2 teaspoons grated ginger
Juice of 1 navel orange	1 teaspoon onion powder
1 tablespoon mirin or dry sherry	1 teaspoon sesame oil
2 tablespoons brown sugar	½ teaspoon white pepper

1. Mix the soy sauce, orange juice, mirin/sherry, brown sugar, garlic, ginger, onion powder, sesame oil, and white pepper in a bowl. 2. Place the tuna steaks in a resealable bag, then pour the garlic mixture over them to coat well, then seal the bag and refrigerate the bowl for 1 hour. 3. At 225 degrees F/ 105 degrees C, preheat your Traeger smoker with its hood closed. Depending on your cooker type, add your choice of wood. 4. Remove the tuna steaks from the prepared marinade, place directly onto the grates, close the lid, and cook them for 1 to 1½ hours until the internal temperature reaches 140 degrees F/ 60 degrees C. 5. Remove the prepared steaks from your cooker and let leave for a few minutes before serving.

Per Serving: Calories 303; Total fat 10.4g; Sodium 703mg; Total Carbs 9.2g; Fiber 0g; Sugars 8.7g; Protein 40.6g

Lemon Buttered Sea Bass

Prep time: 15 minutes | Cook time: 2 hours | Serves: 4

½ teaspoon sea salt	3 tablespoons butter
¼ teaspoon onion powder	Juice of 1 lemon
¼ teaspoon paprika	1 tablespoon chopped flat-leaf
¼ teaspoon black pepper	parsley more for serving
2 pounds sea bass fillets, Chilean	2 garlic cloves
or Atlantic	1½ tablespoons olive oil

1. Preheat the Traeger grill or smoker to 200 degrees F/ 95 degrees C. Depending on your cooker type, add your preferred wood a few minutes before cook time. 2. Mix the sea salt, onion powder, paprika, and pepper in a bowl. 3. Sprinkle the paprika mixture onto the exposed flesh of the fish. Then, place the fish directly on the grill grate, close the lid, and cook for 1½ hours until the internal temperature of the thickest part reaches 140 degrees F/ 60 degrees C. 4. Meanwhile, in a suitable saucepan over medium heat, mix the butter, lemon juice, parsley, and garlic, and cook for 2 minutes. 5. Brush the fish with the butter sauce after 15 minutes of cooking time until it has cooked through. 6. Remove the fish, plate it up, drizzle the olive oil on top, and garnish with the chopped parsley before serving.

Per Serving: Calories 419; Total fat 15.8g; Sodium 3342mg; Total Carbs 0.4g; Fiber 0.2g; Sugars 0g; Protein 65.4g

Herbed Butter Lobster Tails

Prep time: 15 minutes | Cook time: 60 minutes | Serves: 4

4 lobster tails	1 rosemary sprig
1½ sticks butter	1 thyme sprig

1. Flip the Traeger smoker on and set the temperature to 225 degrees F/ 105 degrees C. 2. Put the lobster tails in a cast-iron skillet with the cut side facing up. Along with the rosemary and thyme, cut up one stick of butter into smaller pieces and arrange it around the lobster tails in the pan. 3. Place the pan on the grill grate, and cook them for 45 to 60 minutes. As the lobster tails cook, brush them with the herb butter a few times. 4. Melt the remaining 12 stick of butter and serve it with the lobster for dipping once the lobster is finished cooking.

Per Serving: Calories 423; Total fat 18.4g; Sodium 137mg; Total Carbs 4.6g; Fiber 1.9g; Sugars 0.8g; Protein 56.2g

Juicy Lime Snapper

Prep time: 15 minutes | Cook time: 1 hour | Serves: 4

For Prepared Marinade
- Juice and zest of 1 lime
- ¼ cup olive oil
- ¼ cup white wine
- 2 teaspoons chopped thyme
- 2 teaspoons chopped oregano
- 1 teaspoon salt
- 1 teaspoon black pepper
- ½ teaspoon red pepper flakes

For Snapper
- 1 (4- to 6-pound) whole red snapper
- 2 limes, sliced
- Pinch salt
- Pinch black pepper
- 1 small red onion, sliced
- 1 small orange, sliced

To make the prepared marinade: In a suitable bowl, mix the lime juice and zest, olive oil, wine, thyme, oregano, salt, pepper, and red pepper flakes. Set aside until ready to use.

To make the snapper: 1. Set the snapper on a cutting board. Make diagonal slits inch down the side of the fish starting behind the gills. Stuff lime slices into the slits. Flip the fish over and repeat. Season the snapper inside and out with black pepper and salt. 2. Stuff the inside of the fish with the red onion and orange slices. Place the snapper in a shallow dish and pour the prepared marinade over top. 3. Cover and let it refrigerate the snapper for 4 hours. Turn over halfway through the marinating time. 4. At 250 degrees F/ 120 degrees C, preheat your Traeger smoker with its hood closed. 5. Set the snapper on the indirect portion of the grill, and cook for 1 hour until it reaches an internal temperature of 160 degrees F/ 70 degrees C. 6. Serve.

Per Serving: Calories 347; Total fat 17.7g; Sodium 1655mg; Total Carbs 6.8g; Fiber 1.2g; Sugars 2.8g; Protein 33.3g

Lime–Butter Shrimp

Prep time: 15 minutes | Cook time: 30 minutes | Serves: 4

- 1-pound jumbo shrimp, peeled and deveined
- 1 tablespoon chili powder
- 2 teaspoons salt
- 2 teaspoons onion powder
- 2 teaspoons granulated garlic
- 2 teaspoons black pepper
- 1 teaspoon dried oregano
- ½ cup butter
- 1 tablespoon lime juice
- 2 scallions, green parts only, chopped

1. At 250 degrees F/ 120 degrees C, preheat your Traeger smoker with its hood closed. Depending on your cooker type, add your wood of choice to the fire. 2. Mix the chili powder, salt, onion powder, granulated garlic, black pepper, and oregano in a bowl, then season the shrimp with the rub. 3. Lay the shrimp on an aluminum baking sheet or disposable pan, place it into your grill and cook for 30 minutes. 4. Melt the butter in a saucepan over medium heat.; add the lime juice and stir through. 5. Once the shrimp have cooked, pour the lime-butter mixture into the pan, toss with tongs to coat, garnish with scallions, and serve immediately.

Per Serving: Calories 404; Total fat 19.4g; Sodium 187mg; Total Carbs 5g; Fiber 1.1g; Sugars 0.8g; Protein 52g

Wine–Flavored Oysters

Prep time: 15 minutes | Cook time: 60 minutes | Serves: 6

- 40 oysters in the shell
- 1 cup dry white wine
- 1 cup water
- ¼ cup good-quality olive oil

1. Rinse the oysters in cold water. 2. In a suitable pot, bring the wine and water to a boil. Working in batches, add the oysters to the boiling liquid. Remove the oysters as they open. Any oyster that doesn't open in 3 minutes should be discarded. 3. Once all the oysters are open, strain the boiling liquid through a paper towel, coffee filter, or cheesecloth, and reserve. 4. Cut each oyster from the shell and drop it into the liquid. Leave the oysters to soak for 20 minutes. 5. Preheat the Traeger grill to the lowest temperature you can maintain, around 175 degrees F/ 80 degrees C or lower if possible. Add your choice of wood chips or smoke packet to the fire. 6. Set the oysters on a fine baking rack that won't let the smaller oysters fall through. Transfer them to the smoker and smoke for 1 hour. 7. Remove the oysters from the smoker or grill, toss with the olive oil, and enjoy.

Per Serving: Calories 367; Total fat 22.9g; Sodium 101mg; Total Carbs 8g; Fiber 1.9g; Sugars 3g; Protein 31.8g

Planked Butter Scallops

Prep time: 15 minutes | Cook time: 30 minutes | Serves: 3

- 1 untreated alder or oak plank, soaked in water for 1 hour
- 8 to 10 sea scallops
- 1½ tablespoons olive oil
- ¼ teaspoon salt
- ½ teaspoon black pepper
- ¼ cup butter
- 2 garlic cloves, minced
- Juice of 1 lemon
- ¼ teaspoon onion powder
- Pinch salt
- Pinch red pepper flakes
- 2 tablespoons chopped flat-leaf parsley

1. Preheat the Traeger grill or smoker to 200 degrees F/ 95 degrees C. Depending on the cooker type, add your choice of wood. 2. Remove the plank from the water and blot excess moisture with paper towels. 3. Rinse the scallops under cold water, and trim off the small white muscle tags. Blot dry. 4. In a bowl, mix the olive oil, salt, and black pepper. Add the scallops and toss gently to coat. 5. Arrange the scallops on the plank and place on the grill, close the lid, and cook them for 20 to 30 minutes. 6. Meanwhile, melt the butter in a skillet over medium heat; add the minced garlic and cook for 30 seconds; add the salt, red pepper flakes, onion powder, and lemon juice. and cook the sauce for 2 minutes, or until it starts to decrease. 7. Right away add the smoked scallops to the sauce-filled skillet and gently toss to coat. Serve immediately after adding the chopped parsley to the garnish.

Per Serving: Calories 278; Total fat 15.4g; Sodium 321mg; Total Carbs 1.3g; Fiber 0.5g; Sugars 0.1g; Protein 32.1g

Herbed Catfish with Comeback Sauce

Prep time: 15 minutes | Cook time: 60 minutes | Serves: 4

For Catfish
- ½ cup olive oil
- 3 tablespoons honey
- 3 tablespoons white vinegar
- 2 tablespoons chopped dill
- 1 tablespoon mild chili powder
- 2 teaspoons dried rosemary, crushed
- 4 (6- to 7-ounce) catfish fillets

For Sauce
- 1 cup mayonnaise
- ¼ cup chili sauce
- ¼ cup ketchup
- 2 tablespoons olive oil
- Juice of 1 medium lemon
- 1 teaspoon Creole or spicy mustard
- 1 teaspoon Worcestershire sauce
- 1 garlic clove, minced
- ½ teaspoon Cajun seasoning
- ¼ teaspoon onion powder
- Pinch salt
- Pinch black pepper
- 2 to 3 dashes hot sauce

To make the catfish: 1. Mix the olive oil, honey, vinegar, dill, chili powder, and rosemary in a bowl. 2. Rinse the catfish fillets then pat dry with paper towels, then place them in a resealable bag, and pour the prepared marinade over top. 3. Flip them to coat the fillets with the mixture evenly. Seal the bag and let it refrigerate for 4 hours. 4. At 250 degrees F/ 120 degrees C, preheat your Traeger smoker with its hood closed with indirect cooking. 5. Remove the fillets from the prepared marinade, and blot away any excess with paper towels. Set the fillets directly on the cooking grate and smoke for 1 hour.

To make the sauce: 1. Mix the mayonnaise, chili sauce, ketchup, olive oil, lemon juice, mustard, Worcestershire sauce, garlic, Cajun seasoning, onion powder, salt, pepper, and hot sauce in a separate bowl. Stir to mix well and let it refrigerate until ready to use. 2. When the catfish fillets reach 145 degrees F/ 60 degrees C, remove them from the grill or smoker, and serve immediately with Comeback Sauce on the side.

Per Serving: Calories 340; Total fat 27.7g; Sodium 109mg; Total Carbs 12.6g; Fiber 0.3g; Sugars 3g; Protein 15.7g

Spicy Grilled BBQ Shrimp

Prep time: 15 minutes | Cook time: 40 minutes | Serves: 4

1-pound shrimp, peeled and deveined	2 tablespoons BBQ Dry Rub
1 tablespoon olive oil	Pinch cayenne pepper

1. Flip the Traeger smoker on and set the temperature to 250 degrees F/ 120 degrees C. 2. In a suitable bowl, toss the shrimp with the dry rub, olive oil, and cayenne pepper until the shrimp is coated evenly. 3. Set the shrimp on the grill grate for 30 to 40 minutes, flipping halfway through. 4. Serve warm.

Per Serving: Calories 443; Total fat 16.3g; Sodium 305mg; Total Carbs 37.4g; Fiber 7.8g; Sugars 11.4g; Protein 38.5g

Cajun Garlic Butter Shrimp Pasta

Prep time: 15 minutes | Cook time: 1 hr. 15 minutes | Serves: 6

2½ sticks butter, melted	Salt
6 garlic cloves, minced	Black pepper
2 tablespoons Cajun seasoning	2 pounds jumbo shrimp, peeled and deveined
2 tablespoons lime juice	
½ cup chopped parsley	1-pound pasta of choice

1. Set the Traeger smoker's temperature to 225 degrees F/ 105 degrees C and turn it on. 2. In a cast-iron skillet or a 9 by 13-inch foil pan, combine the butter, garlic, Cajun spice, lime juice, parsley, and a pinch of each black pepper and salt. 3. When the shrimp are evenly coated, add them to the pan and stir. Place this pan on the grill grate and cook for 45 to 1 hour, stirring the shrimp occasionally. 4. Pasta should be cooked as directed on the package, drained, and then added to the pan with the shrimp. Mix everything together and cook everything on the Traeger for an additional 15 minutes.

Per Serving: Calories 348; Total fat 11.1g; Sodium 139mg; Total Carbs 7.9g; Fiber 3g; Sugars 1.6g; Protein 52.8g

Lemon-Herb Whole Trout

Prep time: 15 minutes | Cook time: 16 minutes | Serves: 4

2 whole trout (10 ounces)	wedges
Salt	3 garlic cloves, minced
Black pepper	2 dill sprigs
1 tablespoon lemon pepper seasoning	2 thyme sprigs
	1 tablespoon olive oil
1 lemon, sliced into rounds lemon	

1. Set the Traeger smoker to High (400 degrees F/ 200 degrees C). 2. Season the trout with salt, black pepper, and lemon pepper. Slices of lemon, garlic, dill, and thyme should be placed within each cavity. Each fish should have olive oil applied externally. 3. Cook the trout for 7 to 8 minutes on each side after placing it on the grill grate. 4. Garnish with lemon wedges (optional) and serve.

Per Serving: Calories 348; Total fat 11.1g; Sodium 139mg; Total Carbs 7.9g; Fiber 3g; Sugars 1.6g; Protein 52.8g

Blackened Tilapia Tacos

Prep time: 15 minutes | Cook time: 10 minutes | Serves: 4

4 tilapia fillets, cleaned	12 Tortillas
2 tablespoons blackened seasoning	Toppings:
1 tablespoon olive oil	Lettuce
Salsa	
Pickled jalapeño peppers	Guacamole, etc.

1. On the grill grate, place a baking sheet. Depending on the type of your grill, turn the Traeger smoker on and set the temperature to High. 2. The tilapia is covered in the blackened seasoning on both sides. 3. Wait another 10 minutes after the grill achieves temperature so the baking sheet is nice and hot. 4. Place the tilapia fillets on the baking sheet and drizzle oil over them. Tilapia should be cooked for 5 minutes on each side. To warm the tortillas, place them briefly on the grill grates. 5. Take the fish from the grill, break it up into smaller pieces, and put the dish together.

Per Serving: Calories 402; Total fat 19.9g; Sodium 1387mg; Total Carbs 24g; Fiber 8g; Sugars 12.7g; Protein 32.1g

Sweet Smoked Salmon

Prep time: 15 minutes | Cook time: 4 hours | Serves: 6

1 cup brown sugar	1 (3-pound) salmon fillet
½ cup salt	

1. In a suitable bowl, mix the sugar and salt. 2. Spread a thin layer of this mixture in the bottom of a 9-by-13-inch casserole dish. Set the salmon fillet over the top and then cover the salmon with the rest of the brown sugar mixture. Cover and let it refrigerate for 12 hours. 3. Remove the salmon from the refrigerator then pat dry well. Let it sit out and air-dry for 2 hours. 4. Flip the Traeger smoker on and set the temperature to 180 degrees F/ 80 degrees C. Cook the salmon on the grill grate for 3 to 4 hours. 5. Serve warm

Per Serving: Calories 388; Total fat 21.8g; Sodium 787mg; Total Carbs 5.4g; Fiber 1.5g; Sugars 1.4g; Protein 49.3g

Smoky Buttered Crab Clusters

Prep time: 15 minutes | Cook time: 25 minutes | Serves: 4

1 cup melted butter	2 teaspoons dried oregano
1 teaspoon salt	1 teaspoon garlic powder
1 teaspoon black pepper	2 to 3 pounds snow crab clusters
½ tablespoon ground coriander	

1. At 225 degrees F/ 105 degrees C, preheat your Traeger smoker with its hood closed and set the cooker for indirect grilling. 2. Cook the butter, salt, pepper, coriander, oregano, and garlic powder in a saucepan over low heat, stirring them until melted through, then remove from heat and cover to keep warm. 3. Dip the ends of the crab clusters into the butter sauce and then place directly on the grill. Smoke them for 20 to 25 minutes, basting the clusters with the butter sauce 10 minutes. The shells should be bright in color and the meat should be opaque white. 4. Remove from the cooker and serve hot, or place on ice and serve cold.

Per Serving: Calories 315; Total fat 15g; Sodium 91mg; Total Carbs 0g; Fiber 0g; Sugars 0g; Protein 42.3

Grilled Garlic-Soy Tuna Steaks

Prep time: 15 minutes | Cook time: 12 minutes | Serves: 4

4 yellowfin tuna steaks	3 or 4 garlic cloves, minced
½ cup soy sauce	1 tablespoon honey
2 tablespoons olive oil	

1. With a fork, prick the tuna steaks a few times before placing them in a gallon-sized plastic bag. 2. To prepare the minced garlic-soy marinade, combine the soy sauce, olive oil, garlic, and honey in a suitable bowl and whisk to combine. When the tuna is evenly coated, pour half of this mixture into the bag with the fish. Place the bagged fish and the leftover garlic-soy mixture in the refrigerator for an hour or two to marinate. 3. Set the Traeger smoker's temperature to High (450 degrees F/ 230 degrees C). Take the tuna out of the fridge. Set the tuna on the grill grates and cook it for 4 to 6 minutes on each side after it has heated up. 4. During the final few minutes of cooking, brush the food with the reserved garlic-soy sauce. 5. Any leftover garlic-soy sauce should be served for dipping.

Per Serving: Calories 397; Total fat 19.1g; Sodium 431mg; Total Carbs 16.8g; Fiber 5.3g; Sugars 6.4g; Protein 39.4g

Chapter 3 Pork Recipes

43	Mustard Rubbed Pork Shoulder
43	Smoked Pork Chops
43	Easy Smoked Pork Tenderloin
43	Smoked Teriyaki Pork Tenderloin
43	Cinnamon Pork Tenderloin
43	BBQ Pork Belly Bites
43	Sweet Smoky Bacon
44	Easy Smoked Bacon
44	Cajun Honey-Smoked Ham
44	Flavorful Smoked Ham
44	Savory Pork Chops with Roasted Plums
44	Bacon-Wrapped Pork Chops with Bourbon-Onion Sauce
45	Grilled Pork Chops with Cucumber-Cream Sauce
45	Herbed Cheese Prosciutto Pork Chop Pockets
45	Pork Tacos with Pineapple Salsa
45	Citrus Pork Tenderloins
46	Roasted Pork Loin with Maple-Cream Sauce
46	Apple-Glazed Pork Tenderloins with Mustard Greens
46	Kielbasa-Onion Sauerkraut Sandwiches
46	Grilled Pork Kabobs
47	Pork and Chorizo Burgers with Cabbage Slaw
47	Pork Sliders with Black Bean Salsa
47	Mint Pork Sandwiches
47	Coffee-Spiced Pork Loin
48	Herbed Italian Sausage Pizzas
48	Mushroom-Pepperoni Stuffed Pizza
48	Chorizo Huevos Rancheros
49	Pork Tortas with Guacamole
49	Apple-Flavored Pulled Pork Sandwiches
49	Jerk-Spiced Baby Back Ribs with Pineapple Salsa
50	Slow-Cooked Cinnamon Pork Shoulder
50	Sweet & Spicy Baby Back Ribs with Apple Sauce
50	Delicious Hoisin-Ginger Pulled Pork
51	Grilled Black Forest Ham & Brie Panini
51	Marmalade-Mustard Glazed Ham with Orange-Dill Sauce
51	BBQ Baby Back Ribs with Onion-Beer Sauce
51	Smoked Bacon Kebabs
52	Honey-Orange Glazed Spareribs
52	Apricot-Soy Glazed Country Spareribs
52	BBQ Baby Back Ribs
52	Typical Pork Nachos
53	BBQ Breakfast Pork Grits
53	Cream Cheese Sausage Balls
53	BBQ Candied Spareribs
53	Smoked Pineapple-Pork Kebabs
53	Juicy Pulled Pork Shoulder
54	Smoky Scotch Eggs
54	Bacon-Wrapped Pork Tenderloin
54	Smoked Brats Sliders
54	Lime Garlic Baby Back Ribs
55	Country Pork Roast with Apple & Sauerkraut
55	Jalapeño Pork Chops with Pickled Pepper Relish

Mustard Rubbed Pork Shoulder

Prep time: 15 minutes | Cook time: 20 hours | Serves: 12

1 (6- to 8-pound) bone-in pork shoulder	Not-Just-for-Pork Rub
2 cups Tea Injectable made with	2 tablespoons yellow mustard
	1 batch Not-Just-for-Pork Rub

1. Fill your Traeger Smoker with wood pellets and follow the manufacturer's specific start-up procedure. Preheat the grill at 225 degrees F/ 105 degrees C with the hood closed. 2. Inject the pork shoulder throughout with the tea injectable. 3. Coat the pork shoulder with mustard and season it with the spice rub. 4. Place the shoulder on the grill grate and smoke until its internal temperature reaches 160 degrees F/ 70 degrees C and a dark bark has formed on the exterior. 5. Pull the shoulder from the grill and wrap it completely in aluminum foil or butcher paper. 6. Increase the grill's temperature to 350 degrees F/ 175 degrees C. 7. Flip the pork shoulder to the grill and cook until its internal temperature reaches 195 degrees F/ 90 degrees C. 8. Pull the shoulder from the grill and place it in a cooler. Cover the cooler and let the pork rest for 1 or 2 hours. 9. Remove the pork shoulder from the cooler and unwrap it. Remove the shoulder bone and pull the pork apart using just your fingers. Serve immediately.
Per Serving: Calories 343; Total fat 20.1g; Sodium 903mg; Total Carbs 0.2g; Fiber 0.1g; Sugars 0.2g; Protein 37.1g

Smoked Pork Chops

Prep time: 15 minutes | Cook time: 55 minutes | Serves: 4

4 (8-ounce) pork chops, bone-in or boneless	Salt
	Black pepper

1. Fill your Traeger Smoker with wood pellets and follow the manufacturer's specific start-up procedure. Preheat the grill at 180 degrees F/ 80 degrees C with the hood closed. 2. Season the pork chops with black pepper and salt. 3. Place the chops directly on the grill grate and smoke for 30 minutes. 4. Increase the grill's temperature to 350 degrees F/ 175 degrees C. Continue to cook the chops until their internal temperature reaches 145 degrees F/ 60 degrees C. 5. Before serving, take the pork chops off the grill and let them rest for 5 minutes.
Per Serving: Calories 416; Total fat 23.6g; Sodium 934mg; Total Carbs 6g; Fiber 2g; Sugars 0.6g; Protein 37.9g

Easy Smoked Pork Tenderloin

Prep time: 15 minutes | Cook time: 5 hours | Serves: 6

2 (1-pound) pork tenderloins	1 batch Not-Just-for-Pork Rub

1. Fill your Traeger Smoker with wood pellets and follow the manufacturer's specific start-up procedure. Preheat the grill at 180 degrees F/ 80 degrees C with the hood closed. 2. Apply the rub liberally to the tenderloins. Put the rub on the meat and rub it in with your hands. 3. When the tenderloins' internal temperature reaches 145 degrees F/ 60 degrees C, place them directly on the grill grate and cook for 4 to 5 hours on Smoke setting. 4. Before slicing and serving, take the tenderloins off the grill and give them 10 minutes to rest.
Per Serving: Calories 372; Total fat 16.3g; Sodium 742mg; Total Carbs 6.8g; Fiber 0.8g; Sugars 1.8g; Protein 42.3g

Smoked Teriyaki Pork Tenderloin

Prep time: 15 minutes | Cook time: 2 hours | Serves: 6

2 (1-pound) pork tenderloins	Smoked salt
1 batch Easy Teriyaki Marinade	

1. In a suitable zip-top bag, mix the tenderloins and marinade. Seal the bag, turn to coat, and let it refrigerate the pork for at least 30 minutes or up to overnight. 2. Fill your Traeger Smoker with wood pellets and follow the manufacturer's specific start-up procedure. Preheat the grill, with the hood closed, to 180 degrees F/ 80 degrees C. 3. Remove the tenderloins from the prepared marinade and season them with smoked salt. 4. Place the tenderloins on the grill grate and smoke them for 1 hour. 5. Increase the grill's temperature to 300 degrees F/ 150 degrees C and continue to cook until the pork's internal temperature reaches 145 degrees F/ 60 degrees C. 6. Serve warm.
Per Serving: Calories 326; Total fat 12g; Sodium 779mg; Total Carbs 8.3g; Fiber 2.9g; Sugars 1.3g; Protein 46.9g

Cinnamon Pork Tenderloin

Prep time: 15 minutes | Cook time: 30 minutes | Serves: 6

2 (1-pound) pork tenderloins	Cinnamon Rub
1 batch Sweet and Spicy	

1. Fill your Traeger Smoker with wood pellets and follow the manufacturer's specific start-up procedure. Preheat the grill, with the hood closed, to 350 degrees F/ 175 degrees C. 2. Apply the spice rub liberally to the tenderloins. Put the spice rub on the meat and rub it in with your hands. 3. The tenderloins should be placed directly on the grill grate and smoked until they achieve an internal temperature of 145 degrees F/ 60 degrees C. 4. Prior to slicing and serving, remove the tenderloins from the grill and allow them to rest for 10 minutes.
Per Serving: Calories 412; Total fat 23.6g; Sodium 1495mg; Total Carbs 4.8g; Fiber 1.3g; Sugars 1.7g; Protein 37.9g

BBQ Pork Belly Bites

Prep time: 15 minutes | Cook time: 6 hours | Serves: 8

1 (3-pound) skinless pork belly, cut into 1½- to 2-inch cubes	½ cup honey
1 batch Sweet Brown Sugar Rub	1 cup Bill's Best BBQ Sauce
	2 tablespoons light brown sugar

1. Fill your Traeger Smoker with wood pellets and follow the manufacturer's specific start-up procedure. Preheat the grill at 250 degrees F/ 120 degrees C with the hood closed. 2. Cubes of pork belly should be generously seasoned with the spice rub. Put the spice rub on the meat and rub it in with your hands. 3. The pork cubes should be placed directly on the grill grate and smoked until they reach 195 degrees F/ 90 degrees C inside. 4. Place the grilled cubes in an aluminum pan, and then add the brown sugar, honey, and barbeque sauce. Mix and coat the meat by stirring. 5. Uncovered, smoke the pork for an hour in the grill pan. 6. Serve the pork right away after removing it from the grill.
Per Serving: Calories 408; Total fat 23.1g; Sodium 412mg; Total Carbs 27.7g; Fiber 7.2g; Sugars 19.2g; Protein 24.4g

Sweet Smoky Bacon

Prep time: 15 minutes | Cook time: 2 hours | Serves: 4

1 cup pure maple syrup	1 (1-pound) package thick-sliced bacon
2 tablespoons honey	
1 cup packed light brown sugar	

1. Stir the maple syrup, honey, and ½ cup of brown sugar in an airtight container until well mixed. Add the bacon and turn to coat, then cover the container and let them refrigerate overnight. 2. Fill your Traeger Smoker with wood pellets and follow the manufacturer's specific start-up procedure. Preheat the grill at 225 degrees F/ 105 degrees C with the hood closed. 3. Remove the bacon from the prepared marinade and place them on the grill grate. Add the final ½ cup of brown sugar to the top. Smoke the bacon for 2 hours, or until it is done to your preference. 4. Serve immediately.
Per Serving: Calories 236; Total fat 10.4g; Sodium 713mg; Total Carbs 9.8g; Fiber 0.5g; Sugars 0.1g; Protein 25.7g

Easy Smoked Bacon

Prep time: 15 minutes | Cook time: 30 minutes | Serves: 4

1 (1-pound) package thick-sliced bacon

1. Fill your Traeger Smoker with wood pellets and follow the manufacturer's specific start-up procedure. Preheat the grill at 275 degrees F/ 135 degrees C with the hood closed. 2. Place the bacon strips directly on the grill grate, being careful they do not hang over the drain pan, and smoke for 20 to 30 minutes, or until done to your liking. 3. Serve immediately.
Per Serving: Calories 347; Total fat 15.7g; Sodium 999mg; Total Carbs 11.8g; Fiber 1.1g; Sugars 7g; Protein 39.6g

Cajun Honey–Smoked Ham

Prep time: 15 minutes | Cook time: 5 hours | Serves: 10

1 (5- or 6-pound) bone-in smoked ham	1 batch Cajun Rub
	3 tablespoons honey

1. Fill your Traeger Smoker with wood pellets and follow the manufacturer's specific start-up procedure. Preheat the grill at 225 degrees F/ 105 degrees C with the hood closed. 2. Put the ham on the grill grate, depending on your preference, and generously season it with the rub. Smoke the ham for 1 hour. 3. When the time is up, drizzle the ham with honey and resume cooking until it reaches an internal temperature of 145 degrees F/ 60 degrees C. 4. Before slicing and serving, remove the ham from the grill and allow it to rest for 10 minutes.
Per Serving: Calories 427; Total fat 18.1g; Sodium 676mg; Total Carbs 13.7g; Fiber 7.5g; Sugars 1.7g; Protein 51.2g

Flavorful Smoked Ham

Prep time: 15 minutes | Cook time: 6 hours | Serves: 12

1 (10-pound) ham, skin removed	1 batch Rosemary-Garlic Lamb Seasoning
2 tablespoons olive oil	

1. Fill your Traeger Smoker with wood pellets and follow the manufacturer's specific start-up procedure. Preheat the grill at 180 degrees F/ 80 degrees C with the hood closed. 2. Rub the ham with olive oil and sprinkle it with the seasoning. 3. Set the ham directly on the grill grate and smoke for 3 hours. 4. Increase the grill's temperature to 375 degrees F/ 190 degrees C and continue to smoke the ham until its internal temperature reaches 170 degrees F/ 75 degrees C. 5. Prior to slicing and serving, remove the ham from the grill and allow it to rest for 10 minutes.
Per Serving: Calories 227; Total fat 8.8g; Sodium 302mg; Total Carbs 8.9g; Fiber 2.1g; Sugars 3.3g; Protein 28.5g

Savory Pork Chops with Roasted Plums

Prep time: 15 minutes | Cook time: 1 hr. 30 minutes | Serves: 4

Marinade
¼ cup low-sodium soy sauce	1 tablespoon grated ginger
2 tablespoons red wine vinegar	1 garlic clove, minced
1 tablespoon packed dark brown sugar	Vegetable oil

Pork Chops
4 bone-in pork loin chops	⅓ cup plum jam or preserves
4 firm but ripe plums, about 1-pound total, each cut in half	2 teaspoons red wine vinegar
2 garlic cloves, minced	1 sprig rosemary, about 6 inches long
1 cup fruity, full-bodied red wine, such as Syrah	1½ teaspoons cold unsalted butter
¾ cup low-sodium beef broth	Salt
	Black pepper

1. Mix the prepared marinade ingredients, including 3 tablespoons oil. 2. Place the pork chops in a resealable plastic bag and pour in the prepared marinade. Turn the bag to distribute the prepared marinade, then place it in a suitable bowl, and let the pork chops refrigerate for 2 to 4 hours, turning occasionally. 3. Prepare the Traeger grill for direct cooking over 350 degrees F/ 175 degrees C. 4. Lightly brush the plums with oil on both sides. Grill them for 4 to 8 minutes with the hood closed until they begin to soften, turning once halfway through. 5. Remove them from the hot grill and cut them into ¼-inch slices. 6. Remove the chops from the bag and allow them to leave at room temperature for 15 to 30 minutes before grilling. Discard the prepared marinade. 7. In a saucepan over medium-high heat, Heat 2 teaspoons of oil. Then, add the minced garlic and cook for approximately a minute until fragrant. 8. When the cooking is boiling, add the red wine. Rapidly boil for 7–8 minutes, or until it has been reduced to ¼ cup; add the broth, bring the stew back to a boil, and cook for 8 to 9 minutes longer until it has been reduced to ¼ cup. 9. Reduce the heat to medium-low, add the jam, vinegar, and rosemary sprig, and simmer for 3 minutes while stirring occasionally. Eliminate the rosemary and turn off the heat. Stir in the butter until it is melted; add the plums and season with ¼ teaspoon salt and ⅛ teaspoon pepper. 10. Season the chops with salt and black pepper on both sides. They should be grilled for approximately 10 minutes, flipping once they are halfway done, over direct medium heat with the hood closed. Take the food off the hot grill and give it 5 minutes to rest. 11. Serve the warm plums with it.
Per Serving: Calories 314; Total fat 8.7g; Sodium 337mg; Total Carbs 21.2g; Fiber 4.1g; Sugars 16g; Protein 37.9g

Bacon–Wrapped Pork Chops with Bourbon–Onion Sauce

Prep time: 15 minutes | Cook time: 15 minutes | Serves: 4

Sauce
1 tablespoon unsalted butter	¼ cup bourbon
½ cup chopped yellow onion	1 tablespoon Worcestershire sauce
1 garlic clove, minced	1 tablespoon balsamic vinegar
⅓ cup ketchup	½ teaspoon hot pepper sauce
⅓ cup unsulfured molasses	

Rub
1 teaspoon prepared chili powder	chops, 1 inch thick
½ teaspoon salt	Vegetable oil
½ teaspoon black pepper	4 slices bacon
4 boneless center-cut pork loin	

1. Melt the butter in a good saucepan over medium heat; add the onion, and sauté for 5 minutes until golden brown; add the minced garlic and cook for approximately a minute, or until fragrant. 2. Bring the sauce to a simmer after adding the last few ingredients. Stirring often, reduce its heat to low, and simmer the prepared mixture for 15 minutes or until the sauce is somewhat thickened. 3. Pork chops should be brushed with ¼ cup of the sauce while they are grilling, and the remaining sauce should be served alongside the chops. 4. Mix the spice rub ingredients in a suitable bowl. Oil the chops on both sides, then rub the spice rub on them. Before grilling, let the chops rest at room temperature for 15 to 30 minutes. 5. Prepare the Traeger grill for direct cooking over 350 degrees F/ 175 degrees C. 6. Cook the bacon for 2 minutes on high in a skillet over medium heat until the grease has somewhat rendered. Each chop should have a slice of bacon wrapped around the outside and secured with a toothpick. 7. About 10 minutes into the grilling process, flip the chops once they are halfway done, then brush them with some of the sauce during the final 4 to 5 minutes of grilling. The chops should still be somewhat pink in the center. Take the food off the hot grill and give it 5 minutes to rest. 8. Serve the chops hot with the rest of the sauce.
Per Serving: Calories 344; Total fat 10g; Sodium 251mg; Total Carbs 4.7g; Fiber 0.5g; Sugars 2.2g; Protein 55.7g

Grilled Pork Chops with Cucumber–Cream Sauce

Prep time: 15 minutes | Cook time: 30 minutes | Serves: 4

4 bone-in pork loin chops	½ cup sliced dill gherkins
2 tablespoons olive oil	1½ tablespoons whole-grain mustard
2 tablespoons chopped tarragon leaves	¾ cup low-sodium chicken broth
Salt	3 tablespoons frozen apple juice concentrate, thawed
Black pepper	
3 tablespoons unsalted butter	⅓ cup heavy whipping cream
1½ cups sliced shallots	

1. Oil the pork chops on both sides, then equally sprinkle 1½ tablespoons of tarragon, 1 teaspoon of salt, and ¾ teaspoon of black pepper over the meat. Allow the chops to rest at room temperature for 15 to 30 minutes. 2. Set up the Traeger grill for direct cooking at 350 degrees F/ 175 degrees C. 3. The chops should be grilled for 10 minutes with the hood closed, flipping them once halfway through. 4. Melt 2 tablespoons of the butter in a skillet over medium heat. 5. Add the chopped shallots and sauté for 6 to 7 minutes, or until they are soft and a deep golden color. Add the Gherkins, mustard, broth, and apple juice concentrate, and cook for 1 to 2 minutes until the liquid is reduced and the mixture slightly thickness, then bring to a boil. 6. Add the cream, bring the prepared mixture back to gentle boil, and cook for 3 minutes. Add the final 1 ½ teaspoons of tarragon, ¼ teaspoon of salt, and ¼ teaspoon of pepper to season. Add the final tablespoon of butter and combine. Turn off the heat and cover the area to stay warm. 7. The chops should be taken from the grill and let to rest for 5 minutes to let the liquids cling together. After adding the liquids, mix the sauce to incorporate them. 8. Serve the sauce and the chops warm.

Per Serving: Calories 346; Total fat 18.8g; Sodium 137mg; Total Carbs 13.4g; Fiber 8.5g; Sugars 1g; Protein 36.3g

Herbed Cheese Prosciutto Pork Chop Pockets

Prep time: 15 minutes | Cook time: 18 minutes | Serves: 4

4 double bone-in pork loin chops, 2 inches thick	4 thin slices provolone cheese
	4 thin slices prosciutto
Paste:	
¼ cup olive oil	1 tablespoon grated lemon zest
2 tablespoons chopped rosemary leaves	2 garlic cloves, peeled
	1 teaspoon salt
2 tablespoons oregano leaves	½ teaspoon crushed red pepper flakes
1 tablespoon thyme leaves	

1. In a suitable food processor or a blender mix the paste ingredients and puree until the prepared mixture forms a thick paste. 2. Set the pork chops on a work surface. Using a sharp knife, make a slit in the side of the meat opposite the bone. Cut this slit into a pocket by cutting to the left and right, slowly creating an opening that extends throughout the chop to within ½ inch of the bone. 3. Stuff each chop with one slice of the cheese and one slice of the prosciutto, folding them in half. Spread the paste the chops and marinate at room temperature for 20 to 30 minutes. 4. Prepare the Traeger grill for direct cooking over 350 degrees F/ 175 degrees C. 5. Grill the prepared chops for 16 to 18 minutes with the hood closed until they are still pink in the center, turning occasionally. 6. Remove the chops from the hot grill and let rest for 5 minutes. 7. Serve warm.

Per Serving: Calories 319; Total fat 15.6g; Sodium 99mg; Total Carbs 4.8g; Fiber 0.7g; Sugars 2.9g; Protein 38.5g

Pork Tacos with Pineapple Salsa

Prep time: 15 minutes | Cook time: 13 minutes | Serves: 4

12 corn or flour tortillas (6 inches)	2 limes, cut into wedges

Marinade

½ pineapple, chopped	preferably Mexican
1 medium white onion, chopped	1 teaspoon ground cumin
¼ cup tequila	1 teaspoon salt
2 tablespoons distilled white or cider vinegar	¼ teaspoon ground cinnamon
	2¼ pounds boneless country-style ribs or boneless blade pork chops, about 1 inch thick
1 canned chipotle chili pepper	
2 garlic cloves	
1 teaspoon dried oregano,	

Salsa

½ pineapple, cut crosswise into ½-inch slices, cored	⅓ cup chopped cilantro leaves
	1 jalapeño chili pepper, seeded and minced
½ medium white onion, cut crosswise into ¼-inch slices	Salt

1. Puree the prepared marinade ingredients in the food processor until smooth. 2. Place the pork chops in a resealable plastic bag and pour in the prepared marinade. 3. Turn the bag to distribute the prepared marinade, place the bag in a bowl, and let it refrigerate for 1 hour. 4. Prepare the Traeger grill for direct cooking over 350 degrees F/ 175 degrees C. 5. Grill the pineapple and onion slices for 8 minutes with the hood closed until grill marks appear, flipping once cooked halfway through. Remove them from the hot grill and cut into small dice. 6. Mix all the salsa ingredients. Set aside. 7. Remove the chops from the bag, allowing some of the prepared marinade to cling to the meat. Discard the remaining marinade. Season the chops with salt. 8. Grill the prepared chops for 12 minutes with the hood closed until the meat is still slightly pink in the center, turning once. Remove from the hot grill and let rest for 5 minutes. 9. Heat the tortillas over direct heat for 1 minute and slice. 10. ½Fill each tortilla with pork and salsa, and serve with the lime wedges.

Per Serving: Calories 326; Total fat 12g; Sodium 779mg; Total Carbs 8.3g; Fiber 2.9g; Sugars 1.3g; Protein 46.9g

Citrus Pork Tenderloins

Prep time: 15 minutes | Cook time: 30 minutes | Serves: 2

Marinade

¾ cup cola (not diet)	2 teaspoons mustard powder
¼ cup orange juice	2 teaspoons salt
2 tablespoons lime juice	3 garlic cloves, minced
1½ tablespoons peeled, grated ginger	½ teaspoon ground cardamom
	1 teaspoon black pepper
1 tablespoon packed dark brown sugar	1 teaspoon ground cumin

Pork

2 pork tenderloins	1 tablespoon olive oil

1. Combine the ingredients for the marinade. Put the prepared marinade and the pork in a resealable plastic bag. 2. Place the prepared marinade in a dish, turn the bag to distribute it evenly, and then chill this bowl for 4 hours. 3. Pork should be taken out of the bag, and the marinade should be saved. Before grilling, let the pork rest at room temperature for 15 to 30 minutes. 4. Set up the Traeger grill for direct cooking at 350 degrees F/ 175 degrees C. 5. In the saucepan, pour the prepared marinade and boil them over medium-high heat, then simmer for 4 minutes or until somewhat reduced and thickened. Set aside. 6. Brush the pork with oil. Grill the pork for roughly 5 minutes with the hood closed until nicely marked on both sides, flipping once. Turn and baste the pork every 5 minutes until the outsides are evenly browned and the centers are lightly pink, about 15 minutes more. Lightly baste with the reduced marinade. 7. Take the food off the hot grill and give it 5 minutes to rest. Serve warm

Per Serving: Calories 413; Total fat 24.5g; Sodium 962mg; Total Carbs 6.9g; Fiber 1.1g; Sugars 2.9g; Protein 39.1g

Roasted Pork Loin with Maple-Cream Sauce

Prep time: 15 minutes | Cook time: 30 minutes | Serves: 4

Sauce
- 1½ tablespoons unsalted butter
- ¾ cup chopped shallots
- 3 tablespoons cider vinegar
- 2¼ cups low-sodium beef broth
- 1 cup heavy whipping cream
- ¼ cup maple syrup
- 3 tablespoons country-style Dijon mustard
- ½ teaspoon salt

Rub
- 1 boneless pork loin roast, 3 ½ pounds
- 2 teaspoons smoked paprika
- 1½ teaspoons salt
- 1 teaspoon garlic powder
- ¾ teaspoon black pepper
- 1 tablespoon olive oil
- 2 tablespoons chopped parsley leaves

1. Melt the butter in a saucepan over medium heat; add the shallots and cook for 5 to 6 minutes until just softened; add the vinegar and cook for 1 to 2 minutes to get it to evaporate. 2. Increase the heat to high, then pour in the broth and cream, and bring to a boil, stirring occasionally. Lower the heat to medium and gently simmer the prepared mixture for 20 to 30 minutes, or until it has thickened enough to coat the back of a spoon and has been reduced to 1 ¾ cups. After adding the syrup, boil the prepared mixture for 3 minutes; add the salt and mustard after turning off the heat. Set aside or allow to cool, cover, and refrigerate for 3 hours 3. Mix all the rub ingredients. Oil the roast with a rub before evenly applying the spice rub. Before grilling, let the roast sit at room temperature for 30 minutes. 4. Prepare the Traeger grill for direct and indirect cooking over high heat (450 degrees F/ 230 degrees C to 550 degrees F/ 290 degrees C). 5. For about 10 minutes, turn the roast occasionally as it is seared over direct high heat with the hood closed (watch for flare-ups, especially when searing the fatty side). Move the roast to indirect high heat, cover the hood and cook it for 20 to 30 minutes with fat-side up,, or until an instant-read thermometer inserted into the roast reads 140 to 145 degrees F/ 60 degrees C. 6. Place it on a chopping board, loosely tent with foil, and let it rest for 15 minutes. 7. Add the parsley and slowly reheat the sauce over low heat. Slice the roast diagonally and serve it hot with the sauce.

Per Serving: Calories 412; Total fat 23.6g; Sodium 1495mg; Total Carbs 4.8g; Fiber 1.3g; Sugars 1.7g; Protein 37.9g

Apple-Glazed Pork Tenderloins with Mustard Greens

Prep time: 15 minutes | Cook time: 50 minutes | Serves: 2

Glaze
- 1 jar (12 ounces) apple jelly
- 3 tablespoons cider vinegar
- 2 tablespoons unsalted butter
- 4 teaspoons Dijon mustard

Others
- Salt
- Black pepper
- 4 teaspoons minced thyme leaves
- 2 pork tenderloins
- Olive oil
- 4 garlic cloves, sliced
- ⅛ teaspoon crushed red pepper flakes
- 1-pound mustard greens, stems trimmed and leaves chopped
- ⅓ cup golden raisins
- ½ cup low-sodium chicken broth
- 2 teaspoons cider vinegar
- 4 slices cooked bacon, chopped

1. Add the jelly to the saucepan, and cook them over medium heat for 2 minutes until it melts; add the cider vinegar, Dijon mustard, butter, ½ teaspoon salt and ¼ teaspoon black pepper, and mix until the prepared mixture is smooth. 2. Remove the saucepan from the heat, and reserve ½ cup of the glaze for brushing on the pork during grilling. Leave the remaining glaze in the saucepan. 3. Prepare the Traeger grill for direct cooking over 350 degrees F/ 175 degrees C. 4. Mix the thyme, 1 ½ teaspoons salt, and 1 teaspoon pepper. Rub the pork with oil and season with the spices. 5. Grill the pork for 20 minutes with the hood closed, turning three times. 6. Rub the pork with the reserved glaze, then remove from the hot grill and let rest for 5 minutes. 7. Heat 2 tablespoons of oil in the skillet over medium-high heat; add the minced garlic and the red pepper flakes, cook them for 1 minute until the minced garlic is fragrant; add the greens and toss for 2 minutes until wilted; add the raisins and broth, and bring to a boil, then cook them for 2 to 4 minutes until the broth is completely absorbed and the greens are just tender; add the vinegar, black pepper, and salt. 8. Reheat the glaze in the saucepan. 9. Cut the pork into slices. Divide the greens, pork, and bacon among four plates. Spoon the glaze over the top, and serve right away.

Per Serving: Calories 408; Total fat 23.1g; Sodium 412mg; Total Carbs 27.7g; Fiber 7.2g; Sugars 19.2g; Protein 24.4g

Kielbasa-Onion Sauerkraut Sandwiches

Prep time: 15 minutes | Cook time: 1hr. 30 minutes | Serves: 2

- 6 ounces sauerkraut, rinsed and drained
- 2 red onions, 10–12 ounces total, halved and sliced
- 2 bottles (each 12 ounces) beer
- 1 teaspoon granulated sugar
- ½ teaspoon caraway seed
- ⅛ teaspoon celery seed
- 1-pound kielbasa, halved lengthwise, each half cut crosswise into 2 pieces
- 4 submarine sandwich rolls, each about 6 inches long, split
- Yellow or brown deli mustard

1. Prepare the Traeger grill for direct cooking over 350 degrees F/ 175 degrees C. 2. In a 10-inch cast-iron skillet, mix the sauerkraut, onions, beer, and sugar. Place the skillet over direct medium heat, close the lid, and bring the prepared mixture to a simmer. Simmer the mixture for 25 to 30 minutes, occasionally stirring. 3. After 20 minutes, add the caraway seed and the celery seed. 4. At the same time, grill the kielbasa for 7 to 8 minutes with cut side down first until nicely browned, turning once halfway through. 5. Remove the kielbasa from the grill and cut into 1-inch pieces. After the sauerkraut mixture has simmered for 25 to 30 minutes, add the kielbasa to the skillet and continue to cook for 5 minutes more, stirring occasionally. 6. Toast the rolls, over direct medium heat until warmed through and browned, about 1 minute. 7. Fill the rolls with the onion and kielbasa mixture. Serve the rolls with mustard.

Per Serving: Calories 314; Total fat 8.7g; Sodium 337mg; Total Carbs 21.2g; Fiber 4.1g; Sugars 16g; Protein 37.9g

Grilled Pork Kabobs

Prep time: 15 minutes | Cook time: 10 minutes | Serves: 2

Marinade
- ⅓ cup chopped parsley leaves and tender stems
- ¼ cup olive oil
- 2 tablespoons minced red onion
- 1 tablespoon sherry vinegar
- 1 tablespoon smoked paprika
- 2 teaspoons ground cumin
- 2 teaspoons minced garlic
- ¼ teaspoon ground cayenne pepper

Others
- Salt, to taste
- 2 pork tenderloins, cut into 1¼-inch cubes
- 2 bell peppers, cut into 1¼-inch squares

1. Mix the prepared marinade ingredients, including ½ teaspoon salt. 2. Put the pork cubes in a suitable, resealable plastic bag and pour in the prepared marinade. 3. Flip the bag to distribute the prepared marinade, place in a suitable bowl, and let it refrigerate for 4 to 8 hours, turning occasionally. 4. Prepare the Traeger grill for direct cooking over high heat (450 degrees F/ 230 degrees C to 550 degrees F/ 290 degrees C). 5. Remove the pork from the bag. Thread the pork and bell pepper squares alternately onto skewers. 6. Grill the prepared kabobs for 10 minutes with the hood closed until the pork is barely pink in the center, flipping cooked halfway through. 7. Remove the kabobs from the hot grill and season with salt. Serve warm.

Per Serving: Calories 227; Total fat 8.8g; Sodium 302mg; Total Carbs 8.9g; Fiber 2.1g; Sugars 3.3g; Protein 28.5g

Pork and Chorizo Burgers with Cabbage Slaw

Prep time: 15 minutes | Cook time: 13 minutes | Serves: 4

Patties
14 ounces lean ground pork
10 ounces chorizo
½ cup panko bread crumbs
3 tablespoons minced shallot
2 tablespoons chopped parsley leaves
Slaw
¾ cup cilantro leaves, chopped
½ jalapeño chili pepper, seeded and minced
2 tablespoons lime juice
2 tablespoons sour cream
2 tablespoons mayonnaise
½ teaspoon salt
Mayonnaise
8 thin slices tomato
4 garlic cloves, minced
1 teaspoon ground cumin
½ teaspoon smoked paprika
½ teaspoon dried thyme
½ teaspoon salt
¼ teaspoon black pepper
¼ teaspoon prepared chili powder
12 ounces green cabbage, cored and sliced
1 medium carrot, peeled and grated
4 hamburger buns, split
Olive oil
4 leaves lettuce

1. Gently combine the patty ingredients in a good bowl, then form four patties that are each about 4 inches in diameter and 1-inch-thick using damp hands (they won't be tender if the meat is overly compacted). 2. Create a small indentation in the center of all the patties that is about 1 inch broad with your thumb. This will assist in ensuring equal cooking and stop the prepared patties from blowing up on the grill. Place them in the refrigerator for 30 minutes. 3. In a suitable bowl mix the cilantro, jalapeño, lime juice, sour cream, mayonnaise, salt, and chili powder. Add the cabbage and the carrot and toss to mix. If time allows, cover and let it refrigerate for 1 hour to allow the flavors to develop. Remove from the refrigerator about 20 minutes. 4. Prepare the Traeger grill for direct cooking over 350 degrees F/ 175 degrees C. 5. Rub the cut side of each bun with oil. Grill the prepared patties for 12 to 13 minutes with the hood closed until they have an internal temperature of 145 degrees F/ 60 degrees C, turning once when the prepared patties release easily from the grate without sticking. 6. Looking at the prepared patties will not be an accurate measure of whether they are done since chorizo stays pink when cooked. Toast the buns over direct heat for 1 minute. 7. Remove the prepared patties and the buns from the grill. 8. Cover the cut sides of each bun with mayonnaise. Build each burger with lettuce, a patty, and two tomato slices. 9. Toss the slaw to redistribute the prepared dressing and serve alongside the burgers.

Per Serving: Calories 347; Total fat 15.7g; Sodium 999mg; Total Carbs 11.8g; Fiber 1.1g; Sugars 7g; Protein 39.6g

Pork Sliders with Black Bean Salsa

Prep time: 15 minutes | Cook time: 8 minutes | Serves: 4

Salsa
1 can (15 ounces) black beans, rinsed
¾ cup chopped green bell pepper
¼ cup grated red onion
2 tablespoons olive oil
2 tablespoons minced cilantro
Patties
1½ pounds lean ground pork
¼ cup grated red onion
1 teaspoon mustard powder
1 teaspoon dried oregano
leaves
1 tablespoon red wine vinegar
½ teaspoon dried oregano
¼ teaspoon hot pepper sauce
¼ teaspoon smoked paprika
¼ teaspoon salt
1 teaspoon salt
½ teaspoon smoked paprika
½ teaspoon black pepper
12 small dinner rolls, split

1. Mix all the salsa ingredients. Set aside. 2. Prepare the Traeger grill for direct cooking over 350 degrees F/ 175 degrees C. 3. Mix the patty ingredients lightly, then form 12 patties, each measuring about 3 inches in diameter. The prepared patties won't be tender if the meat is overly compacted. 4. Create a small indentation in the center of the patties that is approximately ½ inch broad with your thumb or the back of a spoon. This will assist in ensuring equal cooking and stop the prepared patties from blowing up on the grill. 5. Grill the patties for 6 to 8 minutes with the hood closed, flipping once halfway through. 6. Toast the rolls in the final minute of cooking. Take the prepared patties off the hot grill and place them in the buns with the salsa you like on top. 7. Serve right away.

Per Serving: Calories 236; Total fat 10.4g; Sodium 713mg; Total Carbs 9.8g; Fiber 0.5g; Sugars 0.1g; Protein 25.7g

Mint Pork Sandwiches

Prep time: 15 minutes | Cook time: 11 minutes | Serves: 2

½ English cucumber, about 6 ounces, sliced
1 red onion, about 4 ounces, cut in half vertically, sliced
1 medium carrot, peeled and grated using the holes of a box grater
1 tablespoon granulated sugar
3 teaspoons salt
¾ teaspoon crushed red pepper flakes
¼ cup white wine vinegar
¼ cup olive oil
2 pork tenderloins
Vegetable oil
1 teaspoon black pepper
¾ cup mayonnaise
1 tablespoon grated lemon zest
1 loaf ciabatta, about 1 pound, cut into 6 equal pieces, each piece halved horizontally
½ cup chopped cilantro leaves
½ cup chopped mint leaves

1. Mix the vegetables with the sugar, 1 teaspoon of the salt, the red pepper flakes, vinegar, and olive oil. Set aside. 2. Cut off the thin, tapered ends from each tenderloin and reserve for another use. Cut each tenderloin crosswise into three equal pieces. Set the pieces of pork, cut side up, on a work surface and, using your hand, pound each piece until it is an even ½-inch thick. Rub the pork pieces with vegetable oil and season them evenly with the remaining 2 teaspoons salt and ½ teaspoon of the pepper. 3. Mix the mayonnaise and the lemon zest. 4. Prepare the Traeger grill for direct cooking over high heat (450 degrees F/ 230 degrees C to 550 degrees F/ 290 degrees C). 5. Grill the prepared pork for 5 to 6 minutes with the hood closed until barely pink in the center, flipping once cooked halfway through. Toast the ciabatta over direct heat. Remove the pork and the ciabatta from the grill. 6. Drain the vegetables and discard the liquid. Build the sandwiches with lemon mayo, pork, pickled vegetables, cilantro, and mint. 7. Serve immediately.

Per Serving: Calories 612; Total fat 38.2g; Sodium 76mg; Total Carbs 39.1g; Fiber 5.8g; Sugars 1.6g; Protein 30.6g

Coffee-Spiced Pork Loin

Prep time: 15 minutes | Cook time: 3 hours | Serves: 4

¼ cup ground coffee
¼ cup paprika
¼ cup garlic powder
2 tablespoons chili powder
1 tablespoon packed light brown sugar
1 tablespoon ground allspice
1 tablespoon ground coriander
1 tablespoon black pepper
2 teaspoons ground mustard
1½ teaspoons celery seeds
1 (1½- to 2-pound) pork loin roast

1. Fill your Traeger Smoker with wood pellets and follow the manufacturer's specific start-up procedure. Preheat the grill at 250 degrees F/ 120 degrees C with the hood closed. 2. Mix the paprika, ground coffee, chili powder, brown sugar, garlic powder, allspice, coriander, pepper, mustard, and celery seeds in a bowl to create a rub, and generously coat the pork loin roast with the rub. 3. Set the pork loin on the grill, fat-side up, close the lid, and grill the roast for 3 hours until it has an internal temperature of 160 degrees F/ 70 degrees C. 4. Let the roast cool for 5 minutes after grilling, then slice and serve.

Per Serving: Calories 385; Total fat 13.2g; Sodium 929mg; Total Carbs 31.6g; Fiber 4.2g; Sugars 2.6g; Protein 36.4g

Chapter 3 Pork Recipes | 47

Herbed Italian Sausage Pizzas

Prep time: 15 minutes | Cook time: 20 minutes | Serves: 6

2 balls premade pizza dough	¼ cup sliced black olives
Olive oil, to cook	2 tablespoons chopped parsley leaves
1 bell pepper, cut into ¼-inch strips	1 tablespoon chopped thyme leaves
½ small yellow onion, sliced	2 teaspoons chopped rosemary leaves
8 ounces mild or spicy Italian sausage	1½ cups shredded mozzarella cheese
All-purpose flour	
1 can (8 ounces) tomato sauce	

1. To make the dough easier to roll out, take the dough balls out of the refrigerator, if required, about an hour before grilling. 2. Heat 1 tablespoon oil in a skillet over medium-high heat; add the bell pepper and onion, and sauté for 3 minutes until they are softened but not browned. Transfer the onion and bell pepper to a bowl, and set aside. 3. After cutting the sausage into medium-sized pieces, add it to the set skillet. About 3 minutes of cooking time over medium-high heat, stirring occasionally and breaking up the sausage into smaller pieces. After turning off the heat, allow the set skillet with the sausage to cool. 4. Prepare the Traeger grill for direct cooking over 350 degrees F/ 175 degrees C, and preheat a pizza stone for at least 15 minutes by following manufacturer's instructions. 5. Roll out the premade dough into circles that are about 12 inches across and ⅓ inch thick on a dusted work surface. Set aside the first round while rolling out the second. 6. Transfer the first round of pizza dough onto a pizza stone (or a rimless baking sheet) coated with flour. Spread ½ cup of the sauce over the dough. 7. Add half of the sausage, half of the onion mixture, half of the parsley, half of the olives, thyme, and rosemary on top. Finish by adding half of the cheese on top of everything. 8. Slide your first pizza onto the preheated pizza stone and cook over direct medium heat, with the hood closed until the crust is golden brown and the cheese is melted, for about 11 minutes. Using a pizza peel or a suitable spatula, remove the pizza from the pizza stone and let rest for a few minutes. 9. Cut the pizza into wedges and serve warm.

Per Serving: Calories 227; Total fat 8.8g; Sodium 302mg; Total Carbs 8.9g; Fiber 2.1g; Sugars 3.3g; Protein 28.5g

Mushroom–Pepperoni Stuffed Pizza

Prep time: 15 minutes | Cook time: 1 hr. 30 minutes | Serves: 4

Filling

1 tablespoon olive oil	1-pound button mushrooms, sliced
3 cups chopped yellow onions	4 garlic cloves, minced
1½ cups chopped green bell pepper	1 teaspoon salt
	½ teaspoon black pepper

Sauce

1 can (8 ounces) tomato sauce	1 garlic clove, minced
¼ cup freshly grated Parmigiano-Reggiano® cheese	¼ teaspoon dried thyme
2 tablespoons tomato paste	olive oil
1 tablespoon olive oil	1½ pounds premade pizza dough
½ teaspoon dried oregano	7 ounces grated mozzarella cheese
½ teaspoon dried basil	5 ounces sliced pepperoni

1. Prepare the Traeger grill for direct and indirect cooking over 350 degrees F/ 175 degrees C. 2. Heat the oil in a good skillet over medium heat. With intermittent turning, add the onions and bell pepper and simmer for 3 minutes until they are slightly softened; add the mushrooms and simmer for 12 minutes until they are soft, browned, and any liquid they have released has evaporated. Add the minced garlic, salt, and black pepper in the last minute. The filling should be taken off the stove and left to cool. 3. Combine the sauce's components. If required, take the dough out of the fridge about an hour prior to grilling so that it will be simpler to roll out. 4. Make two balls out of the prepared dough, one containing two thirds of it and the other the remaining one third. 5. Roll, pat, and spread the larger ball into a 14-inch circle on a surface that has been dusted with flour. 6. Oil a 10-inch cast-iron skillet just enough to coat it. Transfer the dough to the skillet, allowing the excess hang over the sides to prevent the dough from slipping into the skillet. 7. Press the dough into the corners while gently stretching the dough to fit the skillet. 1 cup of the mozzarella should be distributed over the prepared dough. Spread the other half of the filling over the cheese and then top with one-half of the pepperoni, arranging it in a single layer. 8. Make a second layer with the pepperoni and the remaining filling. Sprinkle the top with ½ cup of the mozzarella evenly. A 10-inch circle is formed by rolling, patting, and stretching the final piece of dough. By laying the round on top of the filling and applying pressure, you may eliminate any apparent air pockets. 9. Apply a coating of water to the edges where the top and bottom dough pieces meet, then roll and press the edges to seal them. Several times prick the dough to allow any. To release any newly generated air pockets, prick the dough numerous times. Spread the sauce over the top crust, covering only the sealed edges of the dough. Add the remaining ½ cup mozzarella on top of the sauce. 10. Place the skillet over a direct medium heat, cover it, and cook for 5 minutes, or until the dough's edges appear set and somewhat dry. 11. Close the hood while cooking and move the skillet to indirect medium heat. Cook the food for 35 to 45 minutes. 12. After taking the set skillet off the grill, the pizza should rest for 10 minutes. Slide the pizza onto a serving plate using a broad spatula. Warm wedges after cutting.

Per Serving: Calories 232; Total fat 8.4g; Sodium 300mg; Total Carbs 8.6g; Fiber 0.9g; Sugars 0.1g; Protein 30.1g

Chorizo Huevos Rancheros

Prep time: 15 minutes | Cook time: 25 minutes | Serves: 8

3 poblano chili peppers, about 14 ounces total	tomatoes in juice
1½ teaspoons canola oil	1 can (15 ounces) black beans, rinsed
12 ounces chorizo sausages, casings removed	Salt
	Black pepper
3 garlic cloves, minced	3½ ounces pepper jack cheese, grated
1 cup sliced scallions	4 eggs
2 teaspoons ground cumin	
1 can (28 ounces) chopped plum	8 corn tortillas (6 inches)

1. Prepare the Traeger grill for direct cooking over high heat (450 degrees F/ 230 degrees C to 550 degrees F/ 290 degrees C). 2. Grill the poblanos for 12 minutes with the hood closed until blackened and blistered, turning occasionally. 3. Put the poblanos in a bowl and cover with plastic sheet to trap the steam. Let stand for 10 minutes. Peel away and discard the charred skin. Cut off and discard the stems and seeds, and then chop the poblanos. 4. Place a 10-inch cast-iron skillet over direct high heat, add the oil, and warm for 1 minute. Add the chorizo and break into small pieces using a wooden spoon. Cook them for 5 to 6 minutes until the chorizo pieces are browned, stirring occasionally. 5. Add the minced garlic, scallions, and poblanos and cook for 2 to 3 minutes. Add the cumin, the tomatoes in juice, the beans, ½ teaspoon salt, and ½ teaspoon pepper. Bring to a boil and cook for 12 to 16 minutes until the flavors are blended, the liquid is reduced by two-thirds, and only a small amount of liquid remains in the bottom of the skillet. Top with the cheese and cook for 3 to 4 minutes until most of the cheese is melted. 6. Make four shallow indentations in the chili-bean mixture. Crack one egg into each indentation. Continue cooking over direct high heat, with the hood closed until the egg whites are set for 5 minutes. Season the eggs with some salt and black pepper. Carefully remove the set skillet from the grill. 7. Put four tortillas in each of two foil packets. Warm the packets over direct high heat for 1 minute, turning once. 8. Serve the huevos rancheros with warm tortillas.

Per Serving: Calories 427; Total fat 18.1g; Sodium 676mg; Total Carbs 13.7g; Fiber 7.5g; Sugars 1.7g; Protein 51.2g

Pork Tortas with Guacamole

Prep time: 15 minutes | Cook time: 3 hours | Serves: 8

- 1 tablespoon prepared chili powder
- ¾ teaspoon granulated garlic
- Salt
- 1 bone-in pork shoulder roast (Boston butt), about 3 ½ pounds
- olive oil
- 8 crusty rolls, each about 6 inches long, split

Guacamole
- 2 Hass avocados, cut into ½-inch dice
- 2 plum tomatoes, seeded and ½ diced
- 3 tablespoons minced red onion
- 1 tablespoon chopped cilantro leaves
- 1 tablespoon lime juice
- 1 garlic clove, minced
- ½ teaspoon prepared chili powder
- 8 leaves red lettuce
- 8 slices tomato
- 1 red onion, separated into rings
- Pickled jalapeño chili pepper slices, drained

1. Set the Traeger grill to medium-low heat for indirect grilling (about 325 degrees F/ 160 degrees C). 2. Combine the 2 teaspoons of salt, the chili powder, and the crushed garlic. Oil the roast sparingly, then evenly sprinkles it with the seasonings. 3. Add the roast to a disposable foil pan, and cover the pan, then cook the roast for 1½ hours over indirect medium-low heat. 4. After 45 minutes of cooking times, drain the pan, and add the remaining wood chips. 5. To keep the temperature constant when using a charcoal barbecue, top it off as necessary. After 1½ hours, cover the pan tightly with aluminum foil and continue cooking for 1 to 1 ½ hours more. 6. Remove from the hot grill, cover, and let rest for 15 to 30 minutes. Save the pan juices. Toast the rolls, over direct heat for 1 minute. 7. Mix the guacamole ingredients and mash with a fork. Season with salt. 8. Cut the cooked meat across the grain into thin slices. Skim the fat from the pan juices. 9. Build the tortas on rolls with lettuce, tomato, onion, jalapeño slices, pork, pan juices, and guacamole. Serve warm.

Per Serving: Calories 346; Total fat 18.8g; Sodium 137mg; Total Carbs 13.4g; Fiber 8.5g; Sugars 1g; Protein 36.3g

Apple-Flavored Pulled Pork Sandwiches

Prep time: 15 minutes | Cook time: 3 hours | Serves: 12

Rub
- 1 tablespoon packed dark brown sugar
- 1 tablespoon salt
- 2 teaspoons paprika
- 1 teaspoon chipotle Chile powder
- 1 teaspoon granulated garlic
- 1 bone-in pork shoulder roast, 5 ½–6 pounds, trimmed of excess fat
- 1 teaspoon prepared chili powder

Sauce
- 1 tablespoon unsalted butter
- ½ cup minced yellow onion
- 1 cup ketchup
- 1 cup unsweetened apple juice
- ½ cup cider vinegar
- ½ teaspoon hot pepper sauce
- 2 tablespoons packed dark brown sugar
- 1 tablespoon unsulfured molasses
- 1 tablespoon soy sauce

Slaw
- ⅓ cup mayonnaise
- 3 tablespoons sour cream
- 2 tablespoons cider vinegar
- 1 tablespoon granulated sugar
- ¾ teaspoon salt
- ¼ teaspoon black pepper
- ½ medium head green cabbage, sliced (4 cups)
- 2 medium carrots, peeled, grated (1 cup)
- 12 hamburger buns, split

1. Mix the spice rub ingredients. Apply the spice rub evenly to the roast's surface. Before grilling, let the roast sit at room temperature for 30 minutes. 2. Set up the Traeger grill for low-heat indirect cooking (250 degrees F/ 120 degrees C to 300 degrees F/ 150 degrees C). 3. Put an appropriate disposable foil pan on the charcoal grate's bare side. Warm water should come halfway up the pan. 4. Following the manufacturer's instructions, add 2 handfuls of drained wood chips to the charcoal. 5. Cover the hood, and cook the roast for four hours with the fat side up, until the wood starts to smoke. 6. Drain and add one handful of the wood chips to the charcoal or to the smoker box every 1 hour until they are gone. 7. Check the roast's internal temperature after 4 hours using an instant-read thermometer. Cook it until it reaches 160 degrees F/ 70 degrees C. 8. Set the roast in a disposable foil pan and carefully wrap it in foil. Transfer the pan to the grill, and cook it for an additional 2 to 3 hours. Remove the pan from the hot grill and allow it rest for an hour in the covered foil pan. Make the sauce while the roast is cooling. 9. Melt the butter in a saucepan over medium heat; add the chopped onion and cook for 6 minutes; mix in the remaining sauce ingredients, bring to a simmer, then reduce the heat to medium-low, and occasionally stir for 15 minutes more until slightly thickened. Remove from the heat. 10. Mix the mayonnaise, sour cream, vinegar, sugar, salt, and pepper in a bowl until smooth, then add the cabbage and the carrots, and mix them the vegetables are evenly coated. 11. Pull the meat apart into shreds once the roast has cooled enough to handle. Discard any fat or sinew fragments. Put the pork in a decent saucepan over low heat, add as much sauce as you prefer, and cook until heated through, stirring occasionally. Place the pork on the buns, then add the coleslaw. Serve with any extra sauce.

Per Serving: Calories 344; Total fat 10g; Sodium 251mg; Total Carbs 4.7g; Fiber 0.5g; Sugars 2.2g; Protein 55.7g

Jerk-Spiced Baby Back Ribs with Pineapple Salsa

Prep time: 15 minutes | Cook time: 4 hours 10 minutes | Serves: 8

Paste
- ½ cup chopped white onion
- 1-2 Serrano chili peppers, seeded
- 3 scallions, ends trimmed, chopped
- 2 tablespoons olive oil
- 2 tablespoons lime juice
- 2 tablespoons granulated sugar
- 6 garlic cloves, chopped
- 1 tablespoon ground allspice
- 1 teaspoon dried thyme
- ¾ teaspoon black pepper
- Salt, to taste
- 2 racks baby back ribs, each 1¾–2 ¼ pounds, membrane removed

Salsa
- 2 cups chopped pineapple (about 12 ounces)
- ¼ cup chopped red bell pepper
- ¼ cup chopped white onion
- 2 tablespoons chopped cilantro leaves
- ½ teaspoon hot pepper sauce
- 1 tablespoon lime juice
- 1 tablespoon dark or spiced rum

1. Add the paste ingredients, and 1½ teaspoons salt to the food processor, and process them until fairly smooth. 2. Spread the paste on the racks. Cover and let it refrigerate for 3 to 4 hours, turning occasionally. Allow the ribs to leave at room temperature for 45 minutes before grilling. 3. Prepare the Traeger grill for indirect cooking over low heat (250 degrees F/ 120 degrees C to 350 degrees F/ 175 degrees C). 4. In a nonreactive bowl, mix the salsa ingredients, including 1 teaspoon of salt. Cover the bowl and let the salsa refrigerate until just before serving. 5. Evenly season the racks with salt. Cover the hood, and grill them for 2½ to 3 hours with the bone side down first, turning the racks over and rotating them, and switching their positions about every 40 minutes so that both sides of each rack spend the same amount of time closest to the heat. 6. Additionally, periodically baste them with water to keep the surface damp. 7. When the meat has receded at least ¼-inch from the ends of the majority of the bones, the ribs are finished. 8. Take up one end of the rack to lift it. The meat should rip readily, and it should flex in the middle. Cook the meat for another hour or until it can be readily torn. 9. After transferring, set aside 10 minutes to recover. 10. Rum and lime juice are incorporated into the salsa. 11. Serve the individual ribs from each rack with the salsa.

Per Serving: Calories 307; Total fat 15.5g; Sodium 720mg; Total Carbs 6.6g; Fiber 1g; Sugars 2.8g; Protein 36.6g

Slow-Cooked Cinnamon Pork Shoulder

Prep time: 15 minutes | Cook time: 5 hours | Serves: 12

Marinade
- 2 cans (each 12 ounces) cola (not diet)
- 2 lemons, peel and pith removed, ¼ sliced
- 1 yellow onion, sliced
- ½ cup low-sodium soy sauce
- ⅓ cup packed golden brown sugar
- 3 garlic cloves, chopped
- 3 cinnamon sticks
- 1 canned chipotle Chile pepper in adobo sauce, chopped
- 1 tablespoon dried oregano
- 1 bone-in pork shoulder roast (Boston butt), 6 pounds, trimmed of excess fat

1. Mix the all the ingredients except for the pork shoulder roast in a basin while stirring to dissolve the sugar. 2. Cut slashes through the fat just to the flesh approximately 2 inches apart, scoring the fat on the roast in a crosshatch pattern. Turn the roast to coat with the marinade after placing it in this bowl. It should be covered and chilled for 12 to 24 hours while being turned occasionally. Before grilling, let the roast sit at room temperature for an hour. 3. Prepare the Traeger grill for indirect cooking over low heat (250 degrees F/ 120 degrees C to 350 degrees F/ 175 degrees C). 4. Place the roast in a disposable foil pan with the fat-side down. Pour the prepared marinade and the solids over the roast. 5. Grill the roast for 4 to 5 hours with the hood covered, rotating the meat once every 1½ hours. The roast and the pan should be taken from the grill. 6. Cut the roast into ½-inch slices. Serve warm.

Per Serving: Calories 319; Total fat 15.6g; Sodium 99mg; Total Carbs 4.8g; Fiber 0.7g; Sugars 2.9g; Protein 38.5g

Sweet & Spicy Baby Back Ribs with Apple Sauce

Prep time: 15 minutes | Cook time: 2 hours 30 minutes | Serves: 6

Rub
- 2 tablespoons paprika
- 1½ tablespoons dark brown sugar
- 1 tablespoon prepared chili powder
- 1 tablespoon granulated garlic
- 1 tablespoon salt
- 1½ teaspoons onion powder
- 4 baby back ribs racks, each 2 ½–3 pounds
- 1½ teaspoons black pepper
- ½ teaspoon ground thyme
- ½ teaspoon ground cayenne pepper

Sauce
- 1 cup ketchup
- ⅔ cup unsweetened apple juice
- ⅓ cup cider vinegar
- 2 tablespoons packed dark brown sugar
- 2 tablespoons unsulfured molasses
- 1 tablespoon Worcestershire sauce
- 1 teaspoon prepared chili powder
- 1 teaspoon smoked paprika
- ½ teaspoon ground cumin
- ¼ teaspoon black pepper

Mop
- 1 cup unsweetened apple juice
- 6 tablespoons sauce (from above)
- ¼ cup cider vinegar

1. Mix the spice rub ingredients. Slide the point of a dull knife under the membrane that covers the back of each rack of ribs. When you can pry up the membrane after lifting and loosening it, grasp a corner with a paper towel and peel it off. The spice rub should be applied equally to the racks. Make a rib rack out of the racks by standing them all facing the same way. Before grilling, let the racks rest at room temperature for 45 minutes. 2. Wood chips should be submerged in water for at least 30 minutes. 3. Prepare the Traeger grill for indirect cooking over low heat (300 degrees F/ 150 degrees C to 350 degrees F/ 175 degrees C). Following the manufacturer's instructions, drain and add half of the wood chips to the charcoal. 4. Place the racks on the grill grate, cover the pan when smoke starts to emerge, and cook for one hour. Keep the grill's temperature between 300 degrees F/ 150 degrees C and 350 degrees F/ 175 degrees Cahrenheit. 5. Mix the components for the glaze. Drain the leftover wood chips, then add them to the charcoal or smoker box after the first hour of cooking 6. Close the grill cover and remove the racks from the rib rack after the second hour of cooking. Brush the racks with the remaining mop. Return the racks to the rib rack, this time turning them over so that the ends that were previously facing downward now face upward. Additionally, place any rib racks that seem to be cooking more quickly than the rest in the back of the rack, farthest from the heat. thirty more minutes of cooking. 7. After two and a half hours, most of the bones' meat will have shrunk back by at least a quarter inch. Cooking should continue if it hasn't until it does. After that, take the rib rack off the grill. Shut the hood. After removing the racks from the rib rack, lightly brush some of the sauce over each rack's top and bottom surfaces. 8. Place the racks back on the grill over low, indirect heat. The racks can now be stacked on top of one another. Cook the food for a further 15 to 30 minutes over indirect low heat with the hood covered to achieve tenderness. 9. When you raise a rack with tongs from one end, bone side up, and the rack flexes so much in the middle that the meat readily shreds, the meat is done. 10. Cook the meat longer if it doesn't fall apart readily. 11. Remove off the hot grill and give it ten minutes to cool. 12. Cut the racks into ribs and serve with any extra sauce on the side.

Per Serving: Calories 217; Total fat 5.1g; Sodium 624mg; Total Carbs 6.8g; Fiber 0.8g; Sugars 1.8g; Protein 31.1g

Delicious Hoisin-Ginger Pulled Pork

Prep time: 15 minutes | Cook time: 5 hours 10 minutes | Serves: 8

- 1 bone-in pork shoulder roast (Boston butt), 4–5 pounds
- 1 tablespoon salt
- 1 teaspoon black pepper

Sauce
- 1 tablespoon vegetable oil
- 1 teaspoon toasted sesame oil
- 1 tablespoon peeled, grated ginger
- 3 garlic cloves, minced
- ½ cup hoisin sauce
- 1 tablespoon low-sodium soy sauce
- 2 tablespoons dry sherry
- 2 teaspoons hot chili-garlic sauce
- 3 scallions, ends trimmed, sliced
- ½ teaspoon grated orange zest
- 4 cups cooked white rice
- 3 tablespoons chopped cilantro leaves

1. Trim the roast of excess fat and season with the black pepper and salt. Cover and allow the roast to leave at room temperature for 30 minutes. 2. Prepare the Traeger grill for indirect cooking over low heat (250 degrees F/ 120 degrees C to 350 degrees F/ 175 degrees C). Keep the grill's temperature as close to 300 degrees F/ 150 degrees C as possible. 3. Close the cover after adding half of the wood chips to the smoker box of the charcoal. 4. Cook the roast for one hour with the fat side up. After 30 minutes of cooking time, drain, and add the remaining wood chips. Cook the roast for 4 to 5 hours more until it has an internal temperature of 190 degrees F/ 85 degrees C. 5. After moving the roast to a cutting board, cover it loosely with foil and give it 20 minutes to rest. 6. Heat the oil in a saucepan over medium heat. For about a minute, add the ginger and the minced garlic, and sauté until fragrant and just beginning to brown. 7. Reduce the heat to medium, add the hoisin, soy sauce, sherry, and chili-garlic sauce, and simmer for 2 to 3 minutes, stirring occasionally. 8. Remove the saucepan from the heat, and add half the scallions and the orange zest. Pull the cooked pork apart into shreds, discarding any pieces of fat. Mix the pork and the sauce and toss to moisten. 9. Serve warm, spooned over the rice and topped with the remaining scallions and the cilantro.

Per Serving: Calories 349; Total fat 15.1g; Sodium 157mg; Total Carbs 25.6g; Fiber 2.6g; Sugars 22.5g; Protein 29.7g

Grilled Black Forest Ham & Brie Panini
Prep time: 15 minutes | Cook time: 15 minutes | Serves: 4

- 4 soft French rolls, each about 6 inches long, split
- ¼ cup Dijon mustard
- 8 slices Black Forest ham, each about ⅓ inch thick
- 4 ounces Brie cheese, cut into 8 pieces, each about ¼ inch thick
- 1 ripe pear or apple, cored and cut lengthwise into 8 slices
- 4 crisp leaves romaine lettuce
- ¼ cup (½ stick) butter, melted

1. Prepare the Traeger grill for direct cooking over 350 degrees F/ 175 degrees C and preheat a grill-proof griddle for 10 minutes. 2. Cover the cut side the rolls with the mustard. Top the bottom half of the rolls with two ham slices, two cheese slices, two pear slices, a lettuce leaf, and the top half of the roll. Press down on each sandwich so it is compacted. Brush the sandwiches with the melted butter. 3. Arrange the sandwiches on the grill, and grill for 5 minutes on each side until the rolls are toasted and golden, and the cheese is melted. 4. Remove them from the hot grill and serve immediately.

Per Serving: Calories 271; Total fat 19.2g; Sodium 124mg; Total Carbs 7.2g; Fiber 2.9g; Sugars 0.5g; Protein 18.6g

Marmalade-Mustard Glazed Ham with Orange-Dill Sauce
Prep time: 15 minutes | Cook time: 3 hours | Serves: 12

- 1 bone-in smoked ham, butt end, 6–7 pounds
- **Glaze**
- ⅓ cup whole-grain mustard
- ⅓ cup orange marmalade
- 2 tablespoons lime juice
- ½ teaspoon black pepper
- **Sauce**
- ⅔ cup mayonnaise
- ⅔ cup sour cream
- ¼ cup prepared horseradish
- grated zest and ¼ cup juice of 2 oranges
- 2 tablespoons minced dill
- 1 teaspoon white wine vinegar
- ½ teaspoon salt
- ¼ teaspoon black pepper

1. Before grilling, let the ham sit at room temperature for 30 to 40 minutes. 2. Set the Traeger grill up for indirect cooking at a temperature greater than 350 degrees F/ 175 degrees C. 3. Combine the glaze's components. Place the ham on a suitable disposable foil pan and score it in a suitable crisscross pattern about ½ inch deep on both sides, aside from the sliced side. On the ham's top and sides, Rub half of the glaze. Grill for one hour over indirect medium heat with the hood covered. Grill for a further 45 minutes to 1 ½ hours, basting frequently with the leftover glaze until an instant-read thermometer placed into the thickest part of the ham (but not touching the bone) reads 160 degrees F/ 70 degrees C. For the remainder of the grilling process, cover the ham loosely with aluminum foil if the glaze turns too black. After taking it from the hot grill, cover it loosely with foil and give it 15 to 45 minutes to rest. 4. Mix the sauce components in a basin that is not reactive. Slice the ham, then top with sauce and serve warm.

Per Serving: Calories 309; Total fat 5.1g; Sodium 245mg; Total Carbs 43g; Fiber 9.6g; Sugars 14.2g; Protein 25.8g

BBQ Baby Back Ribs with Onion-Beer Sauce
Prep time: 15 minutes | Cook time: 1 hr. 30 minutes | Serves: 8

- **Rub**
- 2 tablespoons packed golden brown sugar
- 1 tablespoon salt
- 2 teaspoons chipotle chili powder
- 2 teaspoons garlic powder
- 1 teaspoon prepared chili powder
- 1 teaspoon ground cayenne pepper
- 1 teaspoon black pepper
- 2 racks baby back ribs, each 2-2 ½ pounds
- **Sauce**
- 2 tablespoons unsalted butter
- 1 yellow onion, 7–8 ounces, chopped
- 1 cup ketchup
- ¾ cup light molasses (not blackstrap)
- ½ cup beer, preferably lager
- ¼ cup cider vinegar
- 3 tablespoons tomato paste
- 1 ½ teaspoons mustard powder
- 1 teaspoon garlic powder
- 1 cup beer, preferably lager

1. Mix all the rub the ingredients. 2. Slide the point of a dull knife under the membrane that covers the back of each rack of ribs. When you can pry up the membrane after lifting and loosening it, grasp a corner with a paper towel and peel it off. Before grilling, season the racks with the rub and let them leave at room temperature for 45 minutes. 3. Set up the Traeger grill for low-heat indirect cooking (250 degrees F/ 120 degrees C to 350 degrees F/ 175 degrees C). 4. Melt the butter over medium-high heat in a saucepan; add the onion and cook for 3 to 4 minutes until slightly softened, stirring occasionally; add the remaining sauce ingredients and bring to a boil. 5. Reduce the heat to medium-low and cook on a simmer for 18 to 20 minutes with the lid uncovered, until thickened. Remove the saucepan from the heat. 6. Place the racks on the grill with the bone side down, cover the lid, and cook for 3 hours. 7. Baste the racks with beer after the first hour, paying close attention to any areas that appear to be a touch dry. 8. For another hour or so, continue to use beer baste. 9. After three hours, determine if one or both racks can be taken off the grill. When the meat has receded from the ends of the majority of the bones by at least a quarter inch, they are finished. 10. Take up one end of the rack to lift it. The meat should rip readily, and it should flex in the middle. Return the racks to the oven if the meat is difficult to tear. Return the racks to the grill, close the lid, and cook the meat for a further hour or until it is easily torn. 11. After taking the racks from the grill, coat both sides of them with some of the sauce. Return the racks to the grill and cook them for another 10 to 20 minutes with the lid covered, flipping them regularly. 12. Remove them from the hot grill and give it 10 minutes to cool. 13. Slice the racks into individual ribs between the bones, and serve warm with the leftover sauce.

Per Serving: Calories 481; Total fat 14.6g; Sodium 285mg; Total Carbs 57.5g; Fiber 7.3g; Sugars 1g; Protein 31.1g

Smoked Bacon Kebabs
Prep time: 15 minutes | Cook time: 30 minutes | Serves: 8

- Nonstick cooking spray
- 2 pounds thick-cut bacon (24 slices)
- 24 metal skewers
- 1 cup packed light brown sugar
- 2 to 3 teaspoons cayenne pepper
- ½ cup maple syrup

1. Fill your Traeger Smoker with wood pellets and follow the manufacturer's specific start-up procedure. At 350 degrees F/ 175 degrees C, preheat your Traeger smoker with its hood closed. 2. Apply cooking spray, to a baking sheet made of disposable aluminum foil. 3. Each piece of bacon should be threaded onto a metal skewer before being placed on the baking sheet. 4. Combine the cayenne and brown sugar in a medium bowl. 5. ¼ cup of maple syrup should be basted onto the bacon's top sides. 6. Distribute half of the brown sugar mixture over the bacon. 7. Close the grill's cover after placing the baking sheet there to smoke for 15 to 30 minutes. 8. Flip the bacon skewers with tongs. Top with the remaining brown sugar mixture and baste with the final ¼ cup of maple syrup. 9. Cook them for 15 minutes or until the bacon is crispy, keep smoking with the hood closed. The ideal internal temperature for bacon is 155 degrees F/ 70 degrees C 10. Carefully take the bacon skewers from the grill using tongs. Allow to fully cool before handling.

Per Serving: Calories 342; Total fat 13.7g; Sodium 678mg; Total Carbs 32.3g; Fiber 4.5g; Sugars 22.1g; Protein 26.7g

Honey–Orange Glazed Spareribs

Prep time: 15 minutes | Cook time: 2 hours 10 minutes | Serves: 12

Glaze
½ cup honey
2 tablespoons frozen orange juice concentrate, thawed
1 tablespoon balsamic vinegar

Rub
1 tablespoon salt
2 teaspoons ancho chili powder
2 teaspoons ground cumin
2 teaspoons dried oregano
1 teaspoon black pepper
2 racks St. Louis–style spareribs, 3–3 ½ pounds each, membrane removed

1. Soak the wood chips in water for at least 30 minutes. 2. Set up the Traeger grill for direct cooking at 350 degrees F/ 175 degrees Cahrenheit. 3. Combine all the glaze ingredients in a bowl. 4. Mix the rub ingredients. 5. Create two smaller racks by halving each one. Equally rub the racks with the rub. Each half rack should be double wrapped and sealed in its own packet using eight 18 by 24-inch sheets of heavy-quality aluminum foil. 6. Close the grill's cover after placing the foil-wrapped racks on the grate. Cook the racks for 1¼ hours, flipping the packets over once or twice for even cooking. 7. After taking the packets from the grill, give them a 10-minute resting period. Open the packs slowly, take off the racks, and throw away the foil and rendered fat. 8. Following the manufacturer's instructions, drain the wood chips and add them to the charcoal or to the smoker box. Then, cover the grill. Return the racks to the grill once the wood starts to smoke. Smoke the racks for 5 minutes over direct medium heat with the hood closed before flipping them once they are halfway done. Brush them with the glaze on both sides, and cook for 5 minutes until the racks are shiny and crispy, flipping once cooked halfway through and apply more glaze after each turn. 9. Remove from the hot grill and let rest for 10 minutes. Serve warm.

Per Serving: Calories 322; Total fat 15.9g; Sodium 104mg; Total Carbs 5.1g; Fiber 0.9g; Sugars 2.9g; Protein 38.4g

Apricot–Soy Glazed Country Spareribs

Prep time: 15 minutes | Cook time: 2 hours 30 minutes | Serves: 12

Rub
3 tablespoons packed golden brown sugar
2 teaspoons black pepper
1 teaspoon ground ginger
½ teaspoon mustard powder
½ teaspoon Chinese five spice
Salt, to taste

Others
2 racks St. Louis–style spareribs, each 3–3 ½ pounds, membrane removed
2 teaspoons toasted sesame oil
1 tablespoon peeled, grated ginger
3 garlic cloves, minced
½ cup apricot preserves
3 tablespoons low-sodium soy sauce

1. Prepare the Traeger grill for indirect and direct cooking over low heat (250 degrees F/ 120 degrees C to 300 degrees F/ 150 degrees C). 2. Mix the spice rub components and ⅓ teaspoon of salt. 3. Coat the racks with the rub, concentrating more on the meaty side. Before grilling, let the racks rest at room temperature for 45 minutes. 4. Cover the grill's hood, and grill the racks with the bone side down for 2 hours with the hood closed. 5. In the meantime, preheat the oil in a good saucepan over medium-high heat. Stir often for a minute after adding the ginger and the minced garlic, until fragrant and just beginning to brown. Add ¾ teaspoon salt, the preserves, and the soy sauce. Cooking to a boil and cook until thickened, 2 to 3 minutes, with occasional stirring. Remove from the heat. 6. The racks should be taken off the grill and both sides should be coated with three-fourths of the apricot-soy glaze. Reflip the foil-wrapped racks to the grill and cook for a further 1½ hours over indirect low heat with the hood closed, or until the meat is readily torn when you raise each rack and has shrunk back from the ends of most of the bones by at least ¼ inch or more in numerous places. 7. Remove the racks from the hot grill, and allow them to cool until you can handle it. Discard the rendered fat and foil after carefully removing the racks from the foil. Return to the grill over direct low heat, cover it, and cook the racks for 5 minutes. 8. Let them cool for 10 minutes before serving.

Per Serving: Calories 384; Total fat 23.6g; Sodium 80mg; Total Carbs 20.7g; Fiber 8.3g; Sugars 3.5g; Protein 24.6g

BBQ Baby Back Ribs

Prep time: 15 minutes | Cook time: 6 hours | Serves: 8

2 full slabs of baby back ribs, back membranes removed
1 cup prepared table mustard
1 cup House Dry Rub
1 cup apple juice
1 cup packed light brown sugar
1 cup Bill's Best BBQ Sauce

1. Fill your Traeger Smoker with wood pellets and follow the manufacturer's specific start-up procedure. Preheat the grill at 180 degrees F/ 80 degrees C or on Smoke setting with the hood closed. 2. Coat the ribs with the mustard to help the spice rub stick and lock in moisture. 3. Generously coat the ribs with the rub. 4. Place the ribs directly on the grill, close the lid, and smoke for 3 hours. 5. Remove the ribs from the hot grill and wrap each rack individually with aluminum foil, but before sealing tightly, add ½ cup apple juice and ½ cup brown sugar to each package. 6. Return the foil-wrapped ribs to the grill and increase the cooking temperature to 225 degrees F/ 105 degrees C, close the lid, and smoke them for 2 more hours. 7. Carefully unwrap the ribs and remove the foil completely. 8. Coat each slab with ½ cup of barbecue sauce and continue smoking with the hood closed for 1 hour, or until the meat tightens and has a reddish bark. 9. For the perfect rack, the internal temperature should be 190 degrees F/ 85 degrees C.

Per Serving: Calories 314; Total fat 8.7g; Sodium 337mg; Total Carbs 21.2g; Fiber 4.1g; Sugars 16g; Protein 37.9g

Typical Pork Nachos

Prep time: 15 minutes | Cook time: 10 minutes | Serves: 4

2 cups leftover smoked pulled pork
1 small sweet onion, diced
1 medium tomato, diced
1 jalapeño pepper, seeded and diced
1 garlic clove, minced
1 teaspoon salt
1 teaspoon black pepper
1 bag of tortilla chips
1 cup shredded Cheddar cheese
½ cup Bill's Best BBQ Sauce
½ cup shredded jalapeño Monterey Jack cheese
Juice of ½ lime
1 avocado, halved, pitted, and sliced
2 tablespoons sour cream
1 tablespoon chopped cilantro

1. Fill your Traeger Smoker with wood pellets and follow the manufacturer's specific start-up procedure. Preheat the grill at 375 degrees F/ 190 degrees C with the hood closed. 2. Heat the pulled pork in the microwave. 3. Mix the onion, tomato, jalapeño, garlic, salt, and black pepper in a bowl, and set aside. 4. Arrange half of the chips in a suitable cast iron skillet. Spread half of the warmed pork on top and cover with the Cheddar cheese. Top them with half of the onion-jalapeño mixture, then drizzle with ¼ cup of barbecue sauce. 5. Layer on the remaining tortilla chips, then the remaining pork and the Monterey Jack cheese. Top them with the remaining onion-jalapeño mixture and drizzle with the remaining ¼ cup of barbecue sauce. 6. Set the set skillet on the grill, close the lid, and smoke for 10 minutes until the cheese is melted and bubbly. 7. Squeeze the lime juice over the nachos, top with the avocado slices and sour cream, and garnish with the cilantro before serving hot.

Per Serving: Calories 422; Total fat 7.3g; Sodium 1093mg; Total Carbs 26.9g; Fiber 5.9g; Sugars 2.4g; Protein 58.5g

BBQ Breakfast Pork Grits
Prep time: 15 minutes | Cook time: 40 minutes | Serves: 4

2 cups chicken stock	1 tablespoon hot sauce
1 cup water	1 cup shredded Monterey Jack cheese
1 cup quick-cooking grits	1 cup sour cream
3 tablespoons unsalted butter	Salt
2 tablespoons minced garlic	Black pepper
1 medium onion, chopped	2 eggs, beaten
1 jalapeño pepper, stemmed, seeded, and chopped	⅓ cup half-and-half
1 teaspoon cayenne pepper	3 cups leftover pulled pork (preferably smoked)
2 teaspoons red pepper flakes	

1. Fill your Traeger Smoker with wood pellets and follow the manufacturer's specific start-up procedure. At 350 degrees F/ 175 degrees C, preheat your Traeger smoker with its hood closed. 2. Add the chicken stock and water in a suitable saucepan, and boil them over high heat. 3. Add the grits and reduce the heat to low, then add the butter, garlic, onion, jalapeño, cayenne, red pepper flakes, hot sauce, cheese, sour cream, black pepper, and salt, then cook them for 5 minutes. 4. Temper the beaten eggs and incorporate them into the grits. Remove the saucepan from the heat and add the half-and-half and pulled pork. 5. Pour the grits into a greased grill-safe 9-by-13-inch casserole dish or aluminum pan. 6. Transfer this pan to the grill, close the lid, and cook for 30 to 40 minutes, covering with the pan with aluminum foil toward the end of cooking if the grits start to get too brown on top. 7. Serve warm.

Per Serving: Calories 393; Total fat 11.7g; Sodium 591mg; Total Carbs 16.4g; Fiber 4.3g; Sugars 6.6g; Protein 56.4g

Cream Cheese Sausage Balls
Prep time: 15 minutes | Cook time: 30 minutes | Serves: 4

1 pound ground hot sausage, uncooked	8 ounces cream cheese, softened
	1 package mini filo dough shells

1. Fill your Traeger Smoker with wood pellets and follow the manufacturer's specific start-up procedure. At 350 degrees F/ 175 degrees C, preheat your Traeger smoker with its hood closed. 2. In a suitable bowl, using your hands, mix together the sausage and cream cheese until well blended. 3. Place the filo dough shells in a mini muffin tray or on a pizza pan with a rim and perforations. 4. Place the 1-inch balls of the sausage and cheese mixture inside the filo shells. 5. Close the grill cover and place the pizza pan or mini muffin tray on it. Smoke the sausage balls for 30 minutes, or until they are cooked through and the sausage is no longer pink. 6. Serve warm.

Per Serving: Calories 223; Total fat 10.6g; Sodium 646mg; Total Carbs 4.1g; Fiber 2.4g; Sugars 1.6g; Protein 29.5g

BBQ Candied Spareribs
Prep time: 15 minutes | Cook time: 6 hours | Serves: 8

2 racks pork spareribs	1 tablespoon red pepper flakes
2 tablespoons yellow mustard	¼ cup apple juice
2 tablespoons chicken bouillon granules	1 cup Blueberry BBQ Sauce more for serving

1. Fill your Traeger Smoker with wood pellets and follow the manufacturer's specific start-up procedure. Preheat the grill at 250 degrees F/ 120 degrees C with the hood closed. 2. Coat the ribs with the mustard, and then sprinkle the ribs with the bouillon granules and red pepper flakes on all sides. 3. Set the ribs directly on the grill, close the lid, and smoke for 3 hours. 4. Remove the cooked ribs from the grill and wrap each rack individually with aluminum foil, but before sealing tightly, add 2 tablespoons of apple juice to each package. 5. Set the foil-wrapped ribs back on the grill, close the lid, and continue smoking for 2 hours. 6. Carefully unwrap the ribs and remove the foil completely. Baste the ribs with the barbecue sauce, then smoke for 1 hour more with the hood closed. 7. Let the ribs rest for 5 minutes before serving with additional barbecue sauce.

Per Serving: Calories 428; Total fat 29g; Sodium 546mg; Total Carbs 10.8g; Fiber 3.1g; Sugars 0.2g; Protein 30.6g

Smoked Pineapple–Pork Kebabs
Prep time: 15 minutes | Cook time: 12 minutes | Serves: 4

1 (20-ounce) bottle of hoisin sauce	1 teaspoon black pepper
½ cup Sriracha	2 pounds thick-cut pork chops or pork loin, cut into 2-inch cubes
¼ cup honey	10 ounces pineapple, diced
¼ cup apple cider vinegar	1 red onion, diced
2 tablespoons canola oil	1 bag mini sweet peppers, tops removed and seeded
2 teaspoons minced garlic	12 metal or wooden skewers
2 teaspoons onion powder	
1 teaspoon ground ginger	
1 teaspoon salt	

1. In a suitable bowl, stir the Sriracha, hoisin, honey, vinegar, oil, minced garlic, onion powder, ginger, salt, and black pepper to create the prepared marinade. Reserve ¼ cup for basting. 2. Toss the remaining spice marinade with the pork cubes, pineapple pieces, onion wedges, and tiny peppers. Cover them and chill for 6 hours. 3. Fill your Traeger Smoker with wood pellets and follow the manufacturer's specific start-up procedure. At 450 degrees F/ 230 degrees C, preheat your Traeger Smoker with its hood close. 4. Do not rinse after removing the pork, pineapple, and vegetables from the marinade. Throw away the marinade you've made. 5. The kebabs should be put together using the double-skewer method. Make sure the skewer runs through the left side of the ingredients as you thread a piece of pork, a slice of pineapple, an onion chunk, and a sweet little pepper onto each of the 6 skewers. Each skewer must be threaded two more times. 6. By inserting an additional 6 skewers through the ingredients' right side, you can double-skewer the kebabs. 7. Directly place the kebabs on the grill, cover it, and smoke for 12 minutes while rotating them once. 8. Serve hot.

Per Serving: Calories 353; Total fat 18.5g; Sodium 682mg; Total Carbs 2.3g; Fiber 0.8g; Sugars 1g; Protein 45.8g

Juicy Pulled Pork Shoulder
Prep time: 15 minutes | Cook time: 9 hours | Serves: 10

1 (5-pound) Boston butt (pork shoulder)	2 cups apple juice
¼ cup prepared table mustard	½ cup salt
½ cup House Dry Rub	BBQ sauce, for serving

1. Slather the meat with the mustard and coat with ¼ cup of the dry rub. 2. Mix the apple juice and salt and shake in a spray bottle until the salt is dissolved. 3. Fill your Traeger Smoker with wood pellets and follow the manufacturer's specific start-up procedure. Preheat the grill at 225 degrees F/ 105 degrees C with the hood closed. 4. Set the pork fat-side up in an aluminum pan, transfer the pan to the grill, close the lid, and smoke the pork for 8 to 9 hours until the thickest part reaches an internal temperature of 205 degrees F/ 95 degrees C, spritzing well with the salted apple juice every hour. 5. Cover the pork loosely with aluminum foil toward the end of cooking, if necessary, to keep the top from blackening. 6. Drain the liquid from the pan, cover, and allow the meat to cool for a few minutes before using two forks to shred it. 7. Sprinkle the remaining rub over the meat and serve with barbecue sauce.

Per Serving: Calories 282; Total fat 15.4g; Sodium 646mg; Total Carbs 16.4g; Fiber 7g; Sugars 6.5g; Protein 22.5g

Smoky Scotch Eggs

Prep time: 15 minutes | Cook time: 1 hr. 30 minutes | Serves: 4

½ cup all-purpose flour	1 egg, beaten
4 teaspoons poultry seasoning	1 cup panko breadcrumbs
4 hard-boiled eggs, peeled	1 cup mayonnaise
1 pound ground hot sausage	¼ cup Dijon mustard

1. Mix the flour and 2 teaspoons of poultry seasoning in a bowl. 2. Dip the hard-boiled eggs in water, then roll them around in the flour mixture. 3. Divide the sausage into four equal parts and roll it into balls. 4. Flatten the balls and shape them around the hard-boiled eggs until completely covered. 5. Dip each sausage-covered egg in the beaten egg, then dredge in the panko. Transfer to a plate, loosely cover the plate with plastic sheet and l refrigerate them for 2 hours. 6. In a suitable bowl, mix together the mayonnaise, mustard, and the remaining 2 teaspoons of poultry seasoning to create a dipping sauce. Set aside. 7. Fill your Traeger Smoker with wood pellets and follow the manufacturer's specific start-up procedure. Preheat the grill at 180 degrees F/ 80 degrees C or on Smoke mode with the hood closed. 8. Put the chilled eggs directly on the grill, close the lid, and smoke them for 1 hour. Remove from the hot grill. 9. Increase the cooking temperature to 375 degrees F/ 190 degrees C and return the eggs to the grill. Close the hood and smoke them for 30 more minutes. 10. Let the eggs rest for 5 minutes after smoking, then slice them and serve with the dipping sauce you like.
Per Serving: Calories 282; Total fat 15.4g; Sodium 646mg; Total Carbs 16.4g; Fiber 7g; Sugars 6.5g; Protein 22.5g

Bacon–Wrapped Pork Tenderloin

Prep time: 15 minutes | Cook time: 2 hours 30 minutes | Serves: 4

¼ cup yellow mustard	melted
2 (1-pound) pork tenderloins	1 tablespoon minced garlic
¼ cup Our House Dry Rub	2 jalapeño peppers, seeded and diced
8 ounces cream cheese, softened	
1 cup grated Cheddar cheese	1½ pounds bacon
1 tablespoon unsalted butter,	

1. Slather the mustard on the pork tenderloins, then sprinkle generously with the dry rub to coat the meat. 2. Fill your Traeger Smoker with wood pellets and follow the manufacturer's specific start-up procedure. Preheat the grill at 225 degrees F/ 105 degrees C with the hood closed. 3. Set the tenderloins directly on the grill, close the lid, and smoke for 2 hours. 4. After taking the pork off the grill, raise the heat to 375 degrees F/ 190 degrees C. 5. Combine the cheddar cheese, cream cheese, melted butter, garlic, and jalapenos in a bowl. 6. Make a deep cut from top to bottom, end to end, across the center of each tenderloin to create a cavity. 7. In the cavity of one tenderloin, distribute half of the cream cheese mixture. Do the same with the second piece of meat and the remaining mixture. 8. Wrap one tenderloin firmly in half the bacon. Do the same with the other piece of beef and the leftover bacon. 9. Place the tenderloins that have been wrapped in bacon on the grill, cover it, and smoke them for 30 minutes. 10. Ten minutes of resting time is required before cutting and serving the tenderloins.
Per serving: Calories 470; Total fat 41.2g; Sodium 940mg; Total Carbs 6.1g; Fiber 0.9g; Sugars 1.7g; Protein 22.2g

Smoked Brats Sliders

Prep time: 15 minutes | Cook time: 2 hours | Serves: 10

4 (12-ounce) cans of beer	more for the rolls
2 onions, sliced into rings	2 tablespoons red pepper flakes
2green bell peppers, sliced into rings	10 brats, uncooked
	10 hoagie rolls, split
2 tablespoons unsalted butter	Mustard, for serving

1. On your kitchen stove top, in a suitable saucepan over high heat, bring the beer, onions, peppers, butter, and red pepper flakes to a boil. 2. Fill your Traeger Smoker with wood pellets and follow the manufacturer's specific start-up procedure. Preheat, with the hood, closed, to 225 degrees F/ 105 degrees C. 3. Place a disposable pan on one side of the grill, and pour the warmed beer mixture into it, creating a "brat tub". 4. Set the brats on the other side of the grill, directly on the grate, and close the hood and smoke for 1 hour, turning 2 or 3 times during grilling. 5. Add the brats to the pan with the onions and peppers, cover tightly with aluminum foil, and continue smoking for 30 minutes to 1 hour with the hood closed, or until a meat thermometer inserted in the brats reads 160 degrees F/ 70 degrees C. 6. Butter the cut sides of the hoagie rolls and toast cut-side down on the grill. 7. Using any slotted spoon, remove the brats, onions, and peppers from the cooking liquid and discard the liquid. 8. Serve the brats on the toasted buns, topped with the onions and peppers and mustard (ketchup optional).
Per serving: Calories 439; Total fat 38.8g; Sodium 813mg; Total Carbs 11.5g; Fiber 3.7g; Sugars 6g; Protein 16.8g

Lime Garlic Baby Back Ribs

Prep time: 15 minutes | Cook time: 3 hours | Serves: 8

Marinade

⅔ cup peanut or vegetable oil	2 tablespoons minced garlic
¼ cup 2 tablespoons low-sodium soy sauce	2 tablespoons Vietnamese or Thai fish sauce
¼ cup lime juice	2 tablespoons honey
2 tablespoons grated lemon zest	2 teaspoons black pepper

Ribs

2 racks baby back ribs, each 1 ½–2 pounds, membrane removed	2 tablespoons chopped basil leaves
2 limes, cut into wedges	

1. Mix all the marinade ingredients. 2. Arrange the racks on a rimmed sheet pan and pour the prepared marinade over the racks. Turn to coat both sides, then cover the pan and refrigerate the racks for 4 to 6 hours, turning occasionally. 3. Prepare the Traeger grill for indirect cooking over low heat (250 degrees F/ 120 degrees C to 350 degrees F/ 175 degrees C). 4. After removing the racks from the sheet pan, transfer the marinade into the saucepan. After bringing the marinade to a boil, turn down the heat, and simmer the marinade for 2 minutes, stirring every so often. 5. Heavy-duty aluminum foil should be used to wrap each rack, with the seams being well-crimped. Cover the hood, and grill the foil-wrapped racks for 1¼ hours with the bone side down over indirect low heat. 6. Remove from the hot grill and give it a 10-minute rest before returning. Open the sachets when they are cool enough to handle, and then add any accumulated juices to the marinade that has been diluted. 7. Remove any extra fat from the marinade you've made. Place the meaty side of the ribs back on the grill and baste with. Cook for 15 minutes with the hood closed over indirect low heat. After 45 to 1 hour, flip the ribs over and continue to cook until meat is tender. 8. When you raise a rack of ribs with tongs from one end, bone side up, and the rack flexes so much in the middle that the meat readily shreds, the ribs are cooked. Remove off the hot grill and give it ten minutes to cool. 9. Top with basil and serve with lime wedges.
Per Serving: Calories 309; Total fat 17.4g; Sodium 348mg; Total Carbs 4.8g; Fiber 1.9g; Sugars 0.6g; Protein 33.4g

Country Pork Roast with Apple & Sauerkraut

Prep time: 15 minutes | Cook time: 3 hours | Serves: 8

1 (28-ounce) jar or 2 (15 ounces) cans sauerkraut	3 tablespoons Greek seasoning
3 Granny Smith apples, cored and chopped	2 teaspoons dried basil leaves
¾ cup packed light brown sugar	olive oil, for rubbing
	1 (2- to 2½-pound) pork loin roast

1. Fill your Traeger Smoker with wood pellets and follow the manufacturer's specific start-up procedure. Preheat the grill at 250 degrees F/ 120 degrees C with the hood closed. 2. Mix the sauerkraut, chopped apples, and brown sugar in a bowl. 3. Spread the sauerkraut-apple mixture in the bottom of a suitable baking dish. 4. Combine the Greek seasoning and dried basil spice rub in another bowl. 5. Place the pig roast on the baking dish fat-side up on top of the sauerkraut after oiling it and applying the spice rub. 6. Close the grill lid after transferring the baking dish to the grill. 7. Roast the pork for 3 hours, or until the thickest section of the flesh reaches an internal temperature of 160 degrees F/ 70 degrees C. 8. Before slicing, take the pig roast out of the oven dish and let it rest for five minutes. 9. Sliced pork should be placed on top of the sauerkraut-apple combination on each plate.

Per serving: Calories 312; Total fat 25g; Sodium 847mg; Total Carbs 3.1g; Fiber 0.3g; Sugars 0g; Protein 19.3g

Jalapeño Pork Chops with Pickled Pepper Relish

Prep time: 15 minutes | Cook time: 50 minutes | Serves: 4

4 (1-inch-thick) pork chops	¼ cup canned chopped tomatoes, well-drained
½ cup pickled jalapeño juice or pickle juice	¼ cup chopped scallions
¼ cup chopped pickled (jarred) jalapeño pepper slices	2 teaspoons poultry seasoning
¼ cup chopped roasted red peppers	2 teaspoons salt
	2 teaspoons black pepper

1. Pour the jalapeño juice into a container that has a lid. 2. Add the pork chops, cover, and marinate in the refrigerator for at least 4 hours or overnight, supplementing with or substituting pickle juice as desired. 3. Mix the chopped pickled jalapeños, roasted red peppers, tomatoes, scallions, and poultry seasoning in a bowl to make a relish. Set aside. 4. Remove the pork chops from the prepared marinade and shake off any excess. Discard the prepared marinade. Season the chops with black pepper and salt. 5. Fill your Traeger Smoker with wood pellets and follow the manufacturer's specific start-up procedure. Preheat the grill at 325 degrees F/ 160 degrees C with the hood closed. 6. Arrange the pork chops directly on the grill, close the lid, and smoke for 45 to 50 minutes until they have an internal temperature of 160 degrees F/ 70 degrees C. 7. Divide the chops among plates and top with the pickled pepper relish. Enjoy.

Per serving: Calories 353; Total fat 21.8g; Sodium 665mg; Total Carbs 1g; Fiber 0.1g; Sugars 0g; Protein 36.2g

Chapter 4 Beef, Lamb, and Venison Recipes

Page	Recipe
57	Texas Smoked Mustard Brisket
57	BBQ Beef Brisket
57	Grilled Tri-Tip Roast
57	Juicy Lemon-Pepper Tri-Tip Roast
57	Mustard Beef Roast
57	Simple Smoked Top Beef Roast
58	Easy Smoked Beef Burgers
58	Cinnamon-Mustard Beef Ribs
58	Braised Beef Short Ribs
58	Garlic Roast Prime Rib
58	Smoked Corned Beef Brisket
58	Smoked New York Steaks
58	Butter-Seared Steaks
59	Chicago-Style Hot Dog Buns
59	Flavorful T-Bone Steaks
59	Grilled All-Beef Hot Dogs with Avocado Mayo
59	All-Beef Hot Dogs with Pickled Onions
59	Crunch Cheeseburgers
60	BBQ Pickle Beef Burgers
60	Savory Cheeseburgers
60	Texas Cheeseburgers
60	Bacon-Egg Cheeseburgers
61	Spinach Lamb Burgers
61	Kofta Pitas with Cucumber-Tomato Salad
61	Savory Barbecued Meat Loaf
61	Flavorful Flank Steak with Asparagus
62	Balsamic Flank Steak with Baby Arugula
62	Grilled Flank Steak with Black Bean Salad
62	Korean-Style Barbecued Beef
62	Herbed Beef Roast with White Wine–Cream Sauce
63	Tri-Tip Roast with Corn Salsa & Black Beans
63	Barbecue Tri-Tip Sandwiches
63	Steak-Tomato Kabobs with Avocado-Cucumber Sauce
63	Strip Steaks with Horseradish-Cream Sauce
64	Combat Rib- Eye Steaks with Mushrooms
64	Garlic T-Bones with Avocado Salsa
64	Grilled Ginger Porterhouse Steaks
64	Grilled Beef Tenderloin Steaks with Mushrooms
65	Grilled Strip Steaks with Barbecue Sauce
65	New York Strip Steaks with Pesto
65	Smoked Dijon-Herb Rib Eye Steaks
65	Herb-Garlic Leg of Lamb with Zucchini Salad
66	Prime Rib Roast with Hazelnut Pesto
66	Lamb Loin Chops with Mint Salsa Verde
66	Ginger-Curried Lamb Chops with Yogurt Sauce
66	Cheesesteak Meatloaf with Tiger Sauce
67	Garlic-Soy London Broil
67	French Onion Cheeseburgers
67	Sweet Corned Beef with Cabbage
67	Cheeseburger Tomato Hand Pies
68	Garlic Filet Mignons
68	Savory Pastrami
68	Garlic Rump Roast
68	BBQ Chuck Roast
68	Smoked Garlic Prime Rib
68	Herbed Spicy Tri-Tip
69	Cheesy Meat Stuffed Peppers
69	Barbecued Beef Brisket
69	Spicy Beef Shoulder Clod
69	Smoky T-Bone Steak with Blue Cheese Butter

Texas Smoked Mustard Brisket

Prep time: 15 minutes | **Cook time:** 16 to 20 hours | **Serves:** 12-15

1 (12-pound) full packer brisket	Worcestershire Glaze and Spritz, for spritzing
2 tablespoons yellow mustard	
1 batch Espresso Brisket Rub	

1. Fill your Traeger smoker with wood pellets and follow the manufacturer's specific start-up procedure. Preheat the grill at 225 degrees F/ 105 degrees C with the hood closed. 2. Carefully remove the large layer of fat covering one side of the brisket, all but about ½-inch. 3. Coat the brisket with the mustard on all sides and season with the rub, work the rub into the meat. Fill a spray bottle with the mop. 4. Place the brisket directly on the grill grate and smoke it until it has an internal temperature of 195 degrees F/ 90 degrees C, spritzing it with the mop every hour. 5. Remove the brisket from the grill and completely wrap it in aluminum foil. The brisket should be placed in a cooler, cover the cooler, and let to rest for 1 to 2 hours. 6. Unwrap the brisket, separate the brisket point from the flat by cutting along the fat layer and slice the flat. The point can be served for burnt ends.

Per serving: Calories 347; Total fat 11.6g; Sodium 217mg; Total Carbs 46g; Fiber 6g; Sugars 3.1g; Protein 16.3g

BBQ Beef Brisket

Prep time: 30 minutes | **Cook time:** 6 hours | **Serves:** 8-10

1 (6-pound) brisket point	2 tablespoons honey
2 tablespoons yellow mustard	1 cup barbecue sauce
1 batch Sweet Brown Sugar Rub	2 tablespoons light brown sugar

1. Fill your Traeger Smoker with wood pellets and follow the manufacturer's specific start-up procedure. Preheat the grill to 225 degrees F/ 105 degrees C with the lid closed. 2. Carefully remove all but about ½ inch of the large layer of fat covering one side of your brisket point. 3. Coat the brisket with mustard on all sides, and work the rub into it. 4. Smoke the brisket until the interior temperature reaches 165 degrees F/ 75 degrees C. 5. Remove the brisket from the grill and completely wrap it in butcher paper or aluminum foil. 6. Return the wrapped brisket to the grill and raise the temperature to 350 degrees F/ 175 degrees C, then cook it until it reaches an internal temperature of 185 degrees F/ 85 degrees C. 7. Remove the point from the grill, unwrap it, and cut the meat into 1-inch cubes. 8. Place the cubes in an aluminum pan and stir the cubes with the honey, barbecue sauce, and brown sugar. 9. Place the pan on the grill and smoke the meat cubes for 1 hour more with the lid open. 10. Serve warm.

Per serving: Calories 481; Total fat 4.1g; Sodium 1150mg; Total Carbs 70.5g; Fiber 8.7g; Sugars 3.7g; Protein 40.5g

Grilled Tri-Tip Roast

Prep time: 10 minutes | **Cook time:** 2 to 3 hours | **Serves:** 4

1½ pounds tri-tip roast	1 batch Espresso Brisket Rub

1. Fill your Traeger Smoker with wood pellets and follow the manufacturer's specific start-up procedure. Preheat the grill to 180 degrees F/ 80 degrees C with the lid closed. 2. The spice rub is used to season the tri-tip roast. Work the rub into the meat with your hands. 3. The roast should be placed directly on the grill grate and smoked until it reaches an internal temperature of 140 degrees F/ 60 degrees C. 4. Increase the cooking temperature to 450 degrees F/ 230 degrees C, and resume grilling the roast until the internal temperature reaches 145 degrees F/ 60 degrees C. 5. Let the roast rest for 15 minutes before slicing and serving.

Per serving: Calories 463; Total fat 10.1g; Sodium 784mg; Total Carbs 56.8g; Fiber 6.9g; Sugars 5g; Protein 37.5g

Juicy Lemon-Pepper Tri-Tip Roast

Prep time: 25 minutes | **Cook time:** 5 hours | **Serves:** 4

1½ pounds tri-tip roast	2 teaspoons garlic powder
Salt	2 teaspoons lemon pepper
Freshly ground black pepper	½ cup apple juice

1. Fill your Traeger Smoker with wood pellets and follow the manufacturer's specific start-up procedure. Preheat the grill to 180 degrees F/ 80 degrees C with the lid closed. 2. Season the tri-tip roast with salt, pepper, garlic powder, and lemon pepper, working the seasoning into the meat. 3. Place the roast directly on the grill grate and smoke it for 4 hours. 4. Pull the tri-tip from the grill and place it on enough aluminum foil to wrap it completely. 5. Increase the grill's temperature to 375 degrees F/ 190 degrees C. 6. Fold in three sides of the foil around the roast and add the apple juice. Fold in the last side, completely enclosing the tri-tip and liquid. 7. Place the tri-tip back on the hot grill and let it grill for an additional 45 minutes. 8. Before removing, slicing, and serving the tri-tip roast from the grill, allows it to rest for 15 minutes.

Per serving: Calories 311; Total fat 17.4g; Sodium 557mg; Total Carbs 4.8g; Fiber 0.2g; Sugars 4.4g; Protein 34.7g

Mustard Beef Roast

Prep time: 25 minutes | **Cook time:** 12 to 14 hours | **Serves:** 5-8

1 (4-pound) top round roast	1 batch Espresso Brisket Rub
2 tablespoons yellow mustard	½ cup beef broth

1. Fill your Traeger Smoker with wood pellets and follow the manufacturer's specific start-up procedure. Preheat the grill to 225 degrees F/ 105 degrees C with the lid closed. 2. Apply mustard on the top round roast before adding the spice rub for seasoning. Put the spice rub on the meat and rub it in with your hands. 3. The roast should be placed directly on the grill grate and smoked until it reaches an internal temperature of 160 degrees F/ 70 degrees C and develops a brown bark. 4. After removing the roast from the grill, wrap it completely with aluminum foil. 5. Increase the grill to 350 degrees F/ 175 degrees C. 6. Fold in three sides of the foil around the roast and add the beef broth. Fold in the last side, completely enclosing the roast and liquid. 7. Return the roast to the grill and grill until it achieves an internal temperature of 195 degrees F/ 90 degrees C. 8. Transfer the roast in a cooler. Let the roast rest for a couple of hours with the cooler covered. 9. Serve.

Per serving: Calories 516; Total fat 23.7g; Sodium 577mg; Total Carbs 50.9g; Fiber 3.8g; Sugars 6g; Protein 26.8g

Simple Smoked Top Beef Roast

Prep time: 15 minutes | **Cook time:** 14 hours | **Serves:** 8

1 (4-pound) top round roast	1 tablespoon butter
1 batch Espresso Brisket Rub	

1. Fill your Traeger Smoker with wood pellets and follow the manufacturer's specific start-up procedure. Preheat the grill to 180 degrees F/ 80 degrees C with the lid closed. 2. Use the spice rub to season the top round roast, working the rub into the meat. 3. The roast should be placed directly on the grill grate and smoked until it reaches an internal temperature of 140 degrees F/ 60 degrees C. 4. Raise the grill's heat to 450 degrees F/ 230 degrees C and place a cast-iron skillet on it. 5. Place the roast in the set skillet, add the butter, and cook until the internal temperature reaches 145 degrees F/ 60 degrees C, flipping it after 3 minutes of cooking. 6. After taking the roast off the grill, give it 15 minutes to rest, then slice it and enjoy.

Per serving: Calories 289; Total fat 14.3g; Sodium 368mg; Total Carbs 23.3g; Fiber 3.5g; Sugars 2.2g; Protein 18.6g

Easy Smoked Beef Burgers

Prep time: 15 minutes | Cook time: 45 minutes | Serves: 4

1 pound of ground beef	Wood-Fired Burger Shake, for seasoning
1 egg	

1. Fill your Traeger Smoker with wood pellets and follow the manufacturer's specific start-up procedure. Preheat the grill to 180 degrees F/ 80 degrees C with the lid closed. 2. In a suitable bowl, mix together the ground beef and egg, then divide the meat mixture into 4 portions and shape each into a patty. 3. Season the patties with the burger shake. 4. Place the burgers directly on the grill grate and smoke them for 30 minutes. 5. Increase the grill's temperature to 400 degrees F/ 200 degrees C and continue to cook the burgers until their internal temperature reaches 145 degrees F/ 60 degrees C. 6. Serve.
Per serving: Calories 312; Total fat 3.2g; Sodium 654mg; Total Carbs 42g; Fiber 3.4g; Sugars 1.5g; Protein 26.9g

Cinnamon-Mustard Beef Ribs

Prep time: 15 minutes | Cook time: 4 to 6 hours | Serves: 4-8

2 (2- or 3-pound) racks of beef ribs	1 batch Sweet and Spicy Cinnamon Rub
2 tablespoons yellow mustard	

1. Fill your Traeger Smoker with wood pellets and follow the manufacturer's specific start-up procedure. Preheat the grill to 225 degrees F/ 105 degrees C with the lid closed. 2. To remove the membrane from the backside of the ribs, cut through the membrane in an X pattern and work a paper towel between the membrane and the ribs to pull it off. 3. Coat the ribs with mustard on all sides, and work the rub into them. 4. The ribs should be placed directly on the grill grate and smoked until they reach to an internal temperature of between 190 degrees F/ 85 degrees C and 200 degrees F/ 95 degrees C. 5. Cut the rib racks into individual ribs after removing them from the grill. Serve immediately.
Per serving: Calories 425; Total fat 25g; Sodium 408mg; Total Carbs 33.3g; Fiber 10.8g; Sugars 15.1g; Protein 22.3g

Braised Beef Short Ribs

Prep time: 25 minutes | Cook time: 4 hours | Serves: 4

4 beef short ribs	Freshly ground black pepper
Salt	½ cup beef broth

1. Fill your Traeger Smoker with wood pellets and follow the manufacturer's specific start-up procedure. Preheat the grill to 180 degrees F/ 80 degrees C with the lid closed. 2. Season the ribs with black pepper and salt. 3. Place the ribs directly on the grill grate and smoke them for 3 hours. 4. Transfer the ribs to aluminum foil to wrap them completely. Fold in three sides of the foil around the ribs and add the beef broth. Fold in the last side, completely enclosing the ribs and liquid. 5. Increase the grill's temperature to 375 degrees F/ 190 degrees C, and return the ribs to the grill; cook them for an additional 45 minutes. 6. Unwrap them after cooking and serve immediately.
Per serving: Calories 282; Total fat 12.7g; Sodium 378mg; Total Carbs 0.2g; Fiber 0.1g; Sugars 0g; Protein 39.2g

Garlic Roast Prime Rib

Prep time: 15 minutes | Cook time: 4 to 5 hours | Serves: 4-6

1 (3-bone) rib roast	Freshly ground black pepper
Salt	1 garlic clove, minced

1. Fill your Traeger Smoker with wood pellets and follow the manufacturer's specific start-up procedure. Preheat the grill to 360 degrees F / 180 degrees C with the lid closed. 2. Season the roast with black pepper and salt, and rub it with the minced garlic. 3. Set the roast directly on the grill grate and smoke it for 4 or 5 hours. 4. Remove the prepared roast from the grill and let it rest for 15 minutes, then slice it and serve.
Per serving: Calories 209; Total fat 1.8g; Sodium 187mg; Total Carbs 3.3g; Fiber 1.2g; Sugars 0.8g; Protein 43.4g

Smoked Corned Beef Brisket

Prep time: 15 minutes | Cook time: 12-16 hours | Serves: 6-8

1 (8-pound) corned beef brisket	Worcestershire Mop and Spritz, for spritzing
2 tablespoons yellow mustard	
1 batch Espresso Brisket Rub	

1. Fill your Traeger Smoker with wood pellets and follow the manufacturer's specific start-up procedure. Preheat the grill to 225 degrees F/ 105 degrees C with the lid closed. 2. Coat the brisket with mustard, and work the rub into the meat. 3. Pour the mop into a spray bottle. 4. Place the brisket directly on the grill grate and smoke until its internal temperature reaches 195 degrees F/ 90 degrees C, spritzing it with the mop every hour. 5. Wrap the brisket completely with aluminum foil or butcher paper, then place the wrapped brisket in a cooler, cover and let it rest for 1 or 2 hours. 6. Remove the corned beef from the cooler and unwrap it, slice and serve.
Per serving: Calories 362; Total fat 17.6g; Sodium 515mg; Total Carbs 4.5g; Fiber 2g; Sugars 0.2g; Protein 45.8g

Smoked New York Steaks

Prep time: 15 minutes | Cook time: 1-2 hours | Serves: 4

4 (1-inch-thick) New York steaks	Salt
2 tablespoons olive oil	Freshly ground black pepper

1. Fill your Traeger Smoker with wood pellets and follow the manufacturer's specific start-up procedure. Preheat the grill to 180 degrees F/ 80 degrees C with the lid closed. 2. Rub the prepared steaks with olive oil and season with black pepper and salt. 3. Place the steaks directly on the grill grate and smoke them for 1 hour. 4. Increase the grill's temperature to 375 degrees F/ 190 degrees C and continue to cook until the steaks have an internal temperature of 145 degrees F/ 60 degrees C. 5. Remove the prepared steaks and let them rest for 5 minutes, then slice and serve.
Per serving: Calories 338; Total fat 3.6g; Sodium 470mg; Total Carbs 56.1g; Fiber 8.1g; Sugars 44.6g; Protein 22.9g

Butter-Seared Steaks

Prep time: 15 minutes | Cook time: 1 to 2 hours | Serves: 4

4 (4-ounce) sirloin steaks	Freshly ground black pepper
2 tablespoons olive oil	4 tablespoons butter
Salt	

1. Fill your Traeger Smoker with wood pellets and follow the manufacturer's specific start-up procedure. Preheat the grill to 180 degrees F/ 80 degrees C with the lid closed. 2. Rub the prepared steaks all over with olive oil, and season with black pepper and salt on both sides. 3. Place the prepared steaks directly on the grill grate and smoke until they have an internal temperature of 135 degrees F/ 55 degrees C. Remove the steaks from the grill. 4. Raise the grill's heat to 450 degrees F/ 230 degrees C and place a cast-iron skillet on the grates. 5. Place the steaks in the skillet and add 1 tablespoon of butter to each. Flip the prepared steaks once every two or three minutes until they reach an internal temperature of 145 degrees F/ 60 degrees C. 6. Remove the prepared steaks and serve right away.
Per serving: Calories 295; Total fat 12.3g; Sodium 332mg; Total Carbs 11.9g; Fiber 3.2g; Sugars 6.5g; Protein 34.2g

Chicago-Style Hot Dog Buns

Prep time: 10 minutes | Cook time: 5 minutes | Serves: 8

8 tomato slices, each about ¼ inch thick	½ cup chopped white onion, rinsed in a fine-mesh strainer under cold water
8 best-quality all-beef hot dogs with natural casings	½ cup super-green sweet pickle relish
8 poppy seed hot dog buns split	Yellow mustard
16 pickled sport peppers	Celery salt
2 dill pickles cut lengthwise into 4 spears	

1. Prepare the Traeger grill for direct cooking over medium heat (350 degrees F/ 175 degrees C to 450 degrees F/ 230 degrees C). 2. To create half-moon shapes, cut each tomato slice in half. Cut a few well-spaced diagonal shallow slashes crosswise along one side of each hot dog. 3. Grill the hot dogs for 4 to 5 minutes with the lid closed, until they are browned on the outside and heated throughout, turning them occasionally. Remove the hot dogs from the grill. 4. Add a hot dog, two tomato half-moons, two peppers, one pickle spear, some onion, and a teaspoon of relish to each bun. Finish with a dash of celery salt and a dash of mustard. Serve hot.

Per serving: Calories 525; Total fat 23.2g; Sodium 698mg; Total Carbs 6g; Fiber 2.7g; Sugars 0.9g; Protein 69.7g

Flavorful T-Bone Steaks

Prep time: 10 minutes | Cook time: 30 minutes | Serves: 4

4 (1½- to 2-inch-thick) T-bone steaks	2 tablespoons olive oil
	1 batch Espresso Brisket Rub

1. Fill your Traeger Smoker with wood pellets and follow the manufacturer's specific start-up procedure. Preheat the grill at High setting (500 degrees F/ 260 degrees C) with the lid closed. 2. Olive oil should be used to coat the prepared steaks before applying the spice rub to both sides. Put the spice rub on the meat and rub it in with your hands. 3. The prepared steaks should be placed directly on the grill grate and smoked until they reach an internal temperature of 135 degrees F/ 55 degrees C for rare, 145 degrees F/ 60 degrees C for medium-rare, and 155 degrees F/ 70 degrees C for well-done. 4. Serve warm after grilling.

Per serving: Calories 364; Total fat 23.8g; Sodium 534mg; Total Carbs 6.2g; Fiber 5g; Sugars 0.8g; Protein 32.2g

Grilled All-Beef Hot Dogs with Avocado Mayo

Prep time: 20 minutes | Cook time: 5 minutes | Serves: 8

8 all-beef hot dogs with natural casings	1 pound tomatoes, cored, seeded, and chopped
8 hot dog buns split	¼ cup roughly chopped cilantro leaves
1 jar or bag (1 pound) sauerkraut, drained	¼ cup finely chopped red onion
Mayo	
1 Hass avocado, chopped	1 tablespoon lemon juice
⅓ cup mayonnaise	1 garlic clove, minced
½ jalapeño chili pepper, seeded and chopped	¼ teaspoon freshly ground black pepper
1 tablespoon chopped shallot	¼ teaspoon kosher salt

1. Add all the mayo ingredients to the food processor, and puree them until smooth. Cover and refrigerate them for later use. 2. Prepare the Traeger grill for direct cooking over medium heat (350 degrees F/ 175 degrees C to 450 degrees F/ 230 degrees C). 3. Cut a few well-spaced diagonal shallow slashes crosswise along one side of each hot dog. 4. Grill the hot dogs on the clean grates for 4 to 5 minutes with the lid closed, until they are lightly marked on the outside and hot all the way to the center, turn them occasionally during grilling. 5. During the last 30 seconds of grilling time, place the buns on the grill grate with the cut-side done. 6. Generously spread the avocado mayo inside each bun, place a hot dog on each bun and add some sauerkraut, tomatoes, cilantro, and onion. Enjoy.

Per serving: Calories 361; Total fat 23.7g; Sodium 580mg; Total Carbs 10.9g; Fiber 1.8g; Sugars 7.2g; Protein 25.3g

All-Beef Hot Dogs with Pickled Onions

Prep time: 15 minutes | Cook time: 5 minutes | Serves: 4

8 all-beef hot dogs with natural casings (slightly longer than the buns)	8 hot dog buns split
	Mustard
	Ketchup
Pickled Onions	
½ cup cider vinegar	1 teaspoon crushed red pepper flakes
½ cup distilled white vinegar	
½ cup granulated sugar	1 small white or yellow onion ends trimmed
1 tablespoon salt	
2 teaspoons celery seed	1 small red onion ends trimmed

1. Mix all the pickling ingredients except the onions in a glass bowl until the sugar and salt dissolve. 2. Each onion should be split lengthwise. With each half cut side down, cut paper thin slices vertically. 3. Add the onion slices to the glass bowl, and evenly coat them with the vinegar mixture. Then, set them aside at room temperature for 3 hours, stirring the onions occasionally. 4. Drain the pickled onions and set aside. 5. Prepare the Traeger grill for direct cooking over medium heat (350 degrees F/ 175 degrees C to 450 degrees F/ 230 degrees C). 6. Cut a few well-spaced diagonal shallow slashes crosswise along one side of each hot dog. 7. Grill the hot dogs on the clean grill grate for 4 to 5 minutes with the lid closed, until they are lightly marked on the outside and hot all the way to the center; turn them occasionally during grilling. 8. Toast the buns on the grill grate with the cut side down when there are 30 seconds or 1-minute left. 9. Arrange the hot dogs on the buns, squeeze the condiment of your choice alongside the food, and top with the pickled onions, then enjoy.

Per serving: Calories 1444; Total fat 93g; Sodium 6767mg; Total Carbs 90.7g; Fiber 2.3g; Sugars 47.4g; Protein 59g

Crunch Cheeseburgers

Prep time: 10 minutes | Cook time: 6 minutes | Serves: 4

2 slices of cheddar cheese, each about 1 ounce, cut into quarters	16 dill pickle chips
	8 handfuls of thin potato chips, such as Lay's Classic®
8 slider buns split	
Ketchup (optional)	
Patties	
1½ pounds ground chuck (80% lean)	½ teaspoon onion powder
	½ teaspoon salt
1 tablespoon ketchup	¼ teaspoon black pepper
½ teaspoon Worcestershire sauce	

1. Combine all the patty ingredients in a medium bowl, and then make the mixture into 8 patties of equal size, about ½-inch thick. Make a shallow indentation about ½-inch-wide in the center of each patty, cheddar cheese and then chill them in the refrigerator. 2. Prepare the Traeger grill for direct cooking over medium-high heat (400 degrees F/ 200 degrees C to 500 degrees F/ 260 degrees C). 3. Grill the patties on the clean grill grate for 6 minutes with the lid closed until they have an internal temperature of 160 degrees F/ 70 degrees C, turning them halfway through. 4. Toast the buns on the grill grate with the cut side down when there are 30 seconds or 1-minute left. 5. Build a burger on each bun with ketchup, pickles, a patty, and a handful of chips. 6. Cover the burgers with the bun tops and then press down to crunch the chips. Serve right away.

Per serving: Calories 318; Total fat 17.3g; Sodium 310mg; Total Carbs 6.7g; Fiber 1.5g; Sugars 2.8g; Protein 33.5g

BBQ Pickle Beef Burgers

Prep time: 15 minutes | Cook time: 10 minutes | Serves: 4

4 slices of cheddar cheese	4 leaves romaine lettuce, shredded
4 hamburger buns split	16 sweet pickle chips
Sauce	
1 tablespoon vegetable oil	1 tablespoon packed dark brown sugar
½ medium yellow onion, chopped	
1 cup ketchup	1 tablespoon chili powder
¼ cup water	1 tablespoon cider vinegar
2 tablespoons Worcestershire sauce	½ teaspoon garlic powder
Patties	
1½ pounds ground chuck (80% lean)	1 tablespoon chili powder
½ teaspoon salt	½ teaspoon garlic powder

1. Heat the oil in a heavy saucepan over medium heat; add the onion and sauté for 12 to 15 minutes until very soft and as dark as possible without burning; add the remaining sauce ingredients, stir well, and boil them over medium-high heat. 2. Adjust the heat so the sauce simmers gently, and then frequently stir them for 15 to 20 minutes. Set the mixture aside to cool at room temperature. 3. Mix all the patty ingredients in a medium bowl, and then make the mixture into 4 patties, about ¾-inch thick. Make a shallow indentation about ½-inch-wide in the center of each patty, and then chill them in the refrigerator. 4. Set the Traeger grill to medium-high heat for direct cooking (400 degrees F/ 200 degrees C to 500 degrees F/ 260 degrees C). 5. Grill the patties for 8 to 10 minutes with the lid closed until they have an internal temperature of 160 degrees F/ 70 degrees C, turning them halfway through. 6. Toast the buns on the grill grate with the cut side down when there are 30 seconds or 1-minute left. 7. Arrange the lettuce, one patty, some sauce, a bit more sauce, and 4 pickle chips (optional) on each bun, then enjoy. 8. You can store the remaining sauce in a covered container in the refrigerator for up to 7 days.

Per serving: Calories 361; Total fat 23.7g; Sodium 580mg; Total Carbs 10.9g; Fiber 1.8g; Sugars 7.2g; Protein 25.3g

Savory Cheeseburgers

Prep time: 15 minutes | Cook time: 9 to 11 minutes | Serves: 4

Kosher salt and black pepper, to taste	4 slices of sharp cheddar cheese
4 hamburger buns split	4 leaves of butter lettuce
2 tablespoons unsalted butter, softened	Ketchup (optional)
	16 dill pickle chips
Patties	
1½ pounds ground chuck (80% lean)	½ teaspoon Worcestershire sauce
2 tablespoons minced onion	½ teaspoon dried oregano
1 tablespoon ketchup	½ teaspoon salt
1½ teaspoons Dijon mustard	¼ teaspoon black pepper

1. Combine all the patty ingredients in a medium bowl, and then make the mixture into 8 patties of equal size, about 1-inch thick. Make a shallow indentation about 1-inch-wide in the center of each patty, and then chill them in the refrigerator. 2. Prepare the Traeger grill for direct cooking over medium-high heat (400 degrees F/ 200 degrees C to 500 degrees F/ 260 degrees C). 3. Season the patties with salt and black pepper on both sides. Spread the cut side of the buns with butter. 4. Grill the patties on the clean grill grate for 9 to 11 minutes with the lid closed until they have an internal temperature of 160 degrees F/ 70 degrees C, turning them halfway through. 5. Place one cheese slice on each patty to melt them when there are 30 seconds or 1-minute left. 6. Place a lettuce leaf, a patty, ketchup (optional), and four pickle chips on each bread to assemble a burger. Enjoy.

Per serving: Calories 564; Total fat 10.1g; Sodium 366mg; Total Carbs 64g; Fiber 16.4g; Sugars 5.8g; Protein 55.3g

Texas Cheeseburgers

Prep time: 25 minutes | Cook time: 11 minutes | Serves: 4

Kosher salt and black pepper	4 slices sharp cheddar cheese, each about 1 ounce
4 slices thick Texas toast	
Extra-virgin olive oil	Pico de Gallo
4 canned whole green chili peppers, chopped	½ cup sour cream
Patties	
1½ pounds ground chuck (80% lean)	½ teaspoon garlic powder
1 teaspoon onion powder	½ teaspoon chili powder
½ teaspoon ground cumin	½ teaspoon salt
	¼ teaspoon black pepper

1. Combine all the patty ingredients in a medium bowl, and then make the mixture into 8 patties of equal size, about 1-inch thick. Make a shallow indentation about 1-inch-wide in the center of each patty, and then chill the patties in the refrigerator. 2. Prepare the Traeger grill for direct cooking over medium-high heat (400 degrees F/ 200 degrees C to 500 degrees F/ 260 degrees C). 3. Season the patties with salt and black pepper on both side, and slightly spread the bread slices with oil. 4. Grill the patties on the clean grill grate for 5 minutes with the lid closed; turn them over, and equally top them with the green chilies and one cheese slice, then resume grilling them for 4 to 6 minutes until they have an internal temperature of 160 degrees F/ 70 degrees C. 5. Toast the bread slices on the grill grate when there are 30 seconds or 1 minute left. 6. Stir the Pico de Gallo to make sure it is well mixed. Build a burger on each bread slice with 1 tablespoon of the sour cream, a patty, and 1 tablespoon of the Pico de Gallo. 7. Serve warm with the remaining Pico de Gallo and sour cream on the side.

Per serving: Calories 203; Total fat 6.8g; Sodium 313mg; Total Carbs 8.8g; Fiber 1.8g; Sugars 3.6g; Protein 26.2g

Bacon–Egg Cheeseburgers

Prep time: 25 minutes | Cook time: 11 minutes | Serves: 4

8 slices bacon	4 eggs
4 slices of cheddar cheese	Salt and black pepper
¼ teaspoon black pepper	8 tomato slices
4 Kaiser rolls split	
Patties	
1½ pounds ground chuck (80% lean)	2 tablespoons ketchup
	2 teaspoons Worcestershire sauce
¼ cup chopped yellow onion	1 teaspoon salt

1. Mix all the patty ingredients in a medium bowl, and then make the mixture into 8 patties of equal size, about 1-inch thick. Make a shallow indentation about 1-inch-wide in the center of each patty, and then chill the patties in the refrigerator. 2. Fry the bacon slices in the skillet over medium heat for 10 to 12 minutes until crisp, turning them occasionally. Drain the bacon slices with paper towels, reserve 2 tablespoons of bacon fat, keep or discard the remaining fat. 3. Prepare the grill for direct cooking over medium-high heat (400 degrees F/ 200 degrees C to 500 degrees F/ 260 degrees C). 4. Grill the patties on the clean grill grate for 9 to 11 minutes with the lid closed until they have an internal temperature of 160 degrees F/ 70 degrees C, turning them halfway through. 5. Place one cheese slice on each patty when there are 30 seconds or 1 minute left, grill them until the cheese are melted. 6. Heat the reserved 2 tablespoons bacon fat in the skillet over medium heat; add the eggs, adjust the heat to medium-low, and cook the eggs for 2 minutes until the whites are just firm and opaque and the yolks have begun to thicken. 7. Flip the eggs and resume cooking for 30 seconds to 1 minute until the yolks are cooked but still slightly runny. 8. Make a burger on each bun with 2 tomato slices, 2 bacon slices, a patty, and an egg. Enjoy.

Per serving: Calories 319; Total fat 11.7g; Sodium 1026mg; Total Carbs 5.2g; Fiber 0g; Sugars 5.2g; Protein 45.7g

Spinach Lamb Burgers

Prep time: 15 minutes | Cook time: 13 minutes | Serves: 4

8 slices of sourdough bread, each about ½ inch thick	8 slices tomato
Extra-virgin olive oil	¾ cup crumbled blue or feta cheese
1½ cups baby spinach leaves	
Patties	
2 pounds of ground lamb	2 teaspoons minced garlic
⅓ cup minced red onion	1½ teaspoons kosher salt
2 tablespoons extra-virgin olive oil	½ teaspoon freshly ground black pepper
2 tablespoons fresh lemon juice	1 teaspoon dried rosemary (optional)
2 tablespoons chopped Italian parsley leaves	1 teaspoon dried basil (optional)
2 tablespoons chopped oregano leaves	½ teaspoon ground cumin

1. Mix all the patty ingredients in a medium bowl, and then shape the mixture into 8 patties of equal size, about 1-inch thick. Make a shallow indentation about 1-inch-wide in the center of each patty, and then chill the patties in the refrigerator for 2 to 4 hours. 2. Prepare the Traeger grill for direct cooking over medium heat (350 degrees F/ 175 degrees C to 450 degrees F/ 230 degrees C). 3. Lightly brush the bread slices with oil on both sides. 4. Grill the patties on the clean grill grate for 10 to 13 minutes with the lid closed until they have an internal temperature of 160 degrees F/ 70 degrees C, turning them halfway through. 5. Toast the bread slices on the grill grate when there are 30 seconds or 1 minute left, turning them once. 6. Build a burger on each toasted bread slice with some spinach, 2 tomato slices, one patty, and some cheese. Serve warm.
Per serving: Calories 487; Total fat 13.5g; Sodium 293mg; Total Carbs 42.6g; Fiber 20.7g; Sugars 2.9g; Protein 47.4g

Kofta Pitas with Cucumber-Tomato Salad

Prep time: 25 minutes | Cook time: 9 minutes | Serves: 6

3 whole-wheat pita bread	1 cup chopped English cucumber
Extra-virgin olive oil	1 cup quartered cherry tomatoes
Tahini-Yoghurt Dressing	¼ cup chopped red onion
Salad	Kosher salt
Kofta	
1½ pounds ground chuck (80% lean)	1½ teaspoons kosher salt
½ cup minced Italian parsley leaves	½ teaspoon freshly ground black pepper
1 tablespoon minced garlic	½ teaspoon ground allspice
2 teaspoons ground coriander	¼ teaspoon ground cardamom
1½ teaspoons ground cumin	¼ teaspoon ground turmeric

1. Mix the cucumber, tomatoes, and onion in a bowl, and season with salt. Set aside. 2. Combine all the kofta ingredients in another bowl. Gently form the prepared mixture into six patties, each about ¾-inch thick. To keep each patty from doming as it cooks, make a shallow depression in the center of each one with your thumb or the back of a spoon. Before grilling, keep the prepared patties in the refrigerator. 3. Set the Traeger grill to medium-high heat (400 degrees F/ 200 degrees C to 500 degrees F/ 260 degrees C) for both direct and indirect cooking. 4. Lightly sprinkle the pita bread with water and wrap them in aluminum foil, sealing the packet closed. 5. Brush the prepared patties with oil on both sides. 6. Grill the patties over direct heat with the hood closed for 7 to 9 minutes until they have an internal temperature of 160 degrees F/ 70 degrees C (medium doneness), turning once. 7. Warm the pita packet over indirect heat for 5 minutes, turning once. Remove from the hot grill. 8. Cut each pita in half. Scoop about 3 tablespoons of the salad into each pita half. Spoon some of the prepared dressing over the salad. Place a patty into each pita half and spoon in more dressing. Serve warm.
Per serving: Calories 409; Total fat 13.4g; Sodium 285mg; Total Carbs 3.6g; Fiber 1.3g; Sugars 2.2g; Protein 64.5g

Savory Barbecued Meat Loaf

Prep time: 20 minutes | Cook time: 60 minutes | Serves: 8

Meatloaf	
1¼ pounds ground beef (80% lean)	1 teaspoon Worcestershire sauce
1¼ pounds ground pork	1 teaspoon garlic powder
2 cups panko (Japanese-style bread crumbs)	1 teaspoon dried tarragon
1 cup chopped yellow onion	1 teaspoon kosher salt
1 large egg	1 teaspoon freshly ground black pepper
Sauce	
½ cup bottled barbecue sauce	¼ cup ketchup

1. Mix all the meatloaf ingredients in a bowl, and then make the mixture into two loaves about 4 inches wide and 6 to 7 inches long. Set the loaves on a sheet pan. 2. Prepare the Traeger grill for indirect cooking at 300 degrees F/ 150 degrees C. 3. Mix all the sauce ingredients in a separate bowl. 4. Set aside half of the sauce to serve with the meatloaf. 5. Use 3 tablespoons of the remaining sauce to coat the top of each meatloaf evenly. 6. Gently place the loaves on the cooking grates. Close the lid and cook them for 1 hour until their center reaches 155 degrees F/ 70 degrees C. 7. Cut the loaves into slices, and serve with the reserved sauce.
Per serving: Calories 492; Total fat 32g; Sodium 530mg; Total Carbs 16.8g; Fiber 3g; Sugars 2.9g; Protein 32.1g

Flavorful Flank Steak with Asparagus

Prep time: 25 minutes | Cook time: 18 minutes | Serves: 4

1 flank steak, about 1½ pounds	1 tablespoon extra-virgin olive oil
¼ cup sesame seeds	½ teaspoon kosher salt
1 teaspoon sea salt	2 tablespoons chopped cilantro leaves
1-pound asparagus, tough ends removed	
Marinade	
¼ cup plus 1 tablespoon soy sauce	ginger
3 tablespoons rice vinegar	1½ tablespoons sambal Oelek
2 tablespoons sugar	1 tablespoon minced garlic
2 tablespoons toasted sesame oil	1 cup chopped scallions
1½ tablespoons peeled, grated	¼ cup chopped cilantro

1. Mix the soy sauce, vinegar, sugar, sesame oil, ginger, sambal Oelek, and garlic in a bowl until the sugar dissolves, and then add the scallions and cilantro. 2. Set the steak in a glass baking dish, pour in the marinade, and flip the steak to coat evenly. Cover the baking dish and refrigerate them for 3 to 4 hours, turning the steak once or twice. 3. Prepare the Traeger grill for direct cooking over medium heat (350 degrees F/ 175 degrees C to 450 degrees F/ 230 degrees C). 4. Toast the sesame seeds in a nonstick skillet over low heat for 2 to 3 minutes until they are golden brown but have not begun to pop, shaking the pan constantly. Pour the seeds onto a plate and let cool for 10 minutes. Transfer the seeds to a mortar, add the sea salt, and grind the seeds with a pestle. 5. Coat the asparagus with oil and season with salt. 6. Grill the prepared steak with the hood closed for 10 minutes (medium rare) or until cooked to your desired doneness, turning once. 7. Remove the cooked steak from the grill and let rest for 5 minutes. 8. While the steak rests, grill the asparagus for 6 to 8 minutes over direct medium heat with the hood closed until charred and crisp-tender, turning the spears a quarter turn every 1 to 2 minutes. Remove them from the hot grill. 9. Slice the cooked steak across the grain into thin slices. Serve the steak and asparagus warm, topped with the cilantro and some of the sesame seed mixture. The unused mixture will keep in a tightly capped jar in the refrigerator for up to 2 months.
Per Serving: Calories 303; Total fat 10.4g; Sodium 703mg; Total Carbs 9.2g; Fiber 0g; Sugars 8.7g; Protein 40.6g

Chapter 4 Beef, Lamb, and Venison Recipes

Balsamic Flank Steak with Baby Arugula

Prep time: 15 minutes | Cook time: 8 minutes | Serves: 4

1 flank steak, 1½ to 2 pounds Extra-virgin olive oil Kosher salt and freshly ground black pepper ⅓ cup balsamic vinegar ½ teaspoon granulated sugar	6 cups loosely packed baby arugula 1 cup shaved Parmigiano-Reggiano® cheese (about 3 ounces)

1. Light coat the steak with oil on both sides before seasoning with salt and black pepper. Before cooking, let the steak rest at room temperature for 15 to 30 minutes. 2. Prepare the Traeger grill for direct cooking over high heat (450 degrees F/ 230 degrees C to 550 degrees F/ 290 degrees C). 3. Add the vinegar and sugar to the saucepan, then boil them over medium-high heat; cook them on a simmer for 6 minutes until reduced by half, stirring occasionally. Remove the saucepan from the heat and let cool. 4. Grill the steak with the lid closed for 6 to 8 minutes (medium rare), turning once cooked halfway through. When grilled, transfer the steak to a chopping board and allow resting for 5 minutes. 5. Cut the steak in half lengthwise; then cut each half across the grain into thin slices. Divide the slices evenly among individual plates. Pour any juices captured during cutting over the steak and pile the arugula on top. Drizzle the balsamic reduction over the arugula, then season with black pepper and salt and top with the cheese. 6. Serve right away.
Per serving: Calories 478; Total fat 19.2g; Sodium 591mg; Total Carbs 2.6g; Fiber 0.9g; Sugars 0.7g; Protein 69.5g

Grilled Flank Steak with Black Bean Salad

Prep time: 25 minutes | Cook time: 10 minutes | Serves: 6

1 flank steak, 1½ to 2 pounds and ¾-inch thick **Rub** 1 teaspoon chili powder 1 teaspoon ground cumin 1 teaspoon dried oregano 1 teaspoon salt ½ teaspoon black pepper ⅛ teaspoon cinnamon **Salad** 1 can (15 ounces) of black beans	Kosher salt and freshly ground black pepper 1 cup seeded, chopped tomatoes ½ cup chopped yellow bell pepper ⅓ cup chopped red onion ⅓ cup sliced scallions 2 tablespoons olive oil 1 tablespoon lime juice 1 teaspoon minced garlic

1. Mix all the rub ingredients in a bowl. 2. Thoroughly all the salad ingredients and ¾ teaspoon of the rub in a separate bowl. Set aside at room temperature, let leave for at least 1 hour or up to 8 hours to meld the flavors. 3. Coat the steak with oil and season with the remaining rub. Let the steak leave at room temperature for 15 to 30 minutes. 4. Prepare the Traeger grill for direct cooking over high heat (450 degrees F/ 230 degrees C to 550 degrees F/ 290 degrees C). 5. Grill the steak with the hood closed for 10 minutes (medium rare) or until cooked to your desired doneness, turning once halfway through. 6. When grilled, remove the steak from the grill and let rest for 5 minutes. 7. Season the salad with black pepper and salt. 8. Slice the steak and serve over salad.
Per serving: Calories 452; Total fat 29.3g; Sodium 3091mg; Total Carbs 3.2g; Fiber 0.8g; Sugars 1.3g; Protein 40.3g

Korean-Style Barbecued Beef

Prep time: 10 minutes | Cook time: 5 minutes | Serves: 4-6

12 flank-style beef short ribs, about 4 pounds total and ½-inch thick 2 tablespoons sesame seeds, **Marinade** 1 Asian pear, peeled, cored, and	toasted 2 scallions (white and green parts), sliced roughly chopped 3 scallions (white and green parts), roughly chopped 6 garlic cloves 2 cups water ¾ cup soy sauce ⅓ cup granulated sugar ¼ cup rice vinegar

1. Add the pear, chopped scallions, and garlic to a food processor, and pulse until chopped; add the water, soy sauce, sugar, and vinegar, and process them until well mixed. 2. Evenly coat the ribs with the marinade in a suitable bowl, then cover the bowl and refrigerate them for 2 to 4 hours. 3. Prepare the Traeger grill for direct cooking over high heat (450 degrees F/ 230 degrees C to 550 degrees F/ 290 degrees C). 4. Rub the grilling grates with cooking spray. One at a time, lift the ribs from this bowl and let the liquid and solid bits fall back into this bowl. 5. Transfer the ribs to the clean grill grate without liquid and solid buts, then grill them for 3 to 5 minutes (medium or medium-rare doneness) with the lid open, turning them occasionally. 6. Remove the ribs from the hot grill, and sprinkle with the sesame seeds and sliced scallions. Serve warm.
Per Serving: Calories 323; Total fat 17.9g; Sodium 838mg; Total Carbs 4.3g; Fiber 1.5g; Sugars 1g; Protein 35.5g

Herbed Beef Roast with White Wine-Cream Sauce

Prep time: 15 minutes | Cook time: 45 minutes | Serves: 10-12

Rub 1½ tablespoons dried tarragon 1½ teaspoons dried thyme 2½ teaspoons salt 2 teaspoons black pepper **Sauce** ½ cup minced shallot ½ cup rice vinegar 1½ teaspoons dried tarragon ¼ teaspoon dried thyme ½ cup dry white wine	1 teaspoon dried sage 1 whole beef tenderloin, 7 pounds Extra-virgin olive oil ½ cup low-sodium chicken broth 1½ cup heavy whipping cream Kosher salt ½ cup packed minced Italian parsley leaves

1. Mix all the rub ingredients in a bowl. 2. Trim the tenderloin's silver skin and extra fat, and then throw them away. Even if a portion of the thin "tail" end separates, the major muscle will be kept as much as possible attached to it. The smoother side should be up as you lay the tenderloin out straight. To get a uniform thickness, align the narrow sections at the tail end and then fold the tail end under itself (one end of the tenderloin may be larger). 3. At 2-inch intervals, tie butcher's twine snugly around the roast. The folded end is fastened with two cords. Rub the spice rub on the roast after oiling it. Before grilling, allow the roast to sit at room temperature for 30 minutes to 1 hour. 4. Prepare the Traeger grill for direct and indirect cooking over medium heat (350 degrees F/ 175 degrees C to 450 degrees F/ 230 degrees C). 5. Shallot, vinegar, tarragon, and thyme are combined and cooked in a skillet over high heat for 3 to 4 minutes, turning frequently. Boil the prepared mixture for 3 to 4 minutes, until the wine and broth have been reduced to ½ cup. When the sauce has reduced to 1½ cups and the surface is covered with big, sparkling bubbles, add the cream and continue to boil for 5 to 7 minutes while stirring. Salt the seasoning as necessary, then set it aside. 6. Sear the roast over direct medium heat for 15 minutes with the lid closed, rotating it a quarter turn every 3 to 4 minutes. 7. Then place the roast over indirect medium heat, cover the pan, and cook for 20 to 30 minutes, rotating the roast once, until the internal temperature reaches 120 to 125 degrees F/ 50 degrees C for medium rare. 8. Loosely cover the roast with aluminum foil after cooking, and left to rest for 15 minutes. 9. Reheat the prepared sauce over medium heat and stir in the parsley. Slice the meat into ½ to 1-inch thick slices, removing the string from the roast, then season with salt. 10. Serve warm with the sauce.
Per Serving: Calories 423; Total fat 18.4g; Sodium 137mg; Total Carbs 4.6g; Fiber 1.9g; Sugars 0.8g; Protein 56.2g

Tri-Tip Roast with Corn Salsa & Black Beans

Prep time: 30 minutes | Cook time: 45 minutes | Serves: 4-6

3 tablespoons extra-virgin olive oil	excess fat and silver skin removed
1 teaspoon ancho chili powder	1 can (15 ounces) black beans, rinsed
1 teaspoon ground cumin	1½ cups sliced hearts of romaine
Kosher salt and freshly ground black pepper	½ cup crumbled or grated Cotija or queso fresco cheese (2 ounces)
1½ to 2 pounds tri-tip roast,	
Corn Salsa	
2 ears corn, husk removed	3 teaspoons minced Serrano chile pepper
1 cup cherry tomatoes cut into quarters	2 teaspoons lime juice
⅓ cup chopped red onion	½ teaspoon kosher salt
2 tablespoons olive oil	¼ teaspoon freshly ground black pepper
2 tablespoons chopped basil	

1. Prepare the Traeger grill for direct and indirect cooking over medium heat (350 degrees F/ 175 degrees C to 450 degrees F/ 230 degrees C). 2. The corn should be grilled for 15 minutes with the hood closed, flipping it once or twice. 3. Cut the kernels off the cobs, and place the kernels in a suitable bowl; mix them well after adding the remaining salsa ingredients. 4. Mix 2 tablespoons of oil, the cumin, 1 teaspoon of salt, chili powder, and ½ teaspoon pepper in a bowl. Using tri-tip, spread the prepared mixture. Before grilling, let the tri-tip rest at room temperature for 15 to 30 minutes. 5. The tri-tip should be grilled over direct medium heat for 10 minutes with the hood closed, flipping once. 6. Close the lid and cook the tri-tip for the desired doneness—15 to 20 minutes for medium rare—over indirect medium heat. Remove from the hot grill and give it a few minutes to cool. 7. Add the beans and 1 tablespoon oil to a saucepan, and cook them over low heat for 5 minutes, stirring once or twice, season them with salt and black pepper after removing it from the fire. 8. Slice the meat thinly against the grain. Serve immediately with the cheese, lettuce, corn salsa, and black beans.

Per Serving: Calories 419; Total fat 15.8g; Sodium 3342mg; Total Carbs 0.4g; Fiber 0.2g; Sugars 0g; Protein 65.4g

Barbecue Tri-Tip Sandwiches

Prep time: 35 minutes | Cook time: 35 minutes | Serves: 6

2 to 2½ pounds tri-tip roast, about 1½ inches thick	12 slices of French bread
	Tri-Tip Barbecue Sauce
Rub	
1 tablespoon black pepper	1 teaspoon paprika
2 teaspoons garlic salt	¼ teaspoon cayenne pepper
1 teaspoon mustard powder	

1. Mix all the rub ingredients in a bowl. 2. Press the rub into the roast meat, then cover the roast with plastic sheet and let it refrigerate for at least 3 hours or up to 24 hours. 3. Soak a handful of oak, mesquite, or hickory wood chips in water for at least 30 minutes. 4. Prepare the Traeger grill for direct and indirect cooking over medium heat (350 degrees F/ 175 degrees C to 450 degrees F/ 230 degrees C). 5. Drain the wood chips and add to the charcoal or to the smoker box of grill, and close the lid. 6. When smoke appears, set the tri-tip directly over the fire, close the lid, and sear for 5 minutes on both sides, turning once. Move to indirect heat, close the lid, and grill over indirect medium heat for 20 to 30 minutes (medium rare) until the internal temperature reaches about 140 degrees F/ 60 degrees C. 7. During the last 30 seconds to 1 minute of grilling time, toast the bread over direct heat. 8. Remove from the hot grill and let rest for 5 minutes. 9. Cut the meat on the diagonal across the grain into thin slices. Build each sandwich with 2 slices of French bread, meat, and a dollop of sauce. Serve warm or at room temperature.

Per Serving: Calories 347; Total fat 17.7g; Sodium 1655mg; Total Carbs 6.8g; Fiber 1.2g; Sugars 2.8g; Protein 33.3g

Steak-Tomato Kabobs with Avocado-Cucumber Sauce

Prep time: 15 minutes | Cook time: 8 minutes | Serves: 4

2 pounds top sirloin, about 1¼ inches thick, cut into 1¼-inch cubes	24 cherry tomatoes
	Vegetable oil
Sauce	
1 Hass avocado	¼ cup chopped dill
2-inch piece of English cucumber, peeled and chopped	Juice of 1 lime
	About ⅛ teaspoon hot-pepper sauce
¼ cup sour cream	Salt
¼ cup sliced scallions	
Rub	
1 teaspoon minced garlic	½ teaspoon ground coriander
1 teaspoon mustard powder	½ teaspoon ground cumin
1 teaspoon pure chili powder	½ teaspoon salt
½ teaspoon paprika	

1. If you choose the bamboo skewers, soak them in water for at least 30 minutes in advance. 2. Add the avocado, cucumber, sour cream, scallions, dill, and lime juice to a food processor, and process them until smooth, add the hot-pepper sauce to your liking, and then season with salt, stir them well. 3. Pour the sauce into a suitable bowl, cover the bowl, and refrigerate the sauce. Bring to the sauce to room temperature before serving. 4. Prepare the Traeger grill for direct cooking over medium heat (350 degrees F/ 175 degrees C to 450 degrees F/ 230 degrees C). 5. Mix all the spice rub ingredients in a separate bowl, then evenly coat the meat cubes with the rub. 6. Thread the meat onto the wooden skewers, alternating them with the tomatoes. Brush the skewers with oil. 7. Arrange the prepared skewers on the clean grill grate, and close the lid; grill the skewers for 8 minutes (medium rare), turning occasionally. Remove them from the hot grill after cooking. 8. Serve the kabobs warm with the sauce.

Per Serving: Calories 414; Total fat 20.8g; Sodium 156mg; Total Carbs 4.5g; Fiber 0.4g; Sugars 1.6g; Protein 49.8g

Strip Steaks with Horseradish-Cream Sauce

Prep time: 10 minutes | Cook time: 8 minutes | Serves: 4

4 New York strip steaks (each 10 to 12 ounces and about 1-inch thick), trimmed of excess fat	2 tablespoons Dijon mustard
	¾ teaspoon kosher salt
	¾ teaspoon freshly ground black pepper
2 tablespoons extra-virgin olive oil	
Sauce	
¾ cup sour cream	2 teaspoons Dijon mustard
2 tablespoons prepared horseradish	2 teaspoons Worcestershire sauce
	½ teaspoon kosher salt
2 tablespoons chopped Italian parsley leaves	¼ teaspoon freshly ground black pepper black pepper

1. Mix all the sauce ingredients in a bowl, then cover the bowl and place it in the refrigerator. 2. Brush the steaks with oil, mustard, salt, and pepper on both sides. Let the prepared steaks rest at room temperature for 15 to 30 minutes. 3. Set up the Traeger grill for direct cooking over high heat (450 degrees F/ 230 degrees C to 550 degrees F/ 290 degrees C). 4. The prepared steaks should be grilled for 6 to 8 minutes (medium rare) with the lid closed, flipping once. 5. After taking the steaks from the grill, let them rest for 5 minutes. 6. Serve the prepared steaks warm with the sauce.

Per Serving: Calories 305; Total fat 16.7g; Sodium 148mg; Total Carbs 2.5g; Fiber 1.1g; Sugars 0.1g; Protein 36.5g

Combat Rib-Eye Steaks with Mushrooms

Prep time: 15 minutes | Cook time: 8 minutes | Serves: 4

Rub
- ½ teaspoon black pepper
- 1 tablespoon garlic powder
- 1 teaspoon salt
- 4 bone-in rib-eye steaks, each about 10 ounces
- 3 Portobello mushrooms, about 4 ounces
- ½ cup (1 stick) unsalted butter
- 2 teaspoons minced garlic
- ¼ teaspoon salt
- ⅛ teaspoon black pepper
- ¼ cup red wine
- ½ cup crumbled blue cheese (2½ ounces), optional

1. Mix the spice rub ingredients thoroughly in a basin. The spice rub should be applied of the prepared steaks. Let the prepared steaks rest at room temperature for 15 to 30 minutes. 2. Set up the Traeger grill for direct cooking over high-heat (450 degrees F/ 230 degrees C to 550 degrees F/ 290 degrees C). 3. The mushroom stems should be cut off and thrown away. Make use of a damp paper towel to clean the mushroom tops. Scrape out and discard the dark gills with a teaspoon. Slice each mushroom cap crosswise into 12-inch-thick pieces after cutting it in half. 4. Melt half of the butter in a skillet over medium-high heat. Add the minced garlic and mushrooms, arranging them in a single layer, and season with salt and black pepper, and then cook them for 5 minutes, stirring twice or thrice until the mushrooms are just beginning to soften. Cook the wine for three minutes, stirring once, until it almost completely evaporates. Set the skillet aside. 5. The prepared steaks should be grilled for 6 to 8 minutes (medium rare) with the hood closed, flipping once. 6. After taking the prepared steaks from the grill, let them rest for five minutes. 7. Reheat the mushrooms in the skillet over medium heat; add the remaining butter and cooking until it is melted. 8. Serve each steak with a spoonful of the mushrooms, add cheese if desired.

Per Serving: Calories 443; Total fat 16.3g; Sodium 305mg; Total Carbs 37.4g; Fiber 7.8g; Sugars 11.4g; Protein 38.5g

Garlic T-Bones with Avocado Salsa

Prep time: 20 minutes | Cook time: 12 minutes | Serves: 4

- 2 tablespoons roughly chopped garlic
- 2 teaspoons kosher salt, divided
- **Salsa**
- 2 Hass avocados, chopped or mashed
- 1 cup chopped tomato
- 4 scallions, chopped
- 2 tablespoons fresh lime juice
- 1 tablespoon extra-virgin olive oil
- 2 tablespoons chopped basil leaves
- 2 T-bone steaks, each 1 to 1¼ pounds and about 1¼ inches thick
- Extra-virgin olive oil
- 1 teaspoon minced garlic
- 1 teaspoon minced jalapeño chili pepper
- ¾ teaspoon kosher salt
- ¼ teaspoon freshly ground pepper
- ¼ teaspoon Worcestershire sauce
- 1 teaspoon freshly ground black pepper

1. Mix all the salsa components in a basin, and then leave the salsa at room temperature for up to two hours. 2. On a cutting board, arrange the minced garlic in a small pile. Garlic is covered in a teaspoon of salt. Chop the minced garlic and salt with a chef's knife, and then use the side of the knife to press the prepared mixture into a smooth paste. 3. Prepare the Traeger grill for direct and indirect cooking over high heat (450 degrees F/ 230 degrees C to 550 degrees F/ 290 degrees C). 4. Lightly brush the steaks with oil and evenly coat them with the garlic paste on both sides, then season then with the pepper and the remaining salt on both sides. Let the prepared steaks rest at room temperature for 15 to 30 minutes. 5. Arrange the steaks on the clean grill grate, close the lid, and grill the steaks 6 minutes, flipping once. 6. Move the prepared steaks to an indirect high heat source and cook them for an additional 6 minutes for medium rare. 7. After taking the prepared steaks from the grill, let them rest for 5 minutes. 8. Serve the prepared steaks warm with the salsa.

Per Serving: Calories 340; Total fat 27.7g; Sodium 109mg; Total Carbs 12.6g; Fiber 0.3g; Sugars 3g; Protein 15.7g

Grilled Ginger Porterhouse Steaks

Prep time: 20 minutes | Cook time: 8 minutes | Serves: 4

- 3 tablespoons vegetable oil
- 2 tablespoons peeled, grated ginger
- 3 teaspoons salt
- 2 teaspoons black pepper
- 2 porterhouse steaks, about 1¼ pounds and 1-inch thick, trimmed of excess fat
- 3 tablespoons sesame seeds

1. Mix the oil, ginger, 2 teaspoons of salt, and 1½ tablespoons of pepper in a bowl. Coat each steak's top and bottom with the ginger mixture. Let the prepared steaks rest at room temperature for 15 to 30 minutes. 2. Set up the Traeger grill for high-heat direct cooking (450 degrees F/ 230 degrees C to 550 degrees F/ 290 degrees C). 3. Toast the sesame seeds, the remaining salt and the remaining pepper in a 10-inch skillet on medium heat for 10 minutes, until the sesame seeds are deep golden brown. Apportion the roasted sesame salt between four small dipping bowls. 4. The prepared steaks should be grilled for 6 to 8 minutes (medium rare) with the hood closed, flipping once. The prepared steaks should be taken from the grill and rested for 5 minutes after grilling. 5. Cut off the strip from one side of the bone and the filet from the other, and then cut each steak across the grain into slices. Serve warm with the sesame salt. Invite diners to dip an edge of each slice of steak in the salt.

Per Serving: Calories 404; Total fat 19.4g; Sodium 187mg; Total Carbs 5g; Fiber 1.1g; Sugars 0.8g; Protein 52g

Grilled Beef Tenderloin Steaks with Mushrooms

Prep time: 15 minutes | Cook time: 18 minutes | Serves: 4

- 4 beef tenderloin steaks, (6 ounces each) and 1¼ inches thick
- Extra-virgin olive oil
- Kosher salt and freshly ground black pepper
- 3 thick-cut slices bacon, cut into
- **Vinaigrette**
- 3 tablespoons red wine vinegar
- 2 teaspoons Dijon mustard
- 2 garlic cloves, minced
- ¼-inch dice (2 ounces)
- ⅓ cup chopped red onion
- 8 ounces cremini mushrooms, caps cut into quarters
- 2 tablespoons chopped chives
- ¼ teaspoon black pepper
- ¼ cup olive oil
- ½ teaspoon salt

1. Black pepper and salt should be liberally sprinkled of the prepared steaks after brushing them with oil on both sides. Before cooking, let the prepared steaks rest at room temperature for 15 to 30 minutes. 2. Set up the Traeger grill for direct cooking at high and medium heat at 450 degrees F/ 230 degrees C to 550 degrees F/ 290 degrees C ahrenheit. 3. Cook the bacon slices and onion in a pan over medium-low heat for 6 to 8 minutes until crispy and the onion are soft. Get rid of the heat. 4. Mix the vinegar, mustard, and garlic in a bowl; gradually mix in the oil until emulsified, and then mix in the black pepper and salt. 5. Put the mushrooms in a separate bowl, add ¼ cup of the vinaigrette, and mix well. Set aside the remaining vinaigrette. 6. A perforated grill pan should be heated to medium. The mushrooms should be taken out of the marinade and placed on the pan in a single layer, and then grill them over direct medium heat for 6 to 8 minutes with the hood closed until golden brown and tender, flipping halfway through. The mushrooms shouldn't be moved until the undersides are beautifully browned. 7. Grill the prepared steaks over direct high heat for 10 minutes at the same, flipping once, or until done to your preference. 8. Let them stand for 5 minutes after removing them from the grill. 9. Add the mushrooms to the set skillet with the bacon, onions, and heat for approximately a minute on the grill, turning frequently. Stir in the chives completely. With the mushroom mixture spooned on top, serve the prepared steaks warm. Pour some of the reconstituted saved vinaigrette over each steak, if desired.

Per Serving: Calories 392; Total fat 23.4g; Sodium 88mg; Total Carbs 10.4g; Fiber 1.9g; Sugars 3.7g; Protein 34.5g

Grilled Strip Steaks with Barbecue Sauce

Prep time: 35 minutes | Cook time: 8 minutes | Serves: 4

4 New York strip steaks (each 10 to 12 ounces and about 1-inch thick), trimmed of excess fat	2 tablespoons olive oil ¾ teaspoon salt ¾ teaspoon black pepper
Sauce	
1 tablespoon unsalted butter	espresso
2 teaspoons minced shallot	1 tablespoon balsamic vinegar
1 teaspoon minced garlic	1 tablespoon packed light brown sugar
½ cup ketchup	
¼ cup brewed dark-roast coffee or	2 teaspoons ancho chili powder

1. Melt the butter in a saucepan over medium heat; add the shallot and sauté for 3 minutes, or until it starts to color; add the minced garlic and simmer for approximately a minute, or until fragrant; add the remaining ingredients for the sauce, bring to a simmer, and then turn down the heat. Simmer the sauce for 10 minutes until somewhat reduced. 2. Transfer the sauce to a basin to cool. 3. Before seasoning the prepared steaks with salt and black pepper on both sides, brush them with oil on both sides. Let the prepared steaks sit at room temperature for 15 to 30 minutes. 4. Prepare the Traeger grill for direct cooking over high heat (450 degrees F/ 230 degrees C to 550 degrees F/ 290 degrees C). 5. The prepared steaks should be grilled for 6 to 8 minutes (medium rare) with the hood closed, flipping once. After taking the prepared steaks from the grill, let them rest for 5 minutes. 6. Serve the steaks warm with the sauce.

Per Serving: Calories 315; Total fat 15g; Sodium 91mg; Total Carbs 0g; Fiber 0g; Sugars 0g; Protein 42.3g

New York Strip Steaks with Pesto

Prep time: 15 minutes | Cook time: 8 minutes | Serves: 6

6 New York strip steaks (each 8 to 10 ounces and about 1-inch thick), trimmed of excess fat	Extra-virgin olive oil Kosher salt and freshly ground black pepper
Pesto	
1½ cups baby arugula	1 garlic clove
½ cup basil leaves	¼ cup extra-virgin olive oil
2 tablespoons chopped toasted walnuts	Kosher salt and freshly ground black pepper
½ teaspoon grated lemon zest	

1. Arugula, basil, walnuts, lemon zest, and garlic are combined in a food processor and pulsed until finely minced. Add the oil gradually while the machine is running and blend thoroughly. Set aside the pesto after seasoning it with salt and black pepper. 2. Apply a layer of oil to both sides of the prepared steaks before seasoning with salt and black pepper. Before cooking, let the prepared steaks rest at room temperature for 15 to 30 minutes. 3. Set up the Traeger grill for direct cooking high-heat over high heat (450 degrees F/ 230 degrees C to 550 degrees F/ 290 degrees C). 4. The prepared steaks should be grilled for 6 to 8 minutes (medium rare) with the hood closed, flipping once. After taking the prepared steaks from the grill and let them rest for 5 minutes. 5. Serve the heated steaks with a liberal dollop of pesto on top.

Per Serving: Calories 367; Total fat 22.9g; Sodium 101mg; Total Carbs 8g; Fiber 1.9g; Sugars 3g; Protein 31.8g

Smoked Dijon–Herb Rib Eye Steaks

Prep time: 15 minutes | Cook time: 8 minutes | Serves: 4-6

4 boneless rib-eye steaks, each 12 to 16 ounces and about 1-inch thick	½ teaspoon kosher salt ¼ teaspoon freshly ground black pepper
Paste	
1 small handful thyme sprigs	1 tablespoon Dijon mustard
3 tablespoons olive oil	1 tablespoon balsamic vinegar
1 tablespoon minced garlic	½ teaspoon celery seed
1 teaspoon salt	¼ teaspoon black pepper

1. Strip the leaves from the thyme sprigs. Reserve the stems for tossing onto the charcoal later. chop enough leaves to yield 2 tablespoons. 2. Mix the chopped thyme with all the remaining paste ingredients in a bowl to make a paste, add the steaks and evenly rub them with the paste. Cover the bowl and refrigerate them for 2 to 4 hours. 3. Soak 2 small handfuls of hickory or mesquite wood chips in water for at least 30 minutes. 4. Prepare the Traeger Smoker grill for direct cooking over high heat (450 degrees F/ 230 degrees C to 550 degrees F/ 290 degrees C). 5. Season the refrigerated steaks with salt and black pepper on both sides, and then let them rest at room temperature for 15 to 30 minutes. 6. Drain the wood chips, add them to the charcoal along with the thyme stems, and then cover the grill with the hood. 7. When smoke starts to emerge, close the hood and grill the prepared steaks over direct high heat for 6 to 8 minutes for medium rare, flipping once. 8. After taking the prepared steaks from the grill, let them rest for 5 minutes. Serve hot.

Per Serving: Calories 278; Total fat 15.4g; Sodium 321mg; Total Carbs 1.3g; Fiber 0.5g; Sugars 0.1g; Protein 32.1g

Herb–Garlic Leg of Lamb with Zucchini Salad

Prep time: 35 minutes | Cook time: 37 minutes | Serves: 6-8

Marinade	
¼ cup olive oil	1 small red onion, cut into ½-inch-thick slices
1 tablespoon chopped rosemary leaves	Extra-virgin olive oil
1 tablespoon minced garlic	8 ounces cherry tomatoes cut into halves
1 teaspoon salt	
½ teaspoon black pepper	2 tablespoons pitted, chopped Kalamata olives
1 leg of lamb, boneless, 4 pounds, butterflied, trimmed of fat, and cut into 3 or 4 equal sections	2 tablespoons drained, chopped oil-packed sun-dried tomatoes
Salad	2 tablespoons chopped mint leaves
12 ounces small zucchini, trimmed and halved lengthwise	Lemon-Parsley Dressing

1. Mix all the marinade ingredients in a bowl. Set the lamb leg in a resealable plastic bag and pour in the prepared marinade. Flip the bag to distribute the prepared marinade evenly, then place the bag in a suitable bowl, and refrigerate them for 2 to 12 hours, turning the bag occasionally. 2. Prepare the Traeger grill for direct cooking over medium heat (350 degrees F/ 175 degrees C to 450 degrees C/ 230 degrees C). 3. Brush the zucchini and onion evenly with oil, then grill them with the hood closed for 5 to 7 minutes until barely tender, turning them once halfway through. 4. Let them cool slightly after grilling, then cut the zucchini on the diagonal into ½-inch-thick slices and chop the onion. 5. Mix the zucchini, onion, cherry tomatoes, olives, sun-dried tomatoes, and mint in a serving bowl. 6. 3 tablespoons of the prepared dressing should be spooned over the salad. Evenly coat by tossing. Keep the leftover dressing for later. 7. Grill the lamb pieces with the hood closed until cooked to your desired doneness, turning once halfway through. Pieces more than 2 inches thick will take 20 to 30 minutes to reach medium rare (145 degrees F/ 60 degrees C); pieces 1 to 2 inches thick will take 15 to 20 minutes. Remove the lamb from the grill and let rest for 5 minutes. 8. Let the lamb pieces' rest for 5 minutes after grilling. 9. Slice the lamb thinly against the grain. Spoon the reserved dressing over the meat. Serve warm with the salad.

Per Serving: Calories 396; Total fat 11.4g; Sodium 448mg; Total Carbs 30.7g; Fiber 3.7g; Sugars 0.8g; Protein 40.2g

Chapter 4 Beef, Lamb, and Venison Recipes | 65

Prime Rib Roast with Hazelnut Pesto

Prep time: 15 minutes | Cook time: 2 hours 15 minutes | Serves: 8

2 tablespoons crushed black peppercorns	1 three-bone prime rib roast, about 7¼ pounds
1 tablespoon salt	1 tablespoon canola oil
Pesto	
½ cup cilantro leaves	5 garlic cloves, chopped
½ cup Italian parsley leaves	½ teaspoon crushed red pepper flakes
¼ cup oregano leaves	
¼ cup hazelnuts, toasted and skins removed	½ cup olive oil
¼ cup sherry vinegar	Kosher salt and freshly ground black pepper

1. Soak 2 handfuls of apple or oak wood chips in water for at least 30 minutes in advance. 2. Mix the salt and peppercorns in a basin. 3. Brush the roast all over with canola oil, and season it with the peppercorn mixture. Let the roast rest at room temperature for an hour. 4. Add cilantro, parsley, oregano, hazelnuts, vinegar, garlic, and pepper flakes to a food processor, and process them until finely minced; add the oil gradually while the motor is running and process until a thin paste forms. While the roast cooks, season the mixture with salt and black pepper, pour into a serving bowl, then cover the bowl, and let them rest at room temperature. 5. Prepare the Traeger grill for indirect cooking over 350 degrees F/ 175 degrees C. 6. Drained one handful of the wood chips and add to the charcoal, then close the lid. 7. When smoke starts to develop, place the roast on the grill grate with bone-side down. Cook the roast for 2 hours 25 minutes until it has an internal temperature of 120 to 125 degrees F/ 55 degrees C (medium rare). 8. Drain the remaining wood chips and add them to the charcoal after the first hour of cooking. After taking the roast off the grill, give it about 20 minutes to rest. 9. Slice the roast thickly, against the grain. Serve the dish warm with the pesto.

Per Serving: Calories 397; Total fat 19.1g; Sodium 431mg; Total Carbs 16.8g; Fiber 5.3g; Sugars 6.4g; Protein 39.4g

Lamb Loin Chops with Mint Salsa Verde

Prep time: 20 minutes | Cook time: 10 minutes | Serves: 4

8 lamb loin chops, each about 1¼ inches thick	Kosher salt and freshly ground black pepper
Extra-virgin olive oil	
Salsa	
1 cup mint	rinsed
1 cup parsley leaves and	1 garlic clove, chopped
1 teaspoon grated lemon zest	½ teaspoon salt
2 tablespoons lemon juice	¼ teaspoon crushed red pepper flakes
1 tablespoon chopped shallot	
1 tablespoon drained capers,	¼ cup extra-virgin olive oil

1. Add the mint, parsley, lemon zest and juice, shallot, capers, garlic, salt, and pepper flakes to a food processor, and pulse them to chop roughly. 2. When a chunky salsa forms, slowly add the oil while the machine is operating. To prevent discoloration, transfer the mixture to a suitable bowl, then cover the bowl with plastic sheet, pressing it firmly against the surface, and leave at room temperature. 3. Rub the chops with oil and season with black pepper and salt. 4. Let the chops leave at room temperature for 15 to 30 minutes. 5. Prepare the Traeger grill for direct cooking over medium heat (350 degrees F/ 175 degrees C to 450 degrees F/ 230 degrees C). 6. Grill the chops for 8 to 10 minutes (medium rare) with the lid closed or until cooked to your desired doneness, turning them once halfway through. 7. Let the dish rest for 3 to 5 minutes after grilling, and then serve them with the salsa on top.

Per Serving: Calories 348; Total fat 11.1g; Sodium 139mg; Total Carbs 7.9g; Fiber 3g; Sugars 1.6g; Protein 52.8g

Ginger–Curried Lamb Chops with Yogurt Sauce

Prep time: 20 minutes | Cook time: 10 minutes | Serves: 4

8 lamb loin chops, each 1½ inches thick, trimmed	
Sauce	
½ cup plain whole-milk Greek yogurt	1 teaspoon chili-garlic paste
	½ garlic clove, minced
1 tablespoon chopped cilantro leaves	¼ teaspoon salt
	⅛ teaspoon garam masala
2 teaspoons lime juice	
Marinade	
3 tablespoons lime juice	1 teaspoon ground turmeric
2 tablespoons peeled, grated ginger	1 teaspoon cayenne pepper
	1 teaspoon kosher salt
2 tablespoons olive oil	1 teaspoon freshly ground black pepper
2 teaspoons Madras curry powder	
1 teaspoon smoked paprika	

1. In a suitable bowl Mix all the sauce ingredients in a bowl, then cover the bowl and refrigerate the sauce for 30 minutes. 2. Mix all the marinade ingredients in another bowl. 3. Set the lamb chops in a glass baking dish, pour the prepared marinade over them, and flip the chops to coat evenly, cover the dish and refrigerate them for at least 2 hours or up to 4 hours. 4. Let the chops leave at room temperature for 15 to 30 minutes before grilling. 5. Prepare the Traeger grill for direct cooking over 350 degrees F/ 175 degrees C. 6. Take out the lamb chops and place them on the clean grill grates, grill them with the hood closed for 10 minutes (medium rare) or until cooked to your desired doneness for 10 minutes, turning them once halfway through. 7. Let the grilled lamb chops rest for 5 minutes. 8. Serve the chops warm with the yogurt sauce alongside.

Per Serving: Calories 348; Total fat 11.1g; Sodium 139mg; Total Carbs 7.9g; Fiber 3g; Sugars 1.6g; Protein 52.8g

Cheesesteak Meatloaf with Tiger Sauce

Prep time: 15 minutes | Cook time: 2 hours | Serves: 8

1 tablespoon canola oil	1 tablespoon A.1. Steak Sauce
2 garlic cloves, chopped	½ pound bacon, cooked and crumbled
1 medium onion, chopped	
1 poblano chili, stemmed, seeded, and chopped	2 cups shredded Swiss cheese
	1 egg, beaten
2 pounds' extra-lean ground beef	2 cups breadcrumbs
2 tablespoons Montreal steak seasoning	½ cup Tiger Sauce

1. Heat the canola oil in a medium sauté pan over medium-high heat; add the minced garlic, onion, and poblano, and sauté them for 5 minutes until the onion is just barely translucent. 2. Fill your Traeger Smoker with wood pellets and follow the manufacturer's specific start-up procedure. Preheat the grill to 225 degrees F/ 105 degrees C with the lid closed 3. In a suitable bowl, Mix the sautéed vegetables, ground beef, steak seasoning, steak sauce, bacon, Swiss cheese, egg, and breadcrumbs in a large bowl until well incorporated, then shape the mixture into a loaf. 4. Put the meatloaf in a cast iron skillet and place it on the grill. Close the hood and smoke for 2 hours, or until a meat thermometer inserted in the loaf reads 165 degrees F/ 75 degrees C. 5. Top with the meatloaf with the Tiger Sauce, and let rest for 10 minutes before serving.

Per Serving: Calories 402; Total fat 19.9g; Sodium 1387mg; Total Carbs 24g; Fiber 8g; Sugars 12.7g; Protein 32.1g

Garlic–Soy London Broil

Prep time: 20 minutes | Cook time: 16 minutes | Serves: 3-4

1 (1½- to 2-pound) London broil or top round steak	¼ cup chopped scallions
¼ cup soy sauce	2 tablespoons packed brown sugar
2 tablespoons white wine	2 garlic cloves, minced
2 tablespoons extra-virgin olive oil	2 teaspoons red pepper flakes
	1 teaspoon freshly ground black pepper

1. Lightly pound the steak all over to break down its fibers and tenderize with a meat mallet. 2. Mix the soy sauce, white wine, olive oil, scallions, brown sugar, garlic, red pepper flakes, and black pepper in a bowl to make the marinade. 3. Put the steak in a shallow plastic container with a lid, and pour the prepared marinade over the meat, then cover the container and refrigerate them for 4 hours. 4. Remove the steak from the prepared marinade, shaking off any excess. 5. Fill your Traeger Smoker with wood pellets and follow the manufacturer's specific start-up procedure. Preheat the grill to 350 degrees F/ 175 degrees C with the lid closed. 6. Smoke the steak with the lid closed for 6 minutes. Flip, and then smoke for 6 to 10 minutes more. 7. Let the steak rest for 10 minutes before slicing and serving.
Per Serving: Calories 375; Total fat 19.8g; Sodium 2105mg; Total Carbs 29g; Fiber 0.7g; Sugars 24.8g; Protein 24.3g

French Onion Cheeseburgers

Prep time: 35 minutes | Cook time: 25 minutes | Serves: 4

1-pound lean ground beef	1 tablespoon olive oil
1 tablespoon minced garlic	1 teaspoon liquid smoke
1 teaspoon Better Than Bouillon Beef Base	3 medium onions, cut into thick slices but do not separate the rings
1 teaspoon dried chives	1 loaf French bread, cut into 8 slices
1 teaspoon black pepper	
8 slices Gruyère cheese	4 slices provolone cheese
½ cup soy sauce	

1. Mix the ground beef, minced garlic, beef base, chives, and pepper in a bowl. 2. Divide the meat mixture and shape into 8 thin burger patties. 3. Top each of 4 patties with one slice of Gruyère, then top with the remaining 4 patties to create 4 stuffed burgers. 4. Fill your Traeger Smoker with wood pellets and follow the manufacturer's specific start-up procedure. Preheat the grill at High setting (450 degrees F/ 230 degrees C) with the lid closed 5. Arrange the burgers directly on one side of the grill, close the lid, and smoke them for 10 minutes. Flip and smoke them with the hood closed for 15 minutes more, or until a meat thermometer inserted in the burgers reads 160 degrees F/ 70 degrees C. 6. Add another Gruyère slice to the burgers during the last 5 minutes of smoking to melt. 7. Mix the soy sauce, olive oil, and liquid smoke in a separate bowl. 8. Arrange the onion slices on the grill and baste both sides with the soy sauce mixture. Smoke them with the hood closed for 20 minutes, flipping halfway through. 9. Toast the French bread slices on the grill. 10. Layer each of 4 slices with a burger patty, a slice of provolone cheese, and some of the smoked onions. Top each with another slice of toasted French bread. Enjoy.
Per Serving: Calories 388; Total fat 21.8g; Sodium 787mg; Total Carbs 5.4g; Fiber 1.5g; Sugars 1.4g; Protein 49.3g

Sweet Corned Beef with Cabbage

Prep time: 30 minutes | Cook time: 4 to 5 hours | Serves: 6-8

For The Corned Beef

1 gallon water	1 tablespoon black pepper
1 (3- to 4-pound) point cut corned beef brisket with pickling spice packet	1 tablespoon garlic powder
	½ cup molasses
	1 teaspoon ground mustard

For The Cabbage

1 head green cabbage	4 tablespoons (½ stick) butter
2 tablespoons rendered bacon fat	1 chicken bouillon cube, crushed

1. In a suitable container with a lid, mix the water and the corned beef pickling spice packet and submerge the corned beef in it, then cover the container and let it refrigerate overnight, changing the water every 3 hours while you're awake—to soak out some of the curing salt originally added. 2. Fill your Traeger Smoker with wood pellets and follow the manufacturer's specific start-up procedure. Preheat the grill to 275 degrees F/ 135 degrees C with the lid closed. 3. Remove the meat from the brining liquid, pat it dry, and generously rub with the black pepper and garlic powder. 4. Put the seasoned corned beef directly on the grill with the fat-side up, close the lid, and grill for 2 hours. Remove from the hot grill when done. 5. In a suitable bowl, mix the molasses and ground mustard, and pour half of this mixture into the bottom of an aluminum pan. 6. Transfer the meat to the pan with fat-side up, and pour the remaining molasses mixture on top, evenly spreading it over the meat. Cover the pan tightly with aluminum foil. 7. Transfer this pan to the grill, close the hood, and continue smoking the corned beef for 2 to 3 hours, or until a meat thermometer inserted in the thickest part reads 185 degrees F/ 85 degrees C. 8. While the brisket is smoking, core the cabbage and fill the resulting cavity with the butter, rendered bacon fat, and crushed chicken bouillon cube. 9. Wrap the cabbage in foil about two-thirds of the way up the sides to protect the outer leaves, but do not completely cover, and place on the grill alongside the corned beef about an hour before the meat is expected to be finished. 10. Remove both the corned beef and the cabbage from the grill then slice. 11. Carefully unwrap the cabbage and pour the compound butter from the cavity into a suitable casserole dish. 12. Chop the cabbage and add to the casserole dish, then top with the sliced corned beef to serve.
Per Serving: Calories 416; Total fat 23.6g; Sodium 934mg; Total Carbs 6g; Fiber 2g; Sugars 0.6g; Protein 37.9g

Cheeseburger Tomato Hand Pies

Prep time: 35 minutes | Cook time: 10 minutes | Serves: 6

½ pound lean ground beef	pizza dough sheets
1 tablespoon minced onion	2 eggs, beaten with 2 tablespoons water
1 tablespoon steak seasoning	
1 cup Monterey Jack and Colby cheese blend, shredded	24 hamburger dill pickle chips
	2 tablespoons sesame seeds
8 slices white American cheese	6 slices tomato, for garnish
2 (14-ounce) refrigerated prepared	Ketchup and mustard, for serving

1. Fill your Traeger Smoker with wood pellets and follow the manufacturer's specific start-up procedure. Preheat the grill to 325 degrees F/ 160 degrees C with the lid closed. 2. Brown the ground beef for 5 minutes in a medium sauté pan over medium-high heat; add the minced onion and steak seasoning; toss in the shredded cheese blend and 2 slices of American cheese, and stir them until melted and fully incorporated. 3. Remove the cheeseburger mixture from the heat and set aside. 4. Make sure the dough is well chilled for easier handling. Quickly roll out one prepared pizza crust on parchment paper and rub with half of the egg wash. 5. Arrange the remaining 6 slices of American cheese on the dough to outline 6 hand pies. 6. Top each cheese slice with ¼ cup of the cheeseburger mixture, spreading inside the imaginary lines of the hand pies. 7. Place 4 pickle slices on top of the filling for each pie. 8. Top the whole thing with the other prepared pizza crust and cut between the cheese slices to create 6 hand pies. 9. Using kitchen scissors cut the parchment to further separate the pies, but leave them on the paper. 10. Using a fork dipped in egg wash, seal the edges of the pies on all sides. Baste the top of the pies with the remaining egg wash and sprinkle with the sesame seeds. 11. Remove the pies from the parchment paper and gently place on the grill grate. Close the hood and smoke for 5 minutes, then carefully flip and smoke with the hood closed for 5 more minutes, or until browned. 12. Top with the sliced tomato and serve with ketchup and mustard.
Per Serving: Calories 372; Total fat 16.3g; Sodium 742mg; Total Carbs 6.8g; Fiber 0.8g; Sugars 1.8g; Protein 42.3g

Garlic Filet Mignons

Prep time: 10 minutes | Cook time: 14 minutes | Serves: 2

2 (1¼-inch-thick) filet mignons	2 teaspoons minced garlic
2 teaspoons sea salt	2 teaspoons onion powder
2 teaspoons black pepper	

1. Fill your Traeger Smoker with wood pellets and follow the manufacturer's specific start-up procedure. Preheat the grill at High setting (450 degrees F/ 230 degrees C) with the lid closed. 2. In a suitable bowl, mix the salt, pepper, minced garlic, and onion powder to form a rub, and generously apply it to both sides of the prepared steaks. 3. Lay the prepared steaks on the grill grate, close the lid, and smoke for 7 minutes. Flip and continue smoking with the hood closed for 7 minutes, or until the internal temperature reaches 125 degrees F/ 50 degrees C to 130 degrees F/ 55 degrees C for medium-rare. 4. Remove the prepared steaks from the grill. 5. Serve.

Per Serving: Calories 326; Total fat 12g; Sodium 779mg; Total Carbs 8.3g; Fiber 2.9g; Sugars 1.3g; Protein 46.9g

Savory Pastrami

Prep time: 15 minutes | Cook time: 5 hours | Serves: 12

1 gallon water, plus ½ cup	beef brisket with brine mix packet
½ cup packed light brown sugar	2 tablespoons black pepper
1 (3- to 4-pound) point cut corned	¼ cup ground coriander

1. In a suitable container with a lid, mix 1 gallon of water, the brown sugar, and the corned beef spice packet, then submerge the corned beef in it. Then, cover the container and let it refrigerate overnight, changing the water every 3 hours while you're awake—to soak out some of the curing salt originally added. 2. Fill your Traeger Smoker with wood pellets and follow the manufacturer's specific start-up procedure. Preheat the grill to 275 degrees F/ 135 degrees C with the lid closed. 3. In a suitable bowl, mix the black pepper and ground coriander to form a rub. 4. Drain the meat, pat it dry, and generously coat on all sides with the spice rub. 5. Set the corned beef directly on the grill, fat-side up, close the lid, and smoke for 3 hours to 3 hours 30 minutes, or until a meat thermometer inserted in the thickest part reads 175 degrees F/ 75 degrees C to 185 degrees F/ 85 degrees C. 6. Pour the remaining ½ cup of water into the bottom of a disposable roasting pan; add the corned beef, cover the pan tightly with aluminum foil, and smoke on the grill with the hood closed for an additional 30 minutes to 1 hour. 7. Remove the meat from the grill and let cool for 10 minutes. 8. Transfer to a plate and let it refrigerate for at least 1 hour before slicing and serving.

Per Serving: Calories 412; Total fat 23.6g; Sodium 1495mg; Total Carbs 4.8g; Fiber 1.3g; Sugars 1.7g; Protein 37.9g

Garlic Rump Roast

Prep time: 10 minutes | Cook time: 3 to 4 hours | Serves: 6-8

1 (3- to 4-pound) rump roast	2 tablespoons steak seasoning
olive oil, for rubbing	1 tablespoon minced garlic

1. Fill your Traeger Smoker with wood pellets and follow the manufacturer's specific start-up procedure. Preheat the grill at High setting (425 degrees F/ 220 degrees C) with the lid closed. 2. Rub the roast with olive oil and generously apply steak seasoning and minced garlic. 3. Put the meat directly on the grill, and sear all surfaces of the roast for 2 to 5 minutes per side. Remove from the hot grill. 4. Reduce the temperature to 225 degrees F/ 105 degrees C. 5. Set the roast back on the grill, close the lid, and smoke for 3 to 4 hours more. 6. Remove the roast from the grill, tent it with aluminum foil, and let rest for 10 minutes before serving.

Per Serving: Calories 408; Total fat 23.1g; Sodium 412mg; Total Carbs 27.7g; Fiber 7.2g; Sugars 19.2g; Protein 24.4g

BBQ Chuck Roast

Prep time: 15 minutes | Cook time: 8 hours | Serves: 6

1 (3-pound) chuck roast	¾ cup Bill's Best BBQ Sauce
3 tablespoons dry rub	

1. Fill your Traeger Smoker with wood pellets and follow the manufacturer's specific start-up procedure. Preheat the grill to 275 degrees F/ 135 degrees C with the lid closed. 2. Liberally season the chuck roast with the dry rub. 3. Set the meat directly on the grill, close the lid, and smoke for 5 hours. 4. Wrap the meat tightly with a foil, and continue smoking with the hood closed for another hour then cut into cubes. 5. Transfer the cubes to a disposable baking pan and toss with ½ cup of barbecue sauce. 6. Set the pan on the grill, close the lid, and smoke for another 1 hour 30 minutes to 2 hours, or until hot and bubbly, adding the remaining ¼ cup of barbecue sauce in the last 30 minutes of cooking. 7. Serve immediately.

Per Serving: Calories 347; Total fat 15.7g; Sodium 999mg; Total Carbs 11.8g; Fiber 1.1g; Sugars 7g; Protein 39.6g

Smoked Garlic Prime Rib

Prep time: 15 minutes | Cook time: 20 minutes | Serves: 6-8

1 (3- to 4-pound) prime rib	1 tablespoon black pepper
Butcher's string	1 tablespoon garlic powder
1 tablespoon coarse salt	Chimichurri Sauce, for serving

1. Tie the rib with butcher's string in several places to hold it together during the smoking process. 2. Fill your Traeger Smoker with wood pellets and follow the manufacturer's specific start-up procedure. At 450 degrees F/ 230 degrees C, preheat your Traeger Smoker with its hood close. 3. In a suitable bowl, mix the salt, pepper, and garlic powder, and then coat the prime rib with this mixture. 4. Set the rib bone-side down in a roasting pan with a rack, and put the pan on the grill. 5. Close the hood and smoke the prime rib for 30 minutes, then reduce the heat to 300 degrees F/ 150 degrees C. Continue to roast the meat with the hood closed for 25 to 50 minutes, depending on the size and desired internal temperature. Total cook time will be about 20 minutes per pound, but do not remove from the heat before a meat thermometer inserted deep into the middle of the meat reads between 120 degrees F/ 50 degrees C (rare) and 155 degrees F/ 70 degrees C (well-done). 6. Let the prime rib rest for 10 to 20 minutes before removing the string and removing the bones. 7. Slice the steak serve drizzled with chimichurri sauce.

Per Serving: Calories 236; Total fat 10.4g; Sodium 713mg; Total Carbs 9.8g; Fiber 0.5g; Sugars 0.1g; Protein 25.7g

Herbed Spicy Tri-Tip

Prep time: 15 minutes | Cook time: 60 minutes | Serves: 4

2 teaspoons sea salt	1 teaspoon cayenne pepper
2 teaspoons freshly ground black pepper	1 teaspoon ground sage
2 teaspoons onion powder	1 teaspoon chopped rosemary
2 teaspoons garlic powder	1 (1½ – to 2-pound) tri-tip bottom sirloin
2 teaspoons dried oregano	

1. Fill your Traeger Smoker with wood pellets and follow the manufacturer's specific start-up procedure. Preheat, with the hood closed, to 425 degrees F/ 220 degrees C. 2. In a suitable bowl, mix the salt, pepper, onion powder, garlic powder, oregano, cayenne pepper, sage, and rosemary to create a rub. 3. Season the sirloin meat with the spice rub and lay it directly on the grill. 4. Close the hood and smoke the meat for 45 minutes to 1 hour. 5. Remove the tri-tip from the heat, tent with aluminum foil, and let rest for 15 minutes before slicing against the grain.

Per Serving: Calories 227; Total fat 8.8g; Sodium 302mg; Total Carbs 8.9g; Fiber 2.1g; Sugars 3.3g; Protein 28.5g

Cheesy Meat Stuffed Peppers

Prep time: 15 minutes | Cook time: 1 hr. 15 minutes | Serves: 4

4 bell peppers, tops removed, cored, and seeded	and chopped
½ pound ground beef	1 (14-ounce) can tomato paste
½ pound ground sausage	1½ cups grated Cheddar cheese
1 onion, diced	1 teaspoon seasoned salt
1 poblano chili, stemmed, seeded,	1 teaspoon black pepper
	1 tablespoon minced garlic

1. Set the peppers in a disposable aluminum pan, wrapping them at the base with aluminum foil rings, if necessary, to keep them stable. 2. Fill your Traeger Smoker with wood pellets and follow the manufacturer's specific start-up procedure. Preheat the grill to 350 degrees F/ 175 degrees C with the lid closed. 3. Brown the ground beef and ground sausage for 7 minutes in a suitable skillet over medium-high heat, drain off the fat and crumble the meat. 4. Stir the onion, poblano chili, tomato paste, 1 cup of Cheddar cheese, salt, black pepper, and garlic into the meat, mixing well. 5. Stuff the bell peppers in the aluminum pan with the meat mixture. 6. Set the pan on the grill, close the lid, and smoke for 1 hour. 7. Top the stuffed bell peppers with the remaining cheese and continue smoking with the hood closed for 15 minutes, then remove from the heat. 8. Serve hot.

Per Serving: Calories 314; Total fat 8.7g; Sodium 337mg; Total Carbs 21.2g; Fiber 4.1g; Sugars 16g; Protein 37.9g

Barbecued Beef Brisket

Prep time: 35 minutes | Cook time: 8 to 10 hours | Serves: 8-12

1 cup kosher salt	1 cup apple cider vinegar
1 cup ground black pepper	1 cup apple juice
1 (8- to 12-pound) brisket, most fat trimmed off	2 tablespoons salt
	Pink butcher paper
1 cup yellow mustard	

1. Fill your Traeger Smoker with wood pellets and follow the manufacturer's specific start-up procedure. Preheat the grill to 225 degrees F/ 105 degrees C with the lid closed. 2. Mix the black pepper and salt in a bowl. 3. Slather the trimmed brisket with the mustard, and then generously apply the black pepper and salt mixture to the meat until it's well coated. 4. Set the meat in the center of the grill with fat-side up. Close the hood and smoke for 5 hours. 5. While the brisket is smoking, mix the apple cider vinegar, apple juice, and salt in a bowl to make the mop sauce, and pour into a spray bottle. 6. When the brisket has finished the first 4 to 5 hours of cooking, spray it with the glaze sauce and wrap tightly with pink butcher paper to seal in the juices. Close the hood and continue smoking for another 4 to 5 hours (or longer as needed) until the brisket has an internal temperature reaches 195 degrees F/ 90 degrees C to 205 degrees F/ 95 degrees C and has a nice dark bark, spraying with the sauce every hour. 7. Remove the cooked meat from the grill, unwrap it, and let rest for up to an hour before slicing. 8. Separate the point side by dividing at the fat line. Shred or reserve for burnt ends. (Cut into 2-inch cubes, toss in barbecue sauce, and heat in a foil pan until sticky and hot. 9. Cut the flat-shaped half of the brisket against the grain into thin slices.

Per Serving: Calories 346; Total fat 18.8g; Sodium 137mg; Total Carbs 13.4g; Fiber 8.5g; Sugars 1g; Protein 36.3g

Spicy Beef Shoulder Clod

Prep time: 10 minutes | Cook time: 12 to 16 hours | Serves: 16-20

½ cup sea salt	1 tablespoon cayenne pepper
½ cup black pepper	1 tablespoon smoked paprika
1 tablespoon red pepper flakes	1 (13- to 15-pound) beef shoulder clod
1 tablespoon minced garlic	

1. Mix the salt, pepper, red pepper flakes, minced garlic, cayenne pepper, and smoked paprika in a bowl to create a rub. Generously apply it to the beef shoulder. 2. Fill your Traeger Smoker with wood pellets and follow the manufacturer's specific start-up procedure. Preheat the grill to 250 degrees F/ 120 degrees C with the lid closed. 3. Put the meat on the grill grate, close the lid, and smoke for 12 to 16 hours until the food has an internal temperature of 195 degrees F/ 90 degrees C. 4. You may need to cover the clod with aluminum foil toward the end of smoking to prevent over-browning. 5. Slice and serve.

Per Serving: Calories 343; Total fat 20.1g; Sodium 903mg; Total Carbs 0.2g; Fiber 0.1g; Sugars 0.2g; Protein 37.1g

Smoky T–Bone Steak with Blue Cheese Butter

Prep time: 10 minutes | Cook time: 50 minutes | Serves: 4

4 tablespoons (½ stick) unsalted butter	steaks
	2 tablespoons salt
½ cup blue cheese crumbles	1 tablespoon black pepper
4 (14-ounce, 1-inch-thick) T-bone	2 tablespoons minced garlic

1. In a suitable bowl, stir together the butter and blue cheese crumbles and set aside, but do not refrigerate unless making in advance. 2. Fill your Traeger Smoker with wood pellets and follow the manufacturer's specific start-up procedure. Preheat, with the hood closed, to 165 degrees F/ 75 degrees C. 3. Season the prepared steaks with the salt, pepper, and garlic. 4. Arrange the prepared steaks directly on the grill, close the lid, and smoke for 30 minutes. 5. Increase the cooking heat to High (450 degrees F/ 230 degrees C), and smoke for an additional 15 minutes for medium-rare or longer for your desired doneness, turning once, until a meat thermometer inserted in the meat reads 120 degrees F/ 50 degrees C to 155 degrees F/ 70 degrees C. 6. Remove the prepared steaks from the grill, and let rest for 5 minutes before serving topped with the blue cheese butter.

Per Serving: Calories 427; Total fat 18.1g; Sodium 676mg; Total Carbs 13.7g; Fiber 7.5g; Sugars 1.7g; Protein 51.2g

Chapter 4 Beef, Lamb, and Venison Recipes

Chapter 5 Appetizer and Sides Recipes

71	Kidney Beans Chili	73	Lemony Artichokes
71	Smoked Cheese Macaroni	74	Smoked Deviled Eggs with Olives
71	Homemade Smoked Guacamole	74	Smoked Corn on the Cob
71	Sugar-Butter Carrots	74	Smoked Bacon-Cheddar Potato Skins
71	Sweet Smoked Beans & Pineapple	74	Smoked Spaghetti Squash
71	Grilled Potatoes with Onion	74	Smoked Garlic Cauliflower Steaks
72	Cheesy Scalloped Potatoes	74	Cheesy Corn with Chipotle Butter
72	Hassel-back Sweet Potatoes with Pecans	75	Smoked Okra
72	Cilantro-Balsamic Bacon-Wrapped Brussels Sprouts	75	Crispy Sweet Potato Chips
72	Candied Bacon	75	Spaghetti Squash with Garlic-Wine Butter Sauce
72	Bacon-Wrapped Jalapeño Poppers	75	Cheddar Broccoli-Cauliflower Salad
72	Tasty Smoked Onion Bombs	75	Carrot Hot Dogs with Jalapeño Relish
73	Smoked Whole Cabbage	75	Cabbage Slaw Salad
73	Cheesy Hassel-back Russet Potatoes	76	Parmesan Sweet Onion Bake
73	Smoked Sweet & Sour Coleslaw	76	BBQ Beans with Bacon
73	Rosemary-Garlic Potato Wedges	76	Blt Pasta Bacon Salad
73	Smoked Butter Asparagus	76	Vegetable-Cornbread Salad
73	Spicy Bacon-Wrapped Onion Rings	76	Mixed Berries-Watermelon Bowl

Kidney Beans Chili

Prep time: 5 minutes | Cook time: 35 minutes | Serves: 5

1 tablespoon olive oil	chilies
1-pound ground beef	1 packet chili seasoning mix
1 (16-ounce) can kidney beans	14½ ounces water
1 (4-ounce) can chopped green	

1. Fill your Traeger Smoker with wood pellets and follow the manufacturer's specific start-up procedure. Place a suitable cast-iron skillet on the grill grate and Preheat the grill to 400 degrees F/ 200 degrees C with the lid closed. 2. Drizzle the skillet with the olive oil, and then add the beef to the set skillet and cook for 5 minutes until the beef starts to brown. 3. Once the beef is cooked, remove the skillet from the grill and drain off the grease. Return the skillet to the grill. 4. Add the beans, chilies, seasoning mix, and water to the skillet, mix them well and cook them for 30 minutes until the liquid is absorbed, stirring occasionally. 5. Remove the skillet from the grill and serve.
Per Serving: Calories 384; Total fat 23.6g; Sodium 80mg; Total Carbs 20.7g; Fiber 8.3g; Sugars 3.5g; Protein 24.6g

Smoked Cheese Macaroni

Prep time: 5 minutes | Cook time: 30 minutes | Serves: 6

16 ounces elbow macaroni	cheese
4 tablespoons (¼ cup) butter	4 ounces shredded cheddar cheese
¼ cup milk	Salt
4 ounces cream cheese	Black pepper
4 ounces shredded mozzarella	

1. Fill your Traeger Smoker with wood pellets and follow the manufacturer's specific start-up procedure. Place a deep cast-iron pot with a hood or a Dutch oven on the grill and preheat, with the grill hood closed, to 400 degrees F/ 200 degrees C. 2. Cook the pasta according to package directions. Drain and return the pasta to the pot. 3. Set the pot back on the grill grate and adjust the cooking mode to smoke. 4. Add the butter and milk; add the cream cheese, mozzarella, cheddar, and black pepper and salt to the pasta. Stir well to mix. 5. Close the grill hood but uncover the pot, and smoke the food for 15 minutes. 6. Serve.
Per Serving: Calories 314; Total fat 8.7g; Sodium 337mg; Total Carbs 21.2g; Fiber 4.1g; Sugars 16g; Protein 37.9g

Homemade Smoked Guacamole

Prep time: 15 minutes | Cook time: 20 minutes | Serves: 4-6

5 medium avocados	Juice of 1 lime
1 bunch cilantro, stems trimmed and leaves chopped	1 teaspoon garlic powder
1 tablespoon sour cream	Kosher salt
1 teaspoon hot sauce	Freshly ground black pepper

1. Fill your Traeger Smoker with wood pellets and follow the manufacturer's specific start-up procedure. Preheat the grill to 180 degrees F/ 80 degrees C with the lid closed. 2. Cut the avocados in half and remove the seeds. Using a spoon, run it around the edge of the avocado half, separating the flesh from the peel. 3. Set the avocado halves directly on the grill grate, cut-side down. Close the hood and smoke for 20 minutes, or until the halves are soft and buttery. 4. Remove the grilled avocados from the grill and place them in a suitable bowl; add the cilantro, sour cream, hot sauce, lime juice, garlic powder, and black pepper and salt to taste. 5. Mash the prepared mixture until smooth, and serve with tortilla chips.
Per Serving: Calories 228; Total fat 9g; Sodium 546mg; Total Carbs 10.8g; Fiber 3.1g; Sugars 0.2g; Protein 10.6g

Sugar-Butter Carrots

Prep time: 10 minutes | Cook time: 40 minutes | Serves: 4-6

1½ pounds carrots, peeled and halved lengthwise	Freshly ground black pepper
2 tablespoons olive oil	6 tablespoons butter
Kosher salt	4 tablespoons brown sugar

1. Fill your Traeger Smoker with wood pellets and follow the manufacturer's specific start-up procedure. Preheat the grill to 350 degrees F/ 175 degrees C with the lid closed. 2. Set the carrot halves in a suitable bowl, and add the olive oil, salt and black pepper, mix them to coat the carrots well. 3. Set the carrots directly on the grill grate, close the lid, and cook them for 20 minutes. 4. While the carrots cook, mix the butter and brown sugar in a small microwave-safe bowl, and microwave for 25 seconds. 5. After 20 minutes, use a basting to baste the carrots with the brown sugar butter. 6. Cook them for 20 minutes more, or until the carrots are soft when pierced with a fork. 7. Remove the carrots from the grill and serve.
Per Serving: Calories 275; Total fat 2.2g; Sodium 486mg; Total Carbs 27.3g; Fiber 0.4g; Sugars 17.5g; Protein 16.3g

Sweet Smoked Beans & Pineapple

Prep time: 15 minutes | Cook time: 35 minutes | Serves: 4

1 (28-ounce) can baked beans	¼ cup brown sugar
1 (8-ounce) can pineapple chunks, drained	¼ cup ketchup
Worcestershire sauce	Freshly ground black pepper

1. Fill your Traeger Smoker with wood pellets and follow the manufacturer's specific start-up procedure. Place a deep cast-iron skillet with a hood or a Dutch oven onto the grill and preheat the grill to 350 degrees F/ 175 degrees C with the lid closed. 2. In the set skillet, Add the beans, pineapple chunks, 6 to 8 dashes Worcestershire sauce, the brown sugar, ketchup, and pepper to a skillet, mix them well and close the lid, then bring to a soft boil and cook for 30 minutes or until the beans are warmed through. 3. Reduce the grill's temperature to 180 degrees F/ 80 degrees C and smoke them for 5 minutes more. 4. Remove the set skillet from the grill and serve immediately.
Per Serving: Calories 476; Total fat 37.7g; Sodium 742mg; Total Carbs 15.3g; Fiber 6g; Sugars 5g; Protein 2.8g

Grilled Potatoes with Onion

Prep time: 15 minutes | Cook time: 20 minutes | Serves: 4-6

2 pounds baby red or yellow potatoes, washed and chopped into bite-size chunks	1 red bell pepper, cut into ½-inch pieces
3 tablespoons olive oil	Poultry Rub
½ white onion, diced	

1. Fill your Traeger Smoker with wood pellets and follow the manufacturer's specific start-up procedure. Place a cast-iron skillet onto the grill, and preheat the grill at High setting (400 degrees F/ 200 degrees C) with the lid closed. 2. Once the grill has reached temperature, add the potatoes and olive oil into the skillet and mix well. Cook the potatoes for 15 minutes, with occasional stirring. 3. Once the potatoes are semi-soft, add the onion and bell pepper to the skillet, and sprinkle them with the spice rub to taste. Mix well and cook for 5 minutes, or until the onion and pepper are softened. 4. Serve warm.
Per Serving: Calories 254; Total fat 20.1g; Sodium 1mg; Total Carbs 15.4g; Fiber 3.4g; Sugars 9.6g; Protein 3.3g

Chapter 5 Appetizer and Sides Recipes | 71

Cheesy Scalloped Potatoes

Prep time: 15 minutes | Cook time: 50 minutes | Serves: 8-10

2 pounds russet potatoes, washed and sliced into rounds	Nonstick cooking spray
Kosher salt	1 cup shredded cheddar cheese
Freshly ground black pepper	½ cup shredded Parmesan cheese
1 bunch rosemary	2 cups heavy (whipping) cream

1. Fill your Traeger Smoker with wood pellets and follow the manufacturer's specific start-up procedure. Preheat the grill to 375 degrees F/ 190 degrees C with the lid closed. 2. Mix the potatoes, black pepper, salt, and the chopped rosemary in a bowl. 3. Grease a 13-by-9-inch pan and spread half the potatoes in an even layer on the bottom. Cover the potatoes with ½ cup cheddar and ¼ cup Parmesan cheese. 4. Layer on the remaining potatoes and top with the remaining ½ cup cheddar and ¼ cup Parmesan cheese. Pour the heavy cream over the cheese and potatoes evenly. Garnish with the remaining rosemary sprigs. 5. Place the pan on the grill grate, close the lid, and cook the potatoes for 50 minutes with the lid closed until they are soft. 6. Serve hot.

Per Serving: Calories 192; Total fat 6.6g; Sodium 15mg; Total Carbs 34.5g; Fiber 4g; Sugars 27.3g; Protein 2.9g

Hassel-back Sweet Potatoes with Pecans

Prep time: 15 minutes | Cook time: 1 hour 30 minutes | Serves: 4

4 large sweet potatoes, scrubbed	sliced
¼ cup canola oil	1 cup Glazed Spiced Pecans, chopped
2 tablespoons table salt	
½ cup (1 stick) butter	1 tablespoon sea salt
4 Serrano peppers, seeded and	¼ cup honey

1. At 250 degrees F/ 120 degrees C, preheat your Traeger Smoker with the pecan wood. 2. Coat the sweet potatoes with the oil and table salt. 3. Slice into the sweet potatoes, all the way across, making your cuts about ½ inch apart, and being careful not to cut all the way through the bottom of the sweet potato. 4. Set the sweet potatoes on a grill pan and put it into the smoker. Smoke them for 1 hour, then remove from the heat. 5. Place a pat of butter between each slice. 6. Stuff Serrano slices and pecans between the slices. 7. Sprinkle well with the sea salt and drizzle with the honey, getting it between the slices. 8. Smoke the food for 30 to 40 minutes more and remove from the smoker when the potatoes pass the squeeze test.

Per serving: Calories 270; Total fat 6.7g; Sodium 829mg; Total Carbs 40.2g; Fiber 4.7g; Sugars 1.5g; Protein 12g

Cilantro-Balsamic Bacon-Wrapped Brussels Sprouts

Prep time: 15 minutes | Cook time: 60 minutes | Serves: 4-6

16 to 20 long toothpicks	1 tablespoon Cajun seasoning
1 pound Brussels sprouts, trimmed and wilted, leaves removed	¼ cup balsamic vinegar
	¼ cup extra-virgin olive oil
½ pound bacon, cut in half	¼ cup chopped cilantro
1 tablespoon packed brown sugar	2 teaspoons minced garlic

1. Fill your Traeger Smoker with wood pellets and follow the manufacturer's specific start-up procedure. Preheat the grill to 300 degrees F/ 150 degrees C with the lid closed. 2. Use a toothpick to enclose each Brussels sprout with a half-slice of bacon. 3. Combine the brown sugar and Cajun spice in a suitable bowl. Roll each Brussels sprout in this sweet rub after it has been wrapped. 4. Set the sprouts on a parchment paper–lined baking sheet on the grill grate, close the lid, and smoke for 45 minutes to 1 hour, turning as needed, until cooked evenly and the bacon is crisp. 5. Mix the balsamic vinegar, olive oil, cilantro, and garlic in a separate bowl. 6. Remove the toothpicks from the Brussels sprouts, put them on a platter, and drizzle the cilantro-balsamic sauce over them before serving.

Per Serving: Calories 276; Total fat 11.8g; Sodium 888mg; Total Carbs 33.1g; Fiber 6.2g; Sugars 2.6g; Protein 14.4g

Candied Bacon

Prep time: 5 minutes | Cook time: 2 hours | Serves: 4-6

1 (1-pound) package of thick-sliced pork bacon	Sweet Brown Sugar Rub
½ cup brown sugar	

1. Fill your Traeger Smoker with wood pellets and follow the manufacturer's specific start-up procedure. Preheat the grill to 225 degrees F/ 105 degrees C with the lid closed. 2. Arrange the bacon slices directly on the grill grate, making sure they do not hang over the drain pan. Then sprinkle with the brown sugar and rub. 3. Close the grill lid and smoke the bacon to your preferred doneness. 4. Remove the bacon from the grill and serve immediately.

Per Serving: Calories 285; Total fat 28.3g; Sodium 80mg; Total Carbs 27.4g; Fiber 0.7g; Sugars 16.7g; Protein 26g

Bacon-Wrapped Jalapeño Poppers

Prep time: 15 minutes | Cook time: 1 hr. 30 minutes | Serves: 12

8 ounces sharp Cheddar cheese, shredded	lengthwise on one side (not halved), seeded and membranes removed
8 ounces cream cheese	
1 tablespoon red pepper flakes	12 bacon slices
12 jalapeño peppers, sliced	2 teaspoons black pepper

1. At 250 degrees F/ 120 degrees C, close the lid and preheat the Traeger Smoker with the maple wood. 2. Mix the Cheddar, cream cheese, and red pepper flakes in a bowl. 3. Stuff some of the cheese mixture into each jalapeño. 4. Wrap each stuffed pepper with 1 bacon slice and secure it with toothpicks, or tuck the bacon ends in securely. 5. Sprinkle with black pepper. 6. Set the stuffed jalapeños on a grill pan and put them inside the smoker. Smoke for 1 to 1½ hours until the bacon is cooked. 7. You can speed the process by partially cooking the bacon before wrapping the peppers.

Per serving: Calories 293; Total fat 27.1g; Sodium 601mg; Total Carbs 6.2g; Fiber 2.2g; Sugars 0.9g; Protein 11.7g

Tasty Smoked Onion Bombs

Prep time: 15 minutes | Cook time: 2 hours | Serves: 4

4 large Vidalia onions, peeled	½ cup grated Parmesan cheese
½ cup (1 stick) butter 4 chicken bouillon cubes	1 teaspoon black pepper

1. At 225 degrees F/ 105 degrees C, close the lid and preheat your Traeger smoker with maple or mesquite wood. 2. Angle a sharp knife into the onion from the top and cut all the way around, removing the top and creating a deep well in the onion. Repeat with the remaining onions. Save the onion tops. 3. Cut off four pieces of aluminum foil and each about 8 inches square. Place each onion on a sheet of foil. Press 2 tablespoons of butter into the well of each onion and top with a bouillon cube. 4. Mix the Parmesan and pepper in a bowl. Put about 2 tablespoons of the prepared mixture in each onion well. 5. Reset the onion tops tightly (cutting as necessary to fit) and wrap the foil up the sides, but leave the top of the packet open to allow the smoke flavor to permeate the onions. 6. Smoke the onions for 2 hours until tender.

Per serving: Calories 339; Total fat 23.4g; Sodium 195mg; Total Carbs 23.8g; Fiber 6.8g; Sugars 9g; Protein 13.9g

Chapter 5 Appetizer and Sides Recipes

Smoked Whole Cabbage

Prep time: 15 minutes | Cook time: 2 hours | Serves: 4

1 head cabbage, cored completely	melted
4 tablespoons butter	1 chicken bouillon cube
2 tablespoons rendered bacon fat or 2 more tablespoons butter,	1 teaspoon black pepper
	1 garlic clove, minced

1. Preheat the Traeger smoker to 250 degrees F/ 120 degrees C with the apple, maple, or oak wood. 2. Core the cabbage and fill the hole with the butter, bacon fat, bouillon cube, pepper, and garlic. 3. Wrap the cabbage in aluminum foil, two-thirds of the way up the sides to protect the outer leaves, leaving the top open to allow the smoke flavor to permeate the cabbage. 4. Place the cabbage on the grill grate and smoke for 2 hours. 5. Unwrap and enjoy as a side dish.
Per serving: Calories 311; Total fat 26.9g; Sodium 711mg; Total Carbs 9.9g; Fiber 3.4g; Sugars 2.3g; Protein 12.2g

Cheesy Hassel-back Russet Potatoes

Prep time: 20 minutes | Cook time: 1 hour 30 minutes | Serves: 4

4 russet potatoes, cut Hassel-back style	sliced
1 cup olive oil	2 cherry peppers, sliced
2 teaspoons salt	4 ounces block Cheddar cheese, thickly sliced
2 teaspoons black pepper	8 bacon slices, cooked and crumbled
1 small onion, sliced	
2 jalapeño peppers, seeded and	

1. At 250 degrees F/ 120 degrees C, close the lid and preheat your Traeger Smoker with the hickory wood. 2. Place the potatoes on a grill pan, then drizzle ½ cup of oil over the potatoes and sprinkle with the black pepper and salt. 3. Set the pan on the grill grate and smoke for 1 hour. 4. Remove the potatoes from the smoker and place some onion, jalapeños, cherry peppers, Cheddar slices, and crumbled bacon in between each potato slice and on top. 5. Pour the remaining ½ cup of olive oil over all. Reflip the potatoes to the smoker for 30 to 40 minutes or so, until the potatoes are tender in a squeeze test. 6. Serve with sour cream.
Per serving: Calories 380; Total fat 9.5g; Sodium 1092mg; Total Carbs 54.8g; Fiber 17.5g; Sugars 12.1g; Protein 20.6g

Smoked Sweet & Sour Coleslaw

Prep time: 10 minutes | Cook time: 30 minutes | Serves: 10-12

1 head cabbage, shredded	½ teaspoon black pepper
1 carrot, shredded	¼ cup white vinegar
¼ cup sugar	1 cup heavy (whipping) cream
½ teaspoon salt	1 teaspoon paprika

1. Preheat the Traeger smoker to 180 degrees F/ 80 degrees C with the maple wood. 2. Spread the cabbage and carrot in a shallow aluminum foil pan. Set the pan in the smoker and smoke the vegetables for 30 minutes. Remove from the smoker and transfer the vegetables to a suitable bowl. 3. Add the sugar, salt, pepper, vinegar, and heavy cream to mix. Refrigerate the dish for 1 hour before serving with paprika.
Per serving: Calories 364; Total fat 33.4g; Sodium 652mg; Total Carbs 14.5g; Fiber 5.6g; Sugars 6.4g; Protein 7.8g

Rosemary-Garlic Potato Wedges

Prep time: 15 minutes | Cook time: 1 hour 30 minutes | Serves: 6-8

4 to 6 russet potatoes, cut into wedges	2 garlic cloves, minced
	2 tablespoons chopped rosemary leaves, or 1 tablespoon dried rosemary
¼ cup olive oil	
2 teaspoons salt	1 teaspoon sugar
1 teaspoon black pepper	1 teaspoon onion powder

1. At 250 degrees F/ 120 degrees C, preheat your Traeger Smoker with the maple or pecan wood. 2. Coat the potatoes with olive oil. 3. Combine the minced garlic, rosemary, salt, pepper, sugar, and onion powder in a bowl. Sprinkle this prepared mixture on all sides of the potato wedges. 4. Transfer the seasoned wedges to a grill pan and put them into the smoker. 5. Cook the food for 1½ hours until a fork cuts through the wedges easily. 6. Serve warm.
Per serving: Calories 478; Total fat 19.6g; Sodium 316mg; Total Carbs 59.9g; Fiber 17.7g; Sugars 13.8g; Protein 18.4g

Smoked Butter Asparagus

Prep time: 10 minutes | Cook time: 60 minutes | Serves: 4-5

2 tablespoons butter, melted	1 teaspoon salt
2 garlic cloves, minced	½ teaspoon black pepper
2 tablespoons lemon juice	1-pound asparagus (about 18 to 20 stalks), woody ends snapped off
1 tablespoon capers	
1 tablespoon onion powder	

1. Preheat the Traeger smoker to 250 degrees F/ 120 degrees C with the maple wood. 2. Mix the butter, garlic, lemon juice, capers, salt, onion powder, and pepper in a bowl. 3. Place the asparagus in a grill pan and drizzle with the seasoned butter. 4. Put the pan on the grill grate and smoke the food for 1 hour until tender.
Per serving: Calories 245; Total fat 10.5g; Sodium 567mg; Total Carbs 29.2g; Fiber 3.4g; Sugars 1.2g; Protein 8.9g

Spicy Bacon-Wrapped Onion Rings

Prep time: 20 minutes | Cook time: 1 hour 30 minutes | Serves: 16 onion rings

2 onions, peeled and sliced ½ inch thick	1-pound bacon
	1 tablespoon cayenne pepper
¼ cup hot sauce	1 tablespoon sugar
4 tablespoons butter, melted	

1. At 250 degrees F/ 120 degrees C, preheat your Traeger Smoker with the hickory, maple, or mesquite wood. 2. Separate the onion rings and remove the smaller internal rings to save for another use. You should get about eight rings out of one onion, two out of each slice. 3. Mix the hot sauce and melted butter in a shallow bowl. 4. Dip the onion rings in the butter–hot sauce mixture. 5. Wrap each onion ring tightly with a bacon slice. 6. Mix the cayenne and sugar in another shallow bowl. 7. Coat the bacon-wrapped rings well with this mixture. Secure the rings with toothpicks or set them on skewers. 8. Set the onion rings on a grill mat and smoke for 1½ hours until the bacon is done and beyond "chewy" to bite through.
Per serving: Calories 230; Total fat 1.7g; Sodium 318mg; Total Carbs 48.4g; Fiber 2.2g; Sugars 0g; Protein 4.8g

Lemony Artichokes

Prep time: 5 minutes | Cook time: 2 hours | Serves: 8

¼ cup olive oil	Juice of 1 lemon
1 garlic clove, minced	4 artichokes, stemmed and halved lengthwise
1 teaspoon salt	

1. At 225 degrees F/ 105 degrees C, preheat your Traeger smoker with the hickory or maple wood. 2. Mix the olive oil, garlic, salt, and lemon juice in a bowl. 3. Rub the artichoke halves with the seasoned olive oil. Set them directly on the smoker's grate and smoke for 2 hours. 4. The artichoke bottoms should look and feel tender when poked with a fork.
Per serving: Calories 313; Total fat 8.2g; Sodium 512mg; Total Carbs 50.8g; Fiber 2.8g; Sugars 1.2g; Protein 8.4g

Smoked Deviled Eggs with Olives

Prep time: 10 minutes | Cook time: 30 minutes | Serves: 12 deviled eggs

6 hardboiled eggs, peeled	1 teaspoon black pepper
¼ cup mayonnaise	½ teaspoon dry mustard
2 tablespoons sweet pickle–salad cubes, well-drained	2 teaspoons paprika
1 teaspoon salt	4 pimento-stuffed green olives, cut into thirds

1. Preheat the Traeger smoker to 225 degrees F/ 105 degrees C with the hickory wood. 2. Set the eggs in the smoker and smoke for 20 to 30 minutes. Remove from the heat. 3. Halve the eggs lengthwise and scoop the cooked yolk into a suitable bowl, leaving the egg whites intact. 4. Mash the yolks and mix them with the mayonnaise, pickle cubes, salt, pepper, and mustard. 5. Using a small melon baller, drop the yolk mixture into the egg white halves and sprinkle each with the paprika. 6. Top each with an olive slice before serving.
Per serving: Calories 104; Total fat 0.4g; Sodium 129mg; Total Carbs 23.1g; Fiber 1.6g; Sugars 0.9g; Protein 4.4g

Smoked Corn on the Cob

Prep time: 15 minutes | Cook time: 1 hour 30 minutes | Serves: 6-8 ears

½ cup mayonnaise	diced
1 tablespoon chili powder	1 tablespoon adobo sauce
Juice of 1 lime	2 teaspoons salt
6 to 8 ears of corn, silk ends removed and discarded, husks peeled back but still attached	1 tablespoon chopped cilantro leaves
½ cup (1 stick) butter	½ cup queso fresco cheese, crumbled, or Parmesan or Asiago or Romano
2 chipotle peppers in adobo sauce,	

1. At 225 degrees F/ 105 degrees C, preheat your Traeger smoker with the maple wood. 2. Mix the mayonnaise, chili powder, and lime juice in a bowl. 3. Slather the mayo mixture on each corncob and carefully pull the husks back up around the cob. Secure with kitchen twine. Set the corn in the smoker and smoke for 1½ hours. 4. While the corn smokes, melt the butter in a suitable saucepan over medium heat; add the chipotles, adobo sauce, and salt. Mix them well and heat through. 5. Pull down the husks for presentation or remove them completely. Pour the chipotle sauce over the corn and sprinkle with the cilantro and cheese.
Per serving: Calories 281; Total fat 10.1g; Sodium 17mg; Total Carbs 46.6g; Fiber 9.7g; Sugars 1.1g; Protein 3.4g

Smoked Bacon–Cheddar Potato Skins

Prep time: 15 minutes | Cook time: 1 hour 30 minutes | Serves: 5-6

6 small red potatoes, or baby Dutch yellow potatoes	8 bacon slices, cooked and crumbled
¾ cup (1½ sticks) butter, cut into 12 (tablespoon-size) slices	½ cup chopped scallions, white and green parts
1 tablespoon chili powder	1 cup shredded Cheddar cheese
1 tablespoon garlic powder	1 tablespoon dried parsley
2 teaspoons salt	Sour cream, for serving
2 teaspoons freshly black pepper	

1. Prick the potatoes with a fork and microwave on high power for 2 to 3 minutes. They should still be firm. Remove and let them cool. 2. Halve the potatoes and scoop out the centers, leaving enough potato to keep the sides and bottom intact. Discard the extra potato or save for another use. 3. Place a pat of butter in the center of each potato shell. 4. Stir the chili powder, garlic powder, salt, pepper, bacon, and scallion in a bowl. 5. Top each potato with some of this mixture and sprinkle on the Cheddar. Set the potatoes on a smoker rack and smoke for 1½ hours until tender. 6. Sprinkle with the parsley and serve with sour cream.
Per serving: Calories 223; Total fat 1.4g; Sodium 734mg; Total Carbs 42.5g; Fiber 2.6g; Sugars 2g; Protein 8.2g

Smoked Spaghetti Squash

Prep time: 10 minutes | Cook time: 3 hours | Serves: 4

1 spaghetti squash, ends trimmed, halved, seeds discarded	2 teaspoons salt
2 tablespoons olive oil	2 teaspoons freshly ground black pepper

1. Preheat the Traeger smoker to 275 degrees F/ 135 degrees C with the cherry or maple wood. 2. Rub the cut sides of the squash generously with the olive oil and sprinkle with the black pepper and salt. 3. Set the squash, cut-sides down, on a grill pan and smoke for 2½ to 3 hours until the flesh pulls apart into strands easily. 4. Discard the skins and serve the squash as a side dish, or use in place of pasta with marinara or Alfredo sauce.
Per serving: Calories 240; Total fat 4.2g; Sodium 1095mg; Total Carbs 37.4g; Fiber 5g; Sugars 3.2g; Protein 12.8g

Smoked Garlic Cauliflower Steaks

Prep time: 15 minutes | Cook time: 60 minutes | Serves: 4

2 heads cauliflower, leaves removed	2 garlic cloves, minced
¼ cup olive oil	2 teaspoons salt
¼ cup A1 Sauce, or Heinz 57 Steak Sauce more for serving	2 teaspoons freshly ground black pepper

1. At 250 degrees F/ 120 degrees C, preheat your Traeger Smoker with the maple wood. 2. Trim the base off each cauliflower. Save the excess cauliflower florets for another use. 3. Carefully slice each head of cauliflower from top to bottom through the base into 2 thick slices. 4. Mix the olive oil, steak sauce, garlic, black pepper and salt in a sauce bowl. 5. Rub the "steaks" with the garlic mixture and let them marinate on the counter for 10 minutes to absorb the flavors. 6. Set the cauliflower directly on a grill rack and smoke for 45 minutes to 1 hour until tender. 7. Serve the dish with additional steak sauce.
Per serving: Calories 224; Total fat 14.2g; Sodium 1½1mg; Total Carbs 16.8g; Fiber 5.2g; Sugars 4.3g; Protein 9.1g

Cheesy Corn with Chipotle Butter

Prep time: 10 minutes | Cook time: 12 to 14 minutes | Serves: 4

4 ears corn	garnish
½ cup sour cream	Chipotle Butter, for topping
½ cup mayonnaise	1 cup grated Parmesan cheese
¼ cup chopped cilantro more for	

1. Fill your Traeger Smoker with wood pellets and follow the manufacturer's specific start-up procedure. 2. Preheat your Traeger Smoker with its lid close at High setting (450 degrees F/ 230 degrees C). 3. Shuck the corn, removing the silks and cutting off the cores. 4. Tear four squares of aluminum foil enough to completely cover an ear of corn. 5. Mix the sour cream, mayonnaise, and cilantro in a bowl. Slather the prepared mixture the ears of corn. 6. Wrap each ear of corn in foil, sealing tightly. Place on the preheated Traeger grill, close the hood, and smoke for 12 to 14 minutes. 7. Remove the corn from its foil and place in a shallow baking dish. Top the dish with chipotle butter, the Parmesan cheese, and more chopped cilantro. 8. Serve immediately.
Per serving: Calories 272; Total fat 17.3g; Sodium 676mg; Total Carbs 24.3g; Fiber 5.2g; Sugars 3.9g; Protein 8.6g

Smoked Okra

Prep time: 10 minutes | Cook time: 30 minutes | Serves: 3-4

Nonstick cooking spray, for greasing	2 teaspoons seasoned salt
1-pound whole okra	2 teaspoons freshly ground black pepper
2 tablespoons olive oil	

1. Fill your Traeger Smoker with wood pellets and follow the manufacturer's specific start-up procedure. Preheat the grill at High setting (400 degrees F/ 200 degrees C) with the lid closed. 2. Cooking spray should be used to line aluminum foil in a shallow baking dish with a rim. 3. Put the okra in a single layer on the pan. Turn to coat with the olive oil after drizzling. Salt and black pepper should be used to season all surfaces. 4. Close the lid and place the baking pan on the grill grate, and smoke the food for 30 minutes, or until crisp and faintly browned. You can do this step in the oven on roast mode. 5. Serve warm.

Per serving: Calories 384; Total fat 12.5g; Sodium 621mg; Total Carbs 58.3g; Fiber 4.1g; Sugars 7.2g; Protein 10.1g

Crispy Sweet Potato Chips

Prep time: 20 minutes | Cook time: 45 minutes | Serves: 2-3

2 sweet potatoes	1 tablespoon packed brown sugar
1-quart warm water	1 teaspoon ground cinnamon
1 tablespoon cornstarch, plus 2 teaspoons	1 teaspoon freshly ground black pepper
¼ cup extra-virgin olive oil	½ teaspoon cayenne pepper
1 tablespoon salt	

1. Using a Mandoline, slice the sweet potatoes. 2. Pour the warm water into a bowl and add 1 tablespoon of cornstarch and the potato slices. Let them soak for 20 minutes. 3. Fill your Traeger Smoker with wood pellets and follow the manufacturer's specific start-up procedure. Preheat the grill to 375 degrees F/ 190 degrees C with the lid closed. 4. After draining, place the potato slices in a single layer on a baking sheet covered with aluminum foil or a pizza pan with holes. Olive oil should be applied to both sides of the potato slices. 5. Combine the 2 tablespoons of cornstarch with the salt, brown sugar, cinnamon, black pepper, and cayenne pepper in a medium bowl. Sprinkle the potatoes with this seasoning mixture on both sides. 6. Set the pan or baking sheet on the grill grate, close the lid, and smoke for 45 minutes, flipping after 20 minutes, until the chips curl up and become crispy. 7. Store in an airtight container.

Per Serving: Calories 276; Total fat 11.8g; Sodium 888mg; Total Carbs 33.1g; Fiber 6.2g; Sugars 2.6g; Protein 14.4g

Spaghetti Squash with Garlic–Wine Butter Sauce

Prep time: 20 minutes | Cook time: 40 minutes | Serves: 4

Squash

1 spaghetti squash	1 teaspoon freshly ground black pepper
2 tablespoons extra-virgin olive oil	2 teaspoons garlic powder
1 teaspoon salt	

Sauce

4 tablespoons (½ stick) unsalted butter	1 teaspoon red pepper flakes
½ cup white wine	½ teaspoon salt
1 tablespoon minced garlic	½ teaspoon freshly ground black pepper
2 teaspoons chopped parsley	

1. Fill your Traeger Smoker with wood pellets and follow the manufacturer's specific start-up procedure. Preheat the grill to 375 degrees F/ 190 degrees C with the lid closed. 2. Cut off both ends of the squash, then cut it in half lengthwise. Scoop out and discard the seeds. 3. Olive oil should be thoroughly applied to the squash flesh before seasoning with salt, pepper, and garlic powder. Set the squash cut-side up on the grill grate, close the lid, and smoke for 40 minutes, or until tender. 4. On the stove top, add the butter, white wine, minced garlic, parsley, red pepper flakes, salt, and pepper to the saucepan, and cook them for 5 minutes over medium heat, or until heated through. Reduce its heat to low and keep the sauce warm. 5. After taking the squash from the grill, let it cool somewhat before using a fork to mash the flesh; remove the skin. 6. Serve the minced garlic-wine butter sauce immediately after adding the squash shreds.

Per Serving: Calories 161; Total fat 12.4g; Sodium 375mg; Total Carbs 9.8g; Fiber 1.5g; Sugars 2.6g; Protein 3.8g

Cheddar Broccoli–Cauliflower Salad

Prep time: 25 minutes | Cook time: 0 | Serves: 6-8

½ cup sour cream	pieces
¼ cup sugar	1 small red onion, chopped
1½ cups mayonnaise	6 slices bacon, cooked and crumbled
1 bunch broccoli, cut into small pieces	1 cup shredded Cheddar cheese
1 head cauliflower, cut into small	

1. Stir the mayonnaise, sour cream, and sugar in a bowl to make a dressing. 2. Combine the broccoli, cauliflower, onion, bacon, and Cheddar cheese in another bowl. 3. Pour the prepared dressing over the vegetable mixture and toss well to coat. 4. Serve the salad chilled.

Per Serving: Calories 300; Total fat 4.3g; Sodium 1377mg; Total Carbs 45.2g; Fiber 7.7g; Sugars 6.2g; Protein 21.6g

Carrot Hot Dogs with Jalapeño Relish

Prep time: 20 minutes | Cook time: 40 minutes | Serves: 8

8 hot dog-size carrots, peeled	Salt
¼ cup honey	Freshly ground black pepper
¼ cup yellow mustard	8 hot dog buns
Nonstick cooking spray or butter, for greasing	Sweet and Spicy Jalapeño Relish

1. Prepare the carrots by removing the stems and slicing in half lengthwise. 2. Mix the honey and mustard in a bowl. 3. Fill your Traeger Smoker with wood pellets and follow the manufacturer's specific start-up procedure. Preheat the grill to 375 degrees F/ 190 degrees C with the lid closed. 4. Line a suitable baking sheet with aluminum foil and coat with cooking spray. 5. Rub the carrots with the honey mustard and season with black pepper and salt; put them on the baking sheet. 6. Set the baking sheet on the grill grate, close the lid, and smoke for 40 minutes. 7. Lightly toast the hot dog buns on the grill and top each with two slices of carrot and some relish, then enjoy.

Per Serving: Calories 100; Total fat 1.1g; Sodium 741mg; Total Carbs 19.4g; Fiber 5.2g; Sugars 6.2g; Protein 4.3g

Cabbage Slaw Salad

Prep time: 10 minutes | Cook time: 0 minutes | Serves: 10-12

1 head cabbage, shredded	½ teaspoon salt
¼ cup white vinegar	½ teaspoon freshly ground black pepper
¼ cup sugar	
1 teaspoon paprika	1 cup heavy (whipping) cream

1. Set the shredded cabbage in a bowl. 2. Mix the vinegar, sugar, paprika, salt, and pepper in another bowl. 3. Pour the prepared vinegar mixture over the cabbage and mix well. 4. Fold in the heavy cream and let it refrigerate for at least 1 hour before serving.

Per Serving: Calories 253; Total fat 13.9g; Sodium 21mg; Total Carbs 27g; Fiber 9.3g; Sugars 3.8g; Protein 8.3g

Chapter 5 Appetizer and Sides Recipes

Parmesan Sweet Onion Bake

Prep time: 25 minutes | Cook time: 1 hour 15 minutes | Serves: 6-8

Nonstick cooking spray or butter, for greasing	butter, melted
4 Vidalia or other sweet onions	4 chicken bouillon cubes
8 tablespoons (1 stick) unsalted	1 cup grated Parmesan cheese

1. Fill your Traeger Smoker with wood pellets and follow the manufacturer's specific start-up procedure. Preheat the grill to 350 degrees F/ 175 degrees C with the lid closed. 2. Apply butter or cooking spray to a baking dish with high sides. 3. The onions should be peeled before being sliced into quarters and then into individual petals. 4. Place the onions in the preheated pan and cover them with melted butter. 5. Crush the bouillon cubes, sprinkle them over the slices of buttery onion, and then sprinkle cheese on top. 6. Place the pan on the grill, cover it, and let it smoke for a half-hour. 7. Take the pan off the grill, wrap it securely in foil, and make a few vent holes in it. 8. Put the pan back on the grill, close the lid, and smoke for an additional 30 to 45 minutes. 9. Uncover the onions, stir, and serve hot.
Per Serving: Calories 280; Total fat 4.6g; Sodium 271mg; Total Carbs 52.7g; Fiber 7.4g; Sugars 6.3g; Protein 8g

BBQ Beans with Bacon

Prep time: 15 minutes | Cook time: 3 hours | Serves: 12-15

3 (28-ounce) cans of baked beans	Nonstick cooking spray or butter, for greasing
1 onion, chopped	
1 cup Bill's Best BBQ Sauce	1 bell pepper, cut into thin rings
½ cup light brown sugar	½ pound thick-cut bacon, cooked and cut into quarters
¼ cup Worcestershire sauce	
3 tablespoons yellow mustard	

1. Fill your Traeger Smoker with wood pellets and follow the manufacturer's specific start-up procedure. Preheat the grill to 300 degrees F/ 150 degrees C with the lid closed. 2. Stir the beans, onion, barbecue sauce, Worcestershire sauce, brown sugar, and mustard in a bowl until well mixed. 3. Coat a suitable aluminum pan with cooking spray or butter. 4. Pour the beans into the pan and top with the bell pepper rings and bacon pieces, pressing them down into the sauce. 5. Spread a layer of heavy-duty foil on the grill grate to catch drips, and set the pan on top of the foil. Close the hood and cook for 2 hours 30 minutes to 3 hours, or until the beans are hot, thick, and bubbly. 6. Allow the dish cool for 5 minutes before serving. 7. Serve.
Per Serving: Calories 254; Total fat 10.3g; Sodium 514mg; Total Carbs 32.8g; Fiber 3.3g; Sugars 5g; Protein 7.9g

Blt Pasta Bacon Salad

Prep time: 20 minutes | Cook time: 45 minutes | Serves: 10-12

1 pound thick-cut bacon	1 tablespoon chopped basil
16 ounces bowtie pasta, cooked and drained	1 teaspoon salt
	1 teaspoon freshly ground black pepper
2 tomatoes, chopped	
½ cup chopped scallions	1 teaspoon garlic powder
½ cup Italian dressing	1 head lettuce, cored and torn
½ cup ranch dressing	

1. Fill your Traeger Smoker with wood pellets and follow the manufacturer's specific start-up procedure. Preheat, with the hood closed, to 225 degrees F/ 105 degrees C. 2. Arrange the bacon slices on the grill grate, close the lid, and cook for 45 minutes, flipping after 20 minutes, until crisp. 3. Remove the bacon from the grill and chop. 4. Mix the chopped bacon with the cooked pasta, tomatoes, scallions, Italian dressing, ranch dressing, basil, salt, black pepper, and garlic powder in a bowl. Refrigerate them until ready to serve. 5. Toss in the lettuce just before serving to keep it from wilting.
Per Serving: Calories 396; Total fat 8.6g; Sodium 596mg; Total Carbs 65.9g; Fiber 3.4g; Sugars 3.8g; Protein 12.1g

Vegetable-Cornbread Salad

Prep time: 15 minutes | Cook time: 45 minutes | Serves: 8-10

Cornbread

1 cup all-purpose flour	½ cup milk
1 cup yellow cornmeal	½ cup sour cream
1 tablespoon sugar	2 tablespoons dry ranch dressing mix
2 teaspoons baking powder	
1 teaspoon salt	1-pound bacon, cooked and crumbled
1 cup milk	
1 egg, beaten	3 tomatoes, chopped
4 tablespoons (½ stick) unsalted butter, melted and cooled	1 bell pepper, chopped
	1 cucumber, seeded and chopped
Nonstick cooking spray or butter, for greasing	2 stalks celery, chopped (about 1 cup)
Salad	½ cup chopped scallions

1. Mix the flour, cornmeal, sugar, baking powder, and salt in a medium bowl. 2. Stir the milk and egg in another bowl. Pour in the butter, then slowly fold this mixture into the dry ingredients. 3. Fill your Traeger Smoker with wood pellets and follow the manufacturer's specific start-up procedure. Preheat the grill to 375 degrees F/ 190 degrees C with the lid closed. 4. Coat a cast iron skillet with cooking spray or butter. 5. Pour the batter into the set skillet, place on the grill grate, close the lid, and smoke for 35 to 45 minutes, or until the cornbread is browned and pulls away from the side of the set skillet. 6. Remove the cornbread from the grill and let cool, then crumble. 7. Stir the milk, sour cream, and ranch dressing mix in a small bowl. 8. Mix the crumbled bacon, tomatoes, bell pepper, cucumber, celery, and scallions in a separate bowl. 9. Layer half of the crumbled cornbread, half of the bacon-veggie mixture, and half of the prepared dressing in the serving bowl. Toss lightly. 10. Repeat the layering with the remaining cornbread, bacon-veggie mixture, and dressing. Toss again. 11. Refrigerate the salad for at least 1 hour. Serve cold.
Per Serving: Calories 336; Total fat 9.9g; Sodium 1672mg; Total Carbs 42.6g; Fiber 1.7g; Sugars 2.1g; Protein 12.3g

Mixed Berries-Watermelon Bowl

Prep time: 10 minutes | Cook time: 0 | Serves: 4-6

1-pint strawberries, hulled and halved	1 (20-ounce) can of pineapple chunks, drained
1-pint blackberries	4 cups watermelon cubes (1 inch)
1-pint blueberries	Juice of 1 lemon
1-pint raspberries	¼ cup sugar

1. Mix the strawberries, blackberries, blueberries, raspberries, pineapple chunks, and watermelon cubes in a bowl. 2. Add the lemon juice and sugar. 3. Refrigerate this dish for at least 1 hour. 4. Serve.
Per Serving: Calories 241; Total fat 9.8g; Sodium 605mg; Total Carbs 29.8g; Fiber 8.5g; Sugars 1.1g; Protein 9.8g

Chapter 6 Snack and Dessert Recipes

78	Smoked Mac 'N' Cheese	79	Delicious Bacon Brussels Sprouts
78	Cowboy Beans and Beef	80	Delicious Holiday Stuffing
78	Garlic Butter Cauliflower Florets	80	Grilled Cheese Corn Pudding
78	Potato-Egg Salad	80	Grilled Chantilly Potatoes
78	Cinnamon-Honey Sweet Potatoes	80	Easy Smoked Butternut Squash
78	Smoked Plum Tomatoes	80	Grilled S'mores Dip
79	Cheese Beef Stuffed Jalapeños	80	Sweet Candied Pineapple
79	Delicious Cream Onion Dip	81	Cinnamon Chocolate Sauce
79	Bacon-Wrapped Onion Meatloaf Bombs	81	Caramel Apple Crisp
79	Cheesy Hash Browns Casserole		

Smoked Mac 'N' Cheese
Prep time: 15 minutes | Cook time: 1 hour 30 minutes | Serves: 5-6

- 1 stick (8 tablespoons) butter
- ¼ cup all-purpose flour
- 2 teaspoons Dijon mustard
- 2¼ cups half-and-half
- 4 ounces cream cheese
- 2½ cups shredded cheddar cheese
- 1 cup shredded Gouda cheese (not smoked)
- ½ cup shredded Parmesan cheese
- 1 tablespoon ¼ teaspoon salt
- ¼ teaspoon black pepper
- ¼ teaspoon garlic powder
- ¼ teaspoon onion powder
- 12 ounces dry macaroni
- 1 cup panko bread crumbs
- 3 bacon slices, cooked and crumbled

1. Preheat the grill to 225 degrees F/ 105 degrees C with the lid closed. 2. Melt the stick of butter in a suitable saucepan over medium heat. 3. Add the flour and cook until the prepared mixture thickens and forms a roux, 2 minutes. Add the Dijon, then mix in the half-and-half. 4. Add the cream cheese, cheddar, Gouda, Parmesan, ¼ teaspoon of salt, garlic powder, pepper, and onion powder. 5. Meanwhile, bring a suitable pot of water to a boil with the remaining 1 tablespoon of salt and cook the noodles as per the package's directions. 6. Drain the macaroni, add to the cheese mixture, then place into a 19-by-9-inch aluminum pan. 7. Mix the panko, ¼ cup melted butter and crumbled bacon in a bowl. Top the macaroni and cheese with the panko-bacon mixture. 8. Set the pan into the smoker, close the lid, and cook for 1 hour. 9. Once done, remove the pan and serve immediately.
Per Serving: Calories 339; Total fat 14g; Sodium 556mg; Total Carbs 44.6g; Fiber 6.4g; Sugars 3.8g; Protein 10.5g

Cowboy Beans and Beef
Prep time: 20 minutes | Cook time: 2 hours 15 minutes | Serves: 6

- 6 slices raw bacon, diced
- 1 medium yellow onion, diced
- 1 Serrano pepper, seeded and diced
- 3 garlic cloves, minced
- ½ pound ground beef
- 1 (20-ounce) can baked beans
- 1 (15-ounce) can white beans
- 1¾ cups barbecue sauce
- ⅓ cup plain cola
- 3 tablespoons brown sugar
- 3 tablespoons ketchup
- 1 tablespoon Worcestershire sauce
- ½ teaspoon freshly ground black pepper
- ½ teaspoon cayenne pepper (optional)

1. Prepare the Traeger grill or smoker for a 250 degrees F/ 120 degrees C. Add your choice of wood chunks to the fire. 2. Cook the chopped bacon in a cast-iron skillet over medium heat until browned and the fat has rendered. Remove the bacon from the pan, and set it aside, leaving the bacon fat in the skillet. 3. Add the onion and Serrano to the skillet and sauté for 2 minutes. Add the minced garlic and the ground beef and cook for an additional 5 minutes until the ground beef is no longer pink. 4. Turn off the heat, and add the baked beans, white beans, barbecue sauce, cola, brown sugar, ketchup, Worcestershire sauce, black pepper, and cayenne. 5. Transfer the set skillet to the smoker, uncovered. Close the hood and cook for 2 hours at 225 degrees F/ 105 degrees C to 250 degrees F/ 120 degrees C. 6. After 2 hours, use heat-resistant gloves to remove the set skillet from the smoker and serve.
Per Serving: Calories 231; Total fat 2.1g; Sodium 816mg; Total Carbs 38.1g; Fiber 14.4g; Sugars 4.5g; Protein 16.6g

Garlic Butter Cauliflower Florets
Prep time: 15 minutes | Cook time: 50 minutes | Serves: 4-6

- 1 (3- to 4-pound) head of cauliflower
- 2 tablespoons olive oil
- 1½ teaspoons sea salt
- 1 teaspoon garlic powder
- 1 teaspoon lemon pepper
- 3 tablespoons melted butter

1. Preheat the grill to 275 degrees F/ 135 degrees C with the lid closed. Add your choice of wood chunks or smoke packet to the fire. 2. Trim off the leaves, and liberally brush the cleaned cauliflower with the olive oil. 3. Mix the salt, garlic powder, and lemon pepper in a bowl, and season the cauliflower all over. Set it into a suitable skillet or aluminum pan. 4. Place into the smoker, close the lid, and cook for 45 to 50 minutes. 5. Remove the cauliflower from the smoker and either break it into florets or cut into slices. Drizzle the dish with the melted butter and serve.
Per Serving: Calories 173; Total fat 3.1g; Sodium 687mg; Total Carbs 69.2g; Fiber 9.6g; Sugars 3.4g; Protein 1.8g

Potato-Egg Salad
Prep time: 20 minutes | Cook time: 60 minutes | Serves: 6

- 2 pounds russet potatoes
- Olive oil, for brushing
- 1⅔ cups mayonnaise
- 2 scallions, chopped
- 2 tablespoons relish
- 1½ tablespoons Dijon mustard
- 1½ tablespoons white vinegar
- 1½ teaspoons salt
- ½ teaspoon onion powder
- ¼ teaspoon white sugar
- ¼ teaspoon garlic powder
- ¼ teaspoon freshly ground black pepper
- ¼ teaspoon smoked paprika
- 3 hard-boiled eggs, chopped

1. Preheat the Traeger grill or smoker to 225 degrees F/ 105 degrees C. 2. Wash and dry the potatoes, then rub them with the olive oil. Using a skewer or small knife, puncture each potato 5 to 7 times to the center. Place into the smoker for 30 minutes. 3. After 30 minutes, remove the potatoes and finish cooking in a 450 degrees F/ 230 degrees C oven. 4. Once cooked, remove and let cool for 1 hour. Remove the skins and chop into 1-inch pieces. 5. In a large bowl, mix the mayonnaise, scallions, relish, Dijon mustard, white vinegar, salt, onion powder, sugar, garlic powder, pepper, and smoked paprika. Taste and adjust salt as needed. 6. Add the potatoes and eggs, and gently fold to mix. Transfer to a serving bowl, cover tightly, and let it refrigerate for 2 hours before serving.
Per Serving: Calories 283; Total fat 3.6g; Sodium 381mg; Total Carbs 55.4g; Fiber 8.1g; Sugars 3.1g; Protein 8.7g

Cinnamon-Honey Sweet Potatoes
Prep time: 15 minutes | Cook time: 2 hours | Serves: 6

- 6 sweet potatoes
- ½ tablespoon olive oil
- 1 tablespoon kosher salt
- ½ stick (4 tablespoons) salted butter, at room temperature
- 2 tablespoons honey
- 1 teaspoon cinnamon

1. Prepare the Traeger grill or smoker for a 250 degrees F/ 120 degrees C. 2. Wash and dry the sweet potatoes. Pierce each potato 5 to 6 times using a skewer or fork. Rub with the olive oil and rub with the salt. 3. Set the potatoes directly onto the grates, close the lid, and cook for 1½ to 2 hours, or until tender. Remove and let leave for 10 minutes. 4. Mix the butter, honey, and cinnamon in a bowl. 5. Make a lengthwise slit in each sweet potato, open them slightly, and top with 1 to 1½ tablespoons of the honey-cinnamon butter, then serve.
Per Serving: Calories 254; Total fat 2.6g; Sodium 482mg; Total Carbs 49.1g; Fiber 4.8g; Sugars 0.2g; Protein 7.8g

Smoked Plum Tomatoes
Prep time: 15 minutes | Cook time: 45 minutes | Serves: 4-5

- 16 plum tomatoes, halved lengthwise
- Olive oil, for brushing
- 2 tablespoons salt

1. Preheat the Traeger Smoker and grill at 225 degrees F/ 105 degrees C with any additional wood chunks for indirect cooking. 2. Rub tomato halves with olive oil and set them into a suitable aluminum pan. Season them with the salt. 3. Set the pan into the smoker, close the lid, and cook the food for 45 minutes until tender. 4. Let the tomatoes cool before handling.
Per Serving: Calories 128; Total fat 1.7g; Sodium 771mg; Total Carbs 22.1g; Fiber 4.5g; Sugars 3.9g; Protein 7.1g

Cheese Beef Stuffed Jalapeños

Prep time: 30 minutes | Cook time: 2 hours | Serves: 12 jalapeños

12 jalapeños	¼ teaspoon garlic powder
1-pound Beginner's Brisket, chopped	Pinch salt
	Pinch black pepper
12 ounces cream cheese, softened	12 thick-cut bacon slices
½ cup shredded white cheddar cheese	1½ cups barbecue sauce of choice
	Toothpicks
2 tablespoons chopped red onion	
¼ teaspoon ground cumin	

1. Wash and dry each jalapeño. Cut about ⅛ inch under the stem, piercing the jalapeño halfway. Then make a perpendicular cut lengthwise, forming a T shape, exposing the seeds and white flesh. Do not cut all the way through. 2. Carefully scoop out the seeds and white flesh. Do the same with the remaining jalapeños, then set aside. 3. Prepare your grill or smoker for a 250 degrees F/ 120 degrees C. 4. Set the brisket in a suitable food processor and pulse 5 to 6 times. It should resemble cooked ground beef. 5. Remove the brisket and place in a suitable bowl along with the cream cheese, garlic powder, salt, cheddar, onion, cumin, and pepper and stir until mixed. 6. Fill each pepper with as much filling as it can take. Wrap each pepper with a slice of bacon then carefully secure with toothpicks. Place onto a suitable aluminum tray. 7. Set the tray of jalapeños on the grill grate. Close the hood and cook them for 1½ hours. During the last half hour, Rub the barbecue sauce on the jalapeños, close the lid, and cook for 30 minutes. 8. Remove the dish from the smoker and serve immediately.

Per Serving: Calories 244; Total fat 9.1g; Sodium 1399mg; Total Carbs 34.3g; Fiber 8.7g; Sugars 15.7g; Protein 8.3g

Delicious Cream Onion Dip

Prep time: 15 minutes | Cook time: 60 minutes | Serves: 6-8

2 medium yellow onions, halved vertically	2 tablespoons chopped chives
	1 tablespoon chopped parsley
Olive oil, for drizzling	¼ teaspoon salt more as needed
8 ounces cream cheese, softened	¼ teaspoon freshly ground black pepper
¾ cup sour cream	
¼ cup mayonnaise	¼ teaspoon garlic powder
1 tablespoon apple cider vinegar	

1. Preheat the grill to 250 degrees F/ 120 degrees C with the lid closed. 2. Set the onion halves cut-side up into a suitable aluminum pan. 3. Drizzle with the olive oil and set the pan on the smoker. Close the hood and cook for 1 hour, or until the onions are tender and have browned slightly. 4. Once cooked, remove from the smoker and let them cool for 1 hour. Chop into small pieces and set aside. 5. Mix the cream cheese, sour cream, mayonnaise, and apple cider vinegar in a bowl. Fold in the chopped cooked onions, chives, parsley, salt, black pepper, and garlic powder. 6. Mix to incorporate, then serve.

Per Serving: Calories 344; Total fat 3g; Sodium 603mg; Total Carbs 73.8g; Fiber 11.5g; Sugars 8.6g; Protein 9.4g

Bacon–Wrapped Onion Meatloaf Bombs

Prep time: 25 minutes | Cook time: 60 minutes | Serves: 6-7

2 yellow onions, peeled and cut into rings	2 garlic cloves, minced
	1 teaspoon Worcestershire sauce
1-pound ground beef	1 teaspoon salt
½ cup bread crumbs	½ teaspoon dried oregano
½ cup shredded cheddar cheese	½ teaspoon black pepper
½ cup shredded Parmesan cheese	12 thick-cut bacon slices
1 egg	12 to 18 toothpicks
1 tablespoon dried parsley	1 cup barbecue sauce of choice
1 tablespoon ketchup	

1. Preheat the grill to 275 degrees F/ 135 degrees C with the lid closed. 2. Mix the ground beef with the bread crumbs, cheddar, Parmesan, egg, parsley, ketchup, garlic, Worcestershire sauce, salt, oregano, and black pepper in a bowl. 3. Taking about ⅓ cup of the meat mixture, form it into a ball, then press it gently into one of the onion rings. Take the matching onion ring and place on top. 4. Wrap the bomb with 2 strips of bacon and secure with toothpicks. Repeat until all the bombs are assembled. 5. Place onion bombs directly onto the cooking grate. 6. Close hood and cook for 45 minutes. After 45 minutes, rub with barbecue sauce, then cook for another 30 minutes. 7. Remove the bombs from the smoker and serve.

Per Serving: Calories 357; Total fat 16.1g; Sodium 80mg; Total Carbs 26g; Fiber 7.3g; Sugars 9.2g; Protein 9.4g

Cheesy Hash Browns Casserole

Prep time: 15 minutes | Cook time: 75 minutes | Serves: 6-7

2 tablespoons olive oil	cheese
1 small yellow onion, diced	1 cup sour cream
2 garlic cloves, minced	⅓ cup shredded Parmesan cheese
3 cups corn flake cereal, crushed	¼ cup mayonnaise
½ cup melted butter, divided	1 teaspoon salt
1 (30-ounce) bag of frozen hash browns	½ teaspoon black pepper
	1 (4-ounce) can of chopped mild green chilies (optional)
1 (15-ounce) can cream of mushroom soup	
1 cup shredded sharp cheddar	

1. Preheat the grill to 225 degrees F/ 105 degrees C with the lid closed. 2. Heat the oil in a saucepan over medium heat; add the chopped onion and sauté for 3 minutes. 3. Add the cooked garlic and cook for 1 minute. Remove from the heat. 4. Prepare the topping by combining the crushed corn flake cereal with ¼ cup of melted butter in a suitable bowl. 5. In a separate bowl, mix the frozen hash browns with the remaining ¼ cup of melted butter, along with the cream of mushroom soup, sharp cheddar, sour cream, Parmesan, mayonnaise, salt, pepper, and chilies (optional). Fold to mix. 6. Set the hash brown mixture into a suitable aluminum pan and top with the corn flake mixture. 7. Place the pan in the smoker, close the lid, and cook the mixture for 1 hour and 15 minutes, or until the sides of the casserole starts to brown and pull away from the edges and the potatoes are tender. 8. When done, remove the casserole from the smoker and serve immediately.

Per Serving: Calories 194; Total fat 2.6g; Sodium 1257mg; Total Carbs 35.4g; Fiber 3.7g; Sugars 3.1g; Protein 9.4g

Delicious Bacon Brussels Sprouts

Prep time: 15 minutes | Cook time: 55 minutes | Serves: 4-5

6 thick-cut bacon slices	1 tablespoon olive oil
1 small yellow onion, sliced	½ teaspoon salt
2 garlic cloves, chopped	½ teaspoon freshly ground black pepper
1½ pounds Brussels sprouts, washed, steams and excess leaves removed	2 tablespoons balsamic vinegar

1. Preheat the grill to 250 degrees F/ 120 degrees C with the lid closed. 2. Sauté the bacon in a skillet over medium heat for 7 minutes until the fat renders. 3. Once cooked, remove the bacon and use 3 to 4 tablespoons of the bacon fat to sauté the onion. 4. After 2 minutes, add the minced garlic and sauté them for another minute, then remove from heat. 5. Set the Brussels sprouts in a suitable aluminum pan with the onion and garlic. 6. Chop the bacon into small pieces and add to the Brussels sprouts. Add the olive oil, salt, and pepper to the pan and toss to mix. 7. Set the pan on the grill, close the lid, and cook for 45 minutes. 8. Remove and drizzle the dish with balsamic vinegar, then serve.

Per Serving: Calories: 139, Fat: 6.1g, Carbohydrates: 23.6g, Protein: 5.4g, Cholesterol: 0mg, Sodium: 30mg, Fiber: 4.3g, Sugar: 8.7g

Delicious Holiday Stuffing

Prep time: 15 minutes | Cook time: 1 hr. 20 minutes | Serves: 4

2 tablespoons olive oil	chopped
12 ounces chicken-apple sausage, casings removed	2 large eggs
	3 cups vegetable broth
1 small yellow onion, chopped	½ teaspoon dried sage
2 celery stalks, chopped	½ teaspoon salt
2 garlic cloves, minced	½ teaspoon dried rosemary
16 ounces stuffing cubes, homemade or prepackaged	½ teaspoon red pepper flakes (optional)
2 sweet apples, peeled, cored, and	3 tablespoons melted butter

1. At 225 degrees F/ 105 degrees C, preheat your Traeger smoker. 2. Heat the olive oil in a skillet over medium heat; add the sausage and sauté for 3 to 4 minutes. Stir in the chopped onion, celery, and garlic and cook for 2 to 3 minutes, until the vegetables start to become tender. Add the stuffing cubes and apples. Remove from heat and set aside. 3. Mix the eggs, vegetable broth, sage, salt, rosemary, and red pepper flakes (optional) in a bowl. 4. Add the contents of the set skillet to the egg mixture and gently fold to mix. Set the stuffing in a suitable aluminum pan and drizzle with the melted butter. 5. Set the pan on the grill, close the lid, and cook for 1 hour 20 minutes until the stuffing is browned and slightly crispy on top. 6. Serve warm.
Per Serving: Calories 195; Total fat 12.7g; Sodium 1131mg; Total Carbs 27.7g; Fiber 3.5g; Sugars 5.9g; Protein 2.1g

Grilled Cheese Corn Pudding

Prep time: 20 minutes | Cook time: 65 minutes | Serves: 6

2 eggs	½ cup shredded pepper jack cheese
1 (12-ounce) can evaporated milk	
2½ tablespoons all-purpose flour	2 teaspoons white sugar
2 tablespoons melted butter	1 teaspoon salt
1½ cups corn kernels (about 4 medium ears)	½ teaspoon freshly ground black pepper
1 (15-ounce) can creamed corn	1 tablespoon vegetable oil
1 cup shredded cheddar cheese	

1. At 300 degrees F/ 150 degrees C, preheat your Traeger smoker. 2. Mix the eggs, evaporated milk, flour, and melted butter until well mixed. Add the corn kernels, creamed corn, cheddar, pepper jack, sugar, salt, and black pepper in a large bowl. 3. Grease a suitable aluminum pan with the vegetable oil and pour the corn mixture into it. 4. Place the pan on the grill, close the lid, and cook for 50 minutes. After 50 minutes, check to see if the center has set. 5. Cook for an additional 15 minutes. The sides should be golden brown and the center firm. 6. Remove the pan from the smoker and let leave for 10 minutes before serving.
Per Serving: Calories 194; Total fat 10.9g; Sodium 292mg; Total Carbs 21.7g; Fiber 6.4g; Sugars 9g; Protein 6.4g

Grilled Chantilly Potatoes

Prep time: 20 minutes | Cook time: 60 minutes | Serves: 4-5

4 medium russet potatoes, peeled and cut into 1-inch cubes	1 teaspoon salt
	½ teaspoon freshly ground black pepper
1 cup heavy cream	
½ cup butter, melted	¼ teaspoon garlic powder
1 cup shredded Gouda cheese	½ cup shredded Parmesan cheese

1. Bring a pot of water to a boil over high heat; add the potatoes and boil them for 20 minutes until tenders. 2. Drain and mash the potatoes with a fork. 3. At 275 degrees F/ 135 degrees C, preheat your Traeger smoker. 4. Set the cooked potatoes in a large bowl; add the cream, melted butter, Gouda cheese, salt, black pepper, and garlic powder. 5. Taste and adjust salt as needed. 6. Scoop the prepared mixture into a 19-by-9-inch aluminum pan and top with the Parmesan cheese. 7. Place the pan, uncovered, on the grill, close the lid, and cook the mixture for 40 minutes. The cheese will have melted and the potatoes will appear golden brown around the edges when done. 8. Remove the dish from the smoker and serve immediately.
Per Serving: Calories: 139, Fat: 6.1g, Carbohydrates: 23.6g, Protein: 5.4g, Cholesterol: 0mg, Sodium: 30mg, Fiber: 4.3g, Sugar: 8.7g

Easy Smoked Butternut Squash

Prep time: 15 minutes | Cook time: 60 minutes | Serves: 4-5

2 butternut squash	1½ teaspoons coarse salt
3 tablespoons olive oil	

1. At 275 degrees F/ 135 degrees C, preheat your Traeger smoker. 2. Cut off the top inch each squash, then slice them in half lengthwise. 3. Leave the seeds intact. Rub the squash flesh with olive oil, and season with salt. 4. Set the butternut squash on the grill cut-side up, close the lid, and cook for 1 hour. The squash should be tender when done. 5. Remove the food and let it cool for 15 to 20 minutes before handling. 6. Discard the seeds, scoop out the flesh, and use or store as needed.
Per Serving: Calories 344; Total fat 3g; Sodium 603mg; Total Carbs 73.8g; Fiber 11.5g; Sugars 8.6g; Protein 9.4g

Grilled S'mores Dip

Prep time: 15 minutes | Cook time: 15 minutes | Serves: 4-5

12 ounces cookie butter	⅓ cup chopped pecans
1 jar marshmallow fluff	Graham crackers or cookies, for dipping
1 cup chopped milk chocolate	
⅓ cup crushed graham crackers	

1. At 300 degrees F/ 150 degrees C, preheat your Traeger smoker with its hood closed. 2. In a 12-inch cast-iron pan, layer the cookie butter, then the marshmallow fluff, chopped chocolate, crushed graham crackers, and nuts (optional). 3. Set the pan on the preheated grill, close the hood, and cook the food for 15 minutes. 4. Once everything is melted through, remove and serve with graham crackers or cookies of your choice.
Per Serving: Calories 194; Total fat 2.6g; Sodium 1257mg; Total Carbs 35.4g; Fiber 3.7g; Sugars 3.1g; Protein 9.4g

Sweet Candied Pineapple

Prep time: 15 minutes | Cook time: 60 minutes | Serves: 4-6

1 pineapple	1½ teaspoons ground cinnamon
½ cup dark rum	½ teaspoon ground nutmeg
1 cup light brown sugar	

1. Preheat the Traeger grill or smoker to 350 degrees F/ 175 degrees C. 2. Cut the stem and skin off the pineapple, making it as close to a rectangular shape as possible. 3. Put the rum into a suitable bowl. Draw some of it into the injector and slowly inject it into the pineapple in different sections, starting with the core and working around it. 4. Mix the brown sugar, cinnamon, and nutmeg in a separate bowl. 5. Set the pineapple in a suitable aluminum pan and coat the top with half of the sugar mixture. Set in the smoker or grill and cook for 30 minutes. 6. Using heat-resistant gloves, carefully flip the pineapple over and sprinkle the remaining half of the sugar mixture on the opposite side. 7. Close the hood and continue to smoke for 30 more minutes. 8. Transfer to a cutting board and slice into 1-inch-thick rounds. Serve with ice cream on top.
Per Serving: Calories 244; Total fat 9.1g; Sodium 1399mg; Total Carbs 34.3g; Fiber 8.7g; Sugars 15.7g; Protein 8.3g

Cinnamon Chocolate Sauce

Prep time: 15 minutes | Cook time: 20 minutes | Serves: 12

1½ cups heavy cream
¾ cup semisweet chocolate chips
⅛ teaspoon cinnamon
Pinch cayenne pepper (optional)

1. At 250 degrees F/ 120 degrees C, preheat your Traeger smoker. 2. Pour the cream and chocolate chips into a medium cast-iron skillet. 3. Place the skillet on the hot grill and close the lid; cook for 10 minutes. 4. Open the hood and give it a good stir. 5. Place it back into the smoker and cook for an additional 10 minutes. 6. Once the chocolate has melted and has incorporated with the cream, remove and add the cinnamon and cayenne (optional). 7. Remove from heat and serve immediately.

Per Serving: Calories 357; Total fat 16.1g; Sodium 80mg; Total Carbs 26g; Fiber 7.3g; Sugars 9.2g; Protein 9.4g

Caramel Apple Crisp

Prep time: 25 minutes | Cook time: 60 minutes | Serves: 5-6

5 Granny Smith apples, peeled, cored and sliced
1 tablespoon freshly squeezed lemon juice
¼ cup brown sugar, plus ⅓ cup
2 tablespoons white sugar
3 tablespoons melted butter
2 teaspoons vanilla extract
¾ teaspoon ground cinnamon, divided
1¼ cups old-fashioned oats
¼ cup flour
5 tablespoons cold butter, chopped
¼ teaspoon ground nutmeg
Vegetable oil, for greasing

1. Preheat the Traeger grill to 350 degrees F/ 175 degrees C. 2. Mix the apples, lemon juice, ¼ cup of brown sugar, white sugar, melted butter, vanilla, and ¼ teaspoon of cinnamon in a large bowl. 3. Add the oats, flour, remaining ⅓ cup of brown sugar, cold butter, remaining ½ teaspoon of cinnamon, and nutmeg to the food processor, and then pulse them 5 or 6 times. 4. Grease the inside of a medium cast-iron skillet with oil. 5. Arrange the sliced apples in the bottom of the set skillet, then top with the crumble mixture. Set the pan into the grill, close the lid, and cook for 1 hour. 6. Let the dish cool for 15 minutes before serving with a scoop of vanilla ice cream and a drizzle of warm caramel sauce.

Per Serving: Calories 344; Total fat 3g; Sodium 603mg; Total Carbs 73.8g; Fiber 11.5g; Sugars 8.6g; Protein 9.4g

Chapter 7 Rubs, Marinades, and More

83	Quick Beef Brisket Rub	86	Cilantro-Balsamic Sriracha Drizzle
83	Sweet & Spicy Pork Rub	86	Spiced Sweet Potato Mustard
83	Aromatic Rosemary-Garlic Seasoning	86	Delicious Mandarin Glaze
83	Lemon Pepper-Dill Seafood Rub	86	Jamaican Jerk Seasoning Paste
83	BBQ Rub	86	Blueberry Barbecue Sauce
83	Brown Sugar Spice Rub	87	Jalapeño- Cucumber Relish
83	Smoked Garlic Mushroom Tomato Sauce	87	All-Match Spice Rub
84	Easy Carne Asada Marinade	87	Herb Poultry Rub
84	Honey Onion Sauce	87	Spicy Beef and Game Rub
84	Sweet & Spicy BBQ Sauce	87	Dry Cajun Rub
84	Homemade Hickory-Smoked Barbecue Sauce	87	Flavorful Brisket Marinade
84	Maple Mustard Sauce	87	Pork Rib Garlic Marinade
84	Hot Barbecue Sauce	87	Easy Brine
84	Cajun Barbecue Rub	88	Orange BBQ Sauce
85	Bleu Cheese Butter	88	Brown Sugar-Pineapple Glaze
85	Spicy Mayo Sauce	88	Maple Herbed Turkey Brine
85	Savory Plum Sauce	88	Aromatic Pork Marinade
85	Hearty Teriyaki Marinade	88	Asian-Style Marinade
85	Flavorful Pineapple–Brown Sugar Sauce	88	Flavorful Jerk Spice Rub
85	Homemade Java Rub	89	Chinese-Style Beef Rub
85	Delicious BBQ Sauce	89	Blue Cheese Cream Dip
85	All-Purpose Wine Marinade	89	Zesty Lime Guacamole
86	Lime Chipotle Butter	89	Lime Watermelon Salsa
86	Classic Chimichurri Sauce	89	Ruby Port Orange Cranberry Sauce

Quick Beef Brisket Rub
Prep time: 5 minutes | Cook time: 0 | Serves: ½ cup

3 tablespoons coarse salt
1 tablespoon salt
2 tablespoons black pepper
1 tablespoon garlic powder
½ tablespoon onion powder

1. Mix the coarse salt, salt, pepper, garlic powder, and onion powder in a bowl. 2. Store any unused rub in a zip-top bag or airtight container. The spice rub can be stored for several months.
Per Serving: Calories 3; Total fat 0.1g; Sodium 582mg; Total Carbs 0.6g; Fiber 0.2g; Sugars 0.1g; Protein 0.2g

Sweet & Spicy Pork Rub
Prep time: 5 minutes | Cook time: 0 | Serves: ⅓ cup

¼ cup brown sugar
1 teaspoon coarse salt
1 teaspoon garlic powder
1 teaspoon onion powder
1 teaspoon freshly ground black pepper
1 teaspoon paprika
½ teaspoon cayenne pepper
¼ teaspoon cinnamon

1. Mix the brown sugar, salt, garlic powder, onion powder, black pepper, paprika, cayenne pepper, and cinnamon in a bowl. 2. Store any unused rub in a zip-top bag or airtight container. The spice rub can be stored for several months.
Per Serving: Calories 4; Total fat 0.1g; Sodium 567mg; Total Carbs 0.6g; Fiber 0.2g; Sugars 0.1g; Protein 0.2g

Aromatic Rosemary–Garlic Seasoning
Prep time: 5 minutes | Cook time: 0 | Serves: ⅕ cup

3 teaspoons minced rosemary
3 teaspoons coarse kosher salt
1 teaspoon garlic powder
1 teaspoon freshly ground black pepper
½ teaspoon minced garlic
½ teaspoon minced onion

Mix the salt, rosemary, garlic powder, pepper, minced garlic, and minced onion in a bowl. Store any unused rub in a zip-top bag or airtight container. The spice rub can be stored for several months.
Per Serving: Calories 5; Total fat 0.1g; Sodium 452mg; Total Carbs 0.6g; Fiber 0.2g; Sugars 0.1g; Protein 0.2g

Lemon Pepper–Dill Seafood Rub
Prep time: 5 minutes | Cook time: 0 | Serves: ¼ cup

4 tablespoons kosher salt
2 tablespoons freshly ground black pepper
2 tablespoons lemon pepper
2 tablespoons garlic powder
2 teaspoons dried dill weed

1. Mix together the salt, lemon pepper, black pepper, garlic powder, and dill weed in a bowl. 2. Store any unused rub in a zip-top bag or airtight container. The spice rub can be stored for several months.
Per Serving: Calories 3; Total fat 0.1g; Sodium 582mg; Total Carbs 0.6g; Fiber 0.2g; Sugars 0.1g; Protein 0.2g

BBQ Rub
Prep time: 5 minutes | Cook time: 0 | Serves: ½ cup

3 tablespoons coarse kosher salt
2 tablespoons freshly ground black pepper
1 tablespoon brown sugar
1 tablespoon garlic powder
1 tablespoon paprika
½ tablespoon cayenne pepper
½ tablespoon onion powder

1. Mix together the salt, black pepper, brown sugar, garlic powder, paprika, cayenne pepper, and onion powder in a bowl. 2. Store any unused rub in a zip-top bag or airtight container. The spice rub can be stored for several months.
Per Serving: Calories 4; Total fat 0.9g; Sodium 292mg; Total Carbs 0.7g; Fiber 0.4g; Sugars 0 g; Protein 0.4g

Brown Sugar Spice Rub
Prep time: 5 minutes | Cook time: 0 | Serves: ½ cup

¼ cup brown sugar
2 teaspoons coarse kosher salt
1 teaspoon garlic powder
1 teaspoon onion powder
1 teaspoon paprika
1 teaspoon freshly ground black pepper
½ teaspoon cayenne pepper
¼ teaspoon smoked paprika

1. Combine the brown sugar, salt, garlic powder, onion powder, paprika, black pepper, cayenne pepper, and smoked paprika in a bowl. 2. Store any unused rub in a zip-top bag or airtight container. The spice rub can be stored for several months.
Per Serving: Calories 42; Total fat 0.9g; Sodium 1292mg; Total Carbs 7.7g; Fiber 0.3g; Sugars 5.9g; Protein 2.2g

Smoked Garlic Mushroom Tomato Sauce
Prep time: 30 minutes | Cook time: 3 hours | Serves: 8

3 tablespoons olive oil
1 tablespoon unsalted butter
1 garlic bulb, top cut off
Flaked sea salt
Freshly ground black pepper
2 cups cremini mushrooms, or white mushrooms, trimmed and cut into slices
1 cup chopped carrots
1 cup chopped celery
1 cup chopped yellow onions
1 cup leeks, white parts only, quartered lengthwise and sliced
3 tablespoons tomato paste
2 cups Cabernet Sauvignon, Merlot, or Pinot Noir
12 cups or canned chopped Roma tomatoes
3 tablespoons thyme leaves, stripped and chopped
3 tablespoons oregano leaves, minced
3 bay leaves
2 cups chicken (or vegetable) stock
Finely grated Parmesan cheese (optional)
3 tablespoons flat-leaf parsley leaves, minced

1. Preheat the Traeger smoker to 275 degrees F/ 135 degrees C. Ensure the drip tray is clean and in place. Close the door. 2. Set the wood chips in the smoking tray or firebox, get a good smoke rolling, and seal the door. 3. Place a suitable cast iron Dutch oven on the smoking rack to preheat it. Pour in 3 tablespoons of the olive oil and add the butter. 4. Place the garlic whole on a sheet of aluminum foil. 5. Drizzle the garlic with olive oil and season it with black pepper and salt. Wrap the foil to enclose the garlic. Smoke the garlic for 1 hour, or until golden brown and tender. Remove the garlic from the foil and set it aside. 6. Mix the mushrooms, carrots, celery, onions, and leeks in the Dutch oven. Season them with black pepper and salt. Smoke the vegetables, uncovered, for 30 to 45 minutes until golden brown. Move the vegetables to one side of the pan. 7. Stir in the tomato paste to the other side of the pan and smoke for 12 minutes, until browned and fragrant. 8. Pour in the red wine to deglaze the pan, scraping up any browned bits stuck to the bottom. Smoke for 12 minutes more, or until the wine is reduced and the pan is dry. 9. Add the tomatoes, thyme, oregano, bay leaves, and chicken stock. Smoke for 2 hours. 10. Squeeze the smoked garlic cloves from the head and add to the sauce along with the Parmesan cheese. Stir to mix. Remove and discard the bay leaves. Leave the sauce chunky, or purée it using an immersion blender for a smooth sauce. 11. Season them with more black pepper and salt, as needed. Top with the parsley.
Per Serving: Calories 24; Total fat 1.9g; Sodium 382mg; Total Carbs 2g; Fiber 0.2g; Sugars 0.2g; Protein 0.1g

Chapter 7 Rubs, Marinades, and More | 83

Easy Carne Asada Marinade

Prep time: 5 minutes | Cook time: 0 | Serves: 2½ cups

- ½ cup water
- ½ cup soy sauce
- ⅓ cup Worcestershire sauce
- ¼ cup olive oil
- Juice of 1 lime
- ½ bunch cilantro, chopped
- 2 garlic cloves, minced
- 2 tablespoons brown sugar
- 2 tablespoons freshly ground black pepper

1. In a suitable bowl, mix together the water, soy sauce, Worcestershire sauce, olive oil, lime juice, cilantro, garlic, brown sugar, and pepper. 2. You can store the left marinade in an airtight container and refrigerate for up to 7 days.

Per Serving: Calories 72; Total fat 0.5g; Sodium 4292mg; Total Carbs 17.1g; Fiber 0.4g; Sugars 15.8g; Protein 0.5g

Honey Onion Sauce

Prep time: 10 minutes | Cook time: 10 minutes | Serves: 2 cups

- 2 tablespoons olive oil
- ½ white onion, minced
- 1 (8-ounce) can tomato sauce
- ½ cup brown sugar
- ¼ cup white vinegar
- ¼ cup honey
- 1½ tablespoons Worcestershire sauce
- 2 teaspoons chili powder
- ¼ teaspoon dry mustard
- 2 teaspoons kosher salt
- 1 teaspoon freshly ground black pepper

1. Heat the oil in a saucepan over medium-high heat until shimmering. 2. Add the onion and sauté for 1 minute until it is tender and semi-translucent. 3. Add the tomato sauce, brown sugar, vinegar, honey, Worcestershire sauce, chili powder, dry mustard, salt, and pepper, mixing thoroughly. 4. Heat them for 9 minutes until boiling, stirring constantly. 5. Remove the sauce from the stovetop and serve with your favorite cut of meat.

Per Serving: Calories 89; Total fat 0.1g; Sodium 2392mg; Total Carbs 12g; Fiber 0.9g; Sugars 9.3g; Protein 0.5g

Sweet & Spicy BBQ Sauce

Prep time: 10 minutes | Cook time: 10 minutes | Serves: 2 cups

- 2 tablespoons olive oil
- ½ white onion, minced
- 1 (8-ounce) can tomato sauce
- ½ cup brown sugar
- ¼ cup white vinegar
- 1½ tablespoons Worcestershire sauce
- 2 tablespoons hot sauce
- 3 teaspoons chili powder
- ¼ teaspoon dry mustard
- 2 teaspoons kosher salt
- 2 teaspoons freshly ground black pepper

1. Heat the oil in a saucepan over medium-high heat until shimmering. 2. Add the onion and stir for 1 minute until it is tender and semi-translucent. 3. Add the tomato sauce, brown sugar, vinegar, Worcestershire sauce, hot sauce, chili powder, dry mustard, salt, and pepper, mixing thoroughly. 4. Heat them for 9 minutes until boiling, stirring constantly. 5. Remove the sauce from the stovetop and serve with your favorite cut.

Per Serving: Calories 77; Total fat 8.9g; Sodium 292mg; Total Carbs 1g; Fiber 0.3g; Sugars 0.3g; Protein 0.2g

Homemade Hickory-Smoked Barbecue Sauce

Prep time: 30 minutes | Cook time: 30 minutes | Serves: 3 cups

- 1 small onion, chopped
- 2 garlic cloves, minced
- 2 cups ketchup
- 1 cup water
- ½ cup molasses
- ½ cup apple cider vinegar
- 5 tablespoons granulated sugar
- 5 tablespoons brown sugar
- 1 tablespoon Worcestershire sauce
- 1 tablespoon freshly squeezed lemon juice
- 2 teaspoons hickory liquid smoke
- 1½ teaspoons freshly ground black pepper
- 1½ teaspoons dry mustard

1. At 225 degrees F/ 105 degrees C, preheat your Traeger smoker with the hickory wood. 2. Cook the molasses, onion, garlic, ketchup, water, vinegar, granulated sugar, brown sugar, Worcestershire sauce, lemon juice, liquid smoke, pepper, and mustard in the saucepan over medium heat. 3. Bring the sauce to a boil. 4. Transfer the sauce to a small metal or aluminum-foil pan and place it in the smoker, then cook the sauce for 30 minutes to absorb the smoke's flavor. 5. Serve.

Per Serving: Calories 94; Total fat 10.9g; Sodium 292mg; Total Carbs 21.7g; Fiber 6.4g; Sugars 9g; Protein 6.4g

Maple Mustard Sauce

Prep time: 15 minutes | Cook time: 0 | Serves: 1 cup

- ¾ cup prepared yellow mustard
- ¼ cup maple syrup
- ¼ cup apple cider vinegar
- 2 tablespoons brown sugar
- 2 tablespoons ketchup
- 1 tablespoon Worcestershire sauce
- 2 teaspoons hot sauce
- 1 teaspoon pumpkin pie spice
- 1 teaspoon salt
- 1 teaspoon freshly ground black pepper

1. In a suitable bowl, Mix the maple syrup, vinegar, brown sugar, ketchup, Worcestershire sauce, hot sauce, pumpkin-pie spice, salt, and pepper in a bowl. 2. Serve, and the left sauce can be refrigerated in an airtight container for up to 2 weeks.

Per Serving: Calories 44; Total fat 0.9g; Sodium 352mg; Total Carbs 1.7g; Fiber 0.4g; Sugars 0.9g; Protein 0.4g

Hot Barbecue Sauce

Prep time: 30 minutes | Cook time: 30 minutes | Serves: 3 cups

- 2 cups ketchup
- 1 cup light-brown sugar
- 1 cup hot-pepper vinegar sauce
- 2 tablespoons white vinegar
- 2 tablespoons salt
- 1 tablespoon chili powder
- 2 teaspoons freshly ground black pepper
- 1 teaspoon garlic powder
- 1 teaspoon cayenne pepper
- ½ teaspoon ground allspice

1. In a suitable saucepan over medium heat, Stir and cook the ketchup, brown sugar, hot-pepper vinegar sauce, white vinegar, salt, chili powder, pepper, garlic powder, cayenne, and allspice in the saucepan over medium heat. 2. Bring the sauce to a boil, reduce its heat to low, and cook on a simmer, covered, for 25 minutes, stirring occasionally. 3. Serve.

Per Serving: Calories 94; Total fat 10.9g; Sodium 292mg; Total Carbs 21.7g; Fiber 6.4g; Sugars 9g; Protein 1.4g

Cajun Barbecue Rub

Prep time: 10 minutes | Cook time: 0 | Serves: ¾ cup

- ¼ cup paprika
- ¼ cup sugar
- 3 tablespoons Cajun seasoning
- 1 tablespoon brown sugar
- 1½ teaspoons chili powder
- 1½ teaspoons cayenne pepper
- 1½ teaspoons ground cumin

1. In a suitable bowl, Combine the paprika, sugar, Cajun seasoning, brown sugar, chili powder, cayenne, and cumin in a bowl. 2. The left sauce can be refrigerated in an airtight container for up to 2 weeks.

Per Serving: Calories 194; Total fat 10.9g; Sodium 292mg; Total Carbs 21.7g; Fiber 6.4g; Sugars 9g; Protein 6.4g

Bleu Cheese Butter

Prep time: 5 minutes | Cook time: 0 | Serves: 1 cup

- 1 cup unsalted butter, softened
- 4-ounce bleu cheese crumbles, at room temperature
- 1 teaspoon cayenne pepper
- 1 teaspoon garlic powder
- ¼ cup chopped scallions, white and green parts
- 1 tablespoon brown sugar, firmly packed

1. Cream the butter and bleu cheese with a mixer. 2. Add the cayenne pepper, garlic powder, scallions, and brown sugar, and blend well. 3. Using wax paper, roll the prepared mixture into a cylindrical log and wrap well. 4. Refrigerate the mixture for a minimum of 4 hours. 5. When ready to serve, unwrap and cut into 1-inch slices.

Per Serving: Calories 24; Total fat 1.9g; Sodium 382mg; Total Carbs 2g; Fiber 0.2g; Sugars 0.2g; Protein 0.1g

Spicy Mayo Sauce

Prep time: 10 minutes | Cook time: 0 | Serves: 1 cup

- 1 cup mayonnaise
- ¼ cup apple cider vinegar
- 1 tablespoon hot chili powder
- 1 teaspoon Worcestershire sauce
- ½ teaspoon celery seed
- ½ teaspoon red pepper flakes
- ¼ teaspoon cayenne pepper
- Salt
- Freshly ground black pepper

1. Mix the vinegar, mayonnaise, chili powder, Worcestershire sauce, celery seed, red pepper flakes, and cayenne in a bowl until well blended. 2. Season the mixture with black pepper and salt and mix again. 3. Serve with the meat of your choice, and you can refrigerate the left sauce in an airtight container for up to 2 weeks.

Per Serving: Calories 194; Total fat 10.9g; Sodium 292mg; Total Carbs 21.7g; Fiber 6.4g; Sugars 9g; Protein 6.4g

Savory Plum Sauce

Prep time: 30 minutes | Cook time: 20 minutes | Serves: 1 cup

- 12 ounces plum jam
- 2 tablespoons apple cider vinegar
- 1 tablespoon brown sugar
- 1 tablespoon dry minced onion
- 1 teaspoon red pepper flakes
- 1 garlic clove, minced
- ½ teaspoon ground ginger
- Salt
- Freshly ground black pepper

1. Stir and cook the jam, vinegar, brown sugar, onion, red pepper flakes, garlic, and ginger in a saucepan over high heat. Season with black pepper and salt and bring to a boil. 2. Reduce the heat to low and cook on a simmer for 20 minutes. 3. The sauce can be refrigerated in an airtight container for up to 2 weeks.

Per Serving: Calories 73; Total fat 3.1g; Sodium 687mg; Total Carbs 69.2g; Fiber 9.6g; Sugars 3.4g; Protein 1.8g

Hearty Teriyaki Marinade

Prep time: 10 minutes | Cook time: 0 | Serves: 1½ cups

- ½ cup low-sodium soy sauce
- ½ cup teriyaki sauce
- ¼ cup brown sugar
- ¼ cup granulated sugar
- 1 small onion, chopped
- ¼ cup rice wine vinegar
- ¼ cup canola oil
- 3 tablespoons hoisin sauce
- 2 teaspoons ground ginger
- 1 tablespoon minced garlic
- 1 teaspoon liquid smoke

1. Stir the soy sauce, brown sugar, teriyaki sauce, and granulated sugar in a bowl until dissolved and well blended. 2. Add the onion, vinegar, oil, hoisin sauce, ginger, garlic, and liquid smoke. Stir to mix. 3. Pour it over your steak as a marinade, or bring to a boil and serve as a sauce for steak or chicken. 4. The left sauce can be refrigerated in an airtight container for up to 2 weeks.

Per Serving: Calories 28; Total fat 1.7g; Sodium 771mg; Total Carbs 22.1g; Fiber 4.5g; Sugars 3.9g; Protein 7.1g

Flavorful Pineapple–Brown Sugar Sauce

Prep time: 10 minutes | Cook time: 0 | Serves: 2 cups

- 1 (20-ounce) can pineapple chunks, with juice
- 1 cup brown sugar
- 2 tablespoons prepared mustard
- 2 tablespoons tomato paste
- 1 tablespoon ground cloves
- 1 teaspoon ground nutmeg
- 1 teaspoon ground cinnamon
- 1 teaspoon ancho chili powder (or chipotle)

1. Mix the brown sugar, mustard, pineapple chunks and juice, tomato paste, cloves, nutmeg, cinnamon, and chili powder in a bowl. 2. Serve with the meat of your choice, and the left sauce can be refrigerated in an airtight container for up to 2 weeks.

Per Serving: Calories 194; Total fat 10.9g; Sodium 292mg; Total Carbs 21.7g; Fiber 6.4g; Sugars 9g; Protein 6.4g

Homemade Java Rub

Prep time: 10 minutes | Cook time: 0 | Serves: 1 cup

- ¼ cup ground roasted coffee beans
- ¼ cup paprika
- ¼ cup garlic powder
- 2 tablespoons chili powder
- 1 tablespoon light-brown sugar
- 1 tablespoon ground allspice
- 1 tablespoon ground coriander
- 1 tablespoon black pepper
- 2 teaspoons dry mustard
- 1½ teaspoons celery seed

1. Add the coffee beans, paprika, garlic powder, chili powder, brown sugar, allspice, coriander, pepper, mustard, and celery seed to the blender, and then blend them until fine. 2. Store in an airtight container for up to 3 months, after which it starts to lose its flavor.

Per Serving: Calories 194; Total fat 10.9g; Sodium 292mg; Total Carbs 21.7g; Fiber 6.4g; Sugars 9g; Protein 6.4g

Delicious BBQ Sauce

Prep time: 10 minutes | Cook time: 30 minutes | Serves: 3 cups

- 1 small onion, chopped
- 2 garlic cloves, minced
- 2 cups ketchup
- 1 cup water
- ½ cup molasses
- ½ cup apple cider vinegar
- 5 tablespoons granulated sugar
- 5 tablespoons light brown sugar
- 1 tablespoon Worcestershire sauce
- 1 tablespoon lemon juice
- 2 teaspoons liquid smoke
- 1½ teaspoons freshly ground black pepper
- 1 tablespoon yellow mustard

1. Add the onion, garlic, ketchup, water, molasses, apple cider vinegar, granulated sugar, brown sugar, Worcestershire sauce, lemon juice, liquid smoke, pepper, and mustard in the saucepan, and bring to a boil over medium heat. 2. Reduce the heat to low and cook on a simmer for 30 minutes, straining out any bigger chunks. 3. Serve.

Per Serving: Calories 44; Total fat 9.1g; Sodium 1399mg; Total Carbs 4.3g; Fiber 8.7g; Sugars 5.7g; Protein 8.3g

All–Purpose Wine Marinade

Prep time: 10 minutes | Cook time: 0 | Serves: 1 cup

- ⅔ cup red wine vinegar
- 2 garlic cloves, minced
- 1 tablespoon salt
- 2 teaspoons black pepper
- 2 teaspoons onion powder
- 1 teaspoon chopped thyme
- ½ cup olive oil

1. Mix the vinegar, garlic, salt, pepper, onion powder, and thyme in a bowl. Slowly mix in the olive oil to thicken the prepared marinade. 2. Use immediately or store in a closed container in the refrigerator for up to 1 week.

Per Serving: Calories 42; Total fat 0.9g; Sodium 1292mg; Total Carbs 7.7g; Fiber 0.3g; Sugars 5.9g; Protein 2.2g

Lime Chipotle Butter

Prep time: 10 minutes | Cook time: 5 minutes | Serves: 1½ cups

1 cup (2 sticks) salted butter	2 teaspoons adobo sauce
2 chipotle chilies in adobo sauce, chopped	2 teaspoons salt
	Juice of 1 lime

1. Melt the butter in the saucepan over medium heat. 2. Add the chopped chilies, adobo sauce, salt, and lime juice, continuing to stir for 5 minutes until the salt is dissolved. Remove from the heat. 3. Serve the chipotle butter hot or cold. The left sauce can be refrigerated in an airtight container for up to 2 weeks.

Per Serving: Calories 173; Total fat 3.1g; Sodium 687mg; Total Carbs 69.2g; Fiber 9.6g; Sugars 3.4g; Protein 1.8g

Classic Chimichurri Sauce

Prep time: 5 minutes | Cook time: 0 | Serves: 2 cups

½ cup olive oil	Juice of 1 lemon
1 bunch parsley, stems removed	2 tablespoons red wine vinegar
1 bunch cilantro, stems removed	1 teaspoon salt
1 small red onion, chopped	1 teaspoon freshly ground black pepper
3 tablespoons dried oregano	
1 tablespoon minced garlic	1 teaspoon cayenne pepper

1. Add all of recipe ingredients to the food processor and pulse several times until finely chopped. 2. The left sauce can be refrigerated in an airtight container for up to 5 days.

Per Serving: Calories 93; Total fat 1.6g; Sodium 465mg; Total Carbs 15.2g; Fiber 5g; Sugars 3.8g; Protein 4.5g

Cilantro-Balsamic Sriracha Drizzle

Prep time: 5 minutes | Cook time: 0 | Serves: 2 cups

½ cup balsamic vinegar	1 teaspoon salt
½ cup dry white wine	1 teaspoon freshly ground black pepper
¼ cup olive oil	
½ cup chopped cilantro	1 teaspoon red pepper flakes
2 teaspoons garlic powder	Splash of Sriracha

1. Stir the balsamic vinegar, wine, olive oil, cilantro, garlic powder, salt, black pepper, and red pepper flakes in a bowl until well mixed. 2. Add a dash of Sriracha and stir. 3. The left drizzle can be refrigerated in an airtight container for up to 2 weeks.

Per Serving: Calories 48; Total fat 1.7g; Sodium 771mg; Total Carbs 22.1g; Fiber 4.5g; Sugars 3.9g; Protein 7.1g

Spiced Sweet Potato Mustard

Prep time: 25 minutes | Cook time: 20 minutes | Serves: 1½ cups

½ cup apple cider vinegar	¼ cup packed brown sugar
⅓ cup yellow mustard seeds	2 tablespoons ground mustard
1 bay leaf	½ teaspoon smoked paprika
1 cup water	1 teaspoon salt
1 tablespoon molasses	½ teaspoon ground cinnamon
1 tablespoon bourbon	½ teaspoon ground allspice
⅔ cup sweet potato purée	½ teaspoon cayenne pepper

1. Bring the apple cider vinegar to a boil in a saucepan over medium-high heat. 2. Remove from the heat, add the mustard seeds and bay leaf, and let steep, uncovered, for 1 hour. Discard the bay leaf after steeping. 3. Pour the liquid into a suitable food processor or blender, making sure to scrape in the mustard seeds as well. Add the water, molasses, and bourbon, and pulse until smooth. 4. Pour the prepared mixture back into the saucepan over medium heat and add the sweet potato purée. Cooking to a boil, then reduce its heat to low and cook for 5 minutes, with occasional stirring. 5. Mix in the brown sugar, ground mustard, smoked paprika, salt, cinnamon, allspice, and cayenne, and cook on a simmer for 10 minutes until thickened. 6. Remove from the heat and let cool completely before refrigerating. 7. The sweet potato mustard is best served cold. The left sauce can be refrigerated in an airtight container for up to 2 weeks.

Per Serving: Calories 23; Total fat 1.6g; Sodium 465mg; Total Carbs 15.2g; Fiber 5g; Sugars 3.8g; Protein 4.5g

Delicious Mandarin Glaze

Prep time: 5 minutes | Cook time: 15 minutes | Serves: 2 cups

1 (11-ounce) can mandarin oranges, with their juices	1 teaspoon ground cinnamon
	1 teaspoon garlic powder
½ cup ketchup	1 teaspoon onion powder
3 tablespoons brown sugar	1 teaspoon salt
1 tablespoon apple cider vinegar	1 teaspoon freshly ground black pepper
1 tablespoon yellow mustard	
1 teaspoon ground cloves	

1. Add all of the ingredients to the food processor, and pulse them until the oranges are in tiny pieces. 2. Transfer the prepared mixture to a saucepan and bring to a boil over medium heat, stirring occasionally. 3. Reduce its heat to low and cook on a simmer for 15 minutes. 4. Remove from the heat and strain out the orange pieces. Serve the glaze hot. 5. The left glaze can be refrigerated in an airtight container for up to 5 days.

Per Serving: Calories 40; Total fat 5.6g; Sodium 517mg; Total Carbs 5.5g; Fiber 11.2g; Sugars 2.6g; Protein 1g

Jamaican Jerk Seasoning Paste

Prep time: 10 minutes | Cook time: 0 | Serves: ¾ cup

¼ cup cane syrup	2 tablespoons salt
8 whole cloves	2 teaspoons freshly ground black pepper
6 Scotch bonnet or habanero chilies, stemmed and seeded	
	2 teaspoons ground cinnamon
¼ cup chopped scallions	1 teaspoon cayenne pepper
2 tablespoons whole allspice (pimento) berries	1 teaspoon dried thyme
	1 teaspoon ground cumin

1. Blend all of the ingredients in the blender until smooth and sticky. 2. The left paste can be refrigerated in an airtight container for up to 1 week.

Per Serving: Calories 68; Total fat 7g; Sodium 475mg; Total Carbs 1.8g; Fiber 0.3g; Sugars 0g; Protein 0.5g

Blueberry Barbecue Sauce

Prep time: 5 minutes | Cook time: 10 minutes | Serves: 1 cup

2 cups water	1 teaspoon Sriracha
½ cup minced blueberries	1 teaspoon liquid smoke
1 tablespoon balsamic vinegar	1 teaspoon Dijon mustard
½ cup ketchup	Salt
1 tablespoon Worcestershire sauce	Freshly ground black pepper

1. Simmer the water, blueberries, and balsamic vinegar in the saucepan over low heat for 5 minutes. 2. Add the ketchup, Worcestershire sauce, Sriracha, liquid smoke, and Dijon mustard, season with black pepper and salt, and continue simmering for 5 minutes. 3. Remove from the heat and strain out most of the blueberry pulp. 4. The left barbecue sauce can be refrigerated in an airtight container for up to 1 week.

Per Serving: Calories: 139, Fat: 6.1g, Carbohydrates: 23.6g, Protein: 5.4g, Cholesterol: 0mg, Sodium: 30mg, Fiber: 4.3g, Sugar: 8.7g

Jalapeño–Cucumber Relish
Prep time: 10 minutes | Cook time: 0 | Serves: 1 cup

- 6 jalapeño peppers, stemmed, seeded, and cut into pieces
- 1 Serrano chili, stemmed, seeded, and cut into pieces
- 1 red bell pepper, chopped
- 1 cucumber, coarsely chopped
- 1 onion, chopped
- ½ cup rice wine vinegar
- ¼ cup apple cider vinegar
- 2 tablespoons sugar
- 3 teaspoons minced garlic
- 1 teaspoon salt

1. Using a suitable food processor, Blend the jalapeños, Serrano chili, bell pepper, cucumber, and onion in a blender until chopped. 2. Add the rice wine vinegar, cider vinegar, sugar, minced garlic, and salt, and pulse until minced but not puréed. 3. The left relish can be refrigerated in an airtight container for up to 1 week.

Per Serving: Calories 194; Total fat 10.9g; Sodium 292mg; Total Carbs 21.7g; Fiber 6.4g; Sugars 9g; Protein 6.4g

All–Match Spice Rub
Prep time: 10 minutes | Cook time: 0 | Serves: 2¼ cups

- ½ cup brown sugar
- ⅓ cup paprika (not smoked)
- ¼ cup salt
- 3 tablespoons mild chili powder
- 2 tablespoons ground cumin
- 2 tablespoons onion powder
- 2 tablespoons garlic powder
- 2 tablespoons dry mustard
- 1 tablespoon freshly ground black pepper
- 1 tablespoon cayenne pepper
- 2 teaspoons dried marjoram

1. Mix all the recipe ingredients in a medium-sized bowl and use as needed. 2. Store the left rub in an airtight jar in the cupboard for up to 1 year.

Per Serving: Calories 5; Total fat 0.1g; Sodium 452mg; Total Carbs 0.6g; Fiber 0.2g; Sugars 0.1g; Protein 0.2g

Herb Poultry Rub
Prep time: 10 minutes | Cook time: 0 | Serves: ½ cup

- 1 tablespoon paprika (not smoked)
- 1 tablespoon mild chili powder
- 1 tablespoon onion powder
- 1 tablespoon dry mustard
- 1 tablespoon dried parsley
- 1 tablespoon salt
- 1 tablespoon celery salt
- 2 teaspoons Herbes de Provence
- 2 teaspoons white sugar
- 1 teaspoon granulated garlic
- ½ teaspoon dried sage
- ¼ teaspoon allspice

1. Mix all the recipe ingredients in a suitable bowl and use as needed. 2. Make a double or triple batch and store in an airtight container in your pantry for up to a year.

Per Serving: Calories 3; Total fat 0.1g; Sodium 582mg; Total Carbs 0.6g; Fiber 0.2g; Sugars 0.1g; Protein 0.2g

Spicy Beef and Game Rub
Prep time: 15 minutes | Cook time: 0 | Serves: ½ cup

- 2 tablespoons whole peppercorns
- 1 tablespoon cumin seeds
- 1 tablespoon coriander seeds
- 2 tablespoons coarse, kosher, or sea salt
- 1 teaspoon granulated garlic
- ½ teaspoon smoked paprika
- ½ teaspoon cayenne pepper

1. Toast the peppercorns, cumin seeds, and coriander seeds in the skillet over medium heat for 1 minute, or until fragrant. 2. Shake the pan gently during the toasting process to avoid burning the spices. 3. Pour the toasted spices onto a plate and let them cool completely. Grind them in a spice grinder or pulverize them with a mortar and pestle. 4. Mix the ground spices with the salt, granulated garlic, smoked paprika, and cayenne pepper in a bowl. 5. Use immediately or store in a closed container in the cupboard for up to a year.

Per Serving: Calories 4; Total fat 0.9g; Sodium 292mg; Total Carbs 0.7g; Fiber 0.4g; Sugars 0 g; Protein 0.4g

Dry Cajun Rub
Prep time: 10 minutes | Cook time: 0 | Serves: ¾ cup

- ¼ cup paprika
- ¼ cup turbinado sugar
- 3 tablespoons Cajun seasoning
- 1 tablespoon packed brown sugar
- 1½ teaspoons chili powder
- 1½ teaspoons cayenne pepper
- 1½ teaspoons ground cumin

1. Mix the paprika, turbinado sugar, Cajun seasoning, brown sugar, chili powder, cayenne pepper, and cumin in a bowl. 2. Serve. You can store the rub in an airtight container at room temperature for up to 1 month.

Per Serving: Calories 195; Total fat 12.7g; Sodium 1131mg; Total Carbs 27.7g; Fiber 3.5g; Sugars 5.9g; Protein 2.1g

Flavorful Brisket Marinade
Prep time: 10 minutes | Cook time: 0 | Serves: 1 cup

- 1 cup beef broth
- 2 teaspoons Worcestershire sauce
- 2 teaspoons soy sauce
- 2 teaspoons brown sugar
- ½ teaspoon onion powder
- ½ teaspoon garlic powder
- ½ teaspoon salt
- ½ teaspoon freshly ground black pepper

1. Mix the beef broth, Worcestershire sauce, soy sauce, brown sugar, onion powder, garlic powder, salt, and pepper in a bowl until the brown sugar and salt have completely dissolved. 2. Use immediately or make in advance and store in an airtight container in the refrigerator for up to 1 week. Bring the prepared mixture to room temperature before using. 3. To use, draw some of the prepared marinade into the injector syringe. Inject small amounts into the roast. Let the meat marinate for 30 minutes after injecting and before smoking.

Per Serving: Calories 72; Total fat 0.5g; Sodium 4292mg; Total Carbs 17.1g; Fiber 0.4g; Sugars 15.8g; Protein 0.5g

Pork Rib Garlic Marinade
Prep time: 15 minutes | Cook time: 0 | Serves: 1 cup

- ½ cup cooking sherry
- 2 tablespoons tomato paste
- Juice of 2 limes
- 1 tablespoon brown sugar
- 1 tablespoon soy sauce
- ¼ cup 1 tablespoon olive oil
- 6 garlic cloves, minced
- 1 teaspoon salt
- ½ teaspoon red pepper flakes
- ½ teaspoon dried oregano
- ½ teaspoon smoked paprika
- ½ teaspoon freshly ground black pepper

1. Mix the sherry, tomato paste, lime juice, brown sugar, soy sauce, and olive oil in a medium nonreactive bowl. 2. Add the minced garlic, salt, red pepper flakes, oregano, paprika, and black pepper until the salt and sugar have dissolved. 3. Use immediately or make ahead of time and store in the fridge for up to 1 week.

Per Serving: Calories 89; Total fat 0.1g; Sodium 2392mg; Total Carbs 12g; Fiber 0.9g; Sugars 9.3g; Protein 0.5g

Easy Brine
Prep time: 10 minutes | Cook time: 0 | Serves: 1 quart

- 4 cups cold water
- ¼ cup salt
- ¼ cup white sugar

In a suitable bowl enough to accommodate both the brine and the meat, mix the salt, water, and sugar and stir until the salt and sugar dissolve.

Per Serving: Calories 77; Total fat 8.9g; Sodium 292mg; Total Carbs 1g; Fiber 0.3g; Sugars 0.3g; Protein 0.2g

Chapter 7 Rubs, Marinades, and More

Orange BBQ Sauce

Prep time: 10 minutes | Cook time: 10 minutes | Serves: 1-1¼ cups

Juice of 2 blood oranges	2 teaspoons soy sauce
Juice of 2 oranges	½ teaspoon mild chili powder
½ cup maple syrup	Pinch salt
2 teaspoons bourbon	Pinch freshly ground black pepper
⅓ cup ketchup	
2 tablespoons butter	

1. Stir and cook the blood orange juice, other orange juice, and maple syrup in a saucepan over medium heat. Simmer them for 2 minutes, stirring often. 2. Add the bourbon and let the sauce cook on a simmer for an additional minute, then add the ketchup, butter, soy sauce, chili powder, salt, and pepper. 3. Reduce the heat to low and cook on a simmer for an additional 5 to 7 minutes. 4. Once the sauce starts to thicken and take on the consistency of syrup. 5. Remove the saucepan from heat, cover, and keep warm. If making the sauce for later use, cool completely and store in the refrigerator for up to 1 week.

Per Serving: Calories 44; Total fat 0.9g; Sodium 352mg; Total Carbs 1.7g; Fiber 0.4g; Sugars 0.9g; Protein 0.4g

Brown Sugar–Pineapple Glaze

Prep time: 10 minutes | Cook time: 10 minutes | Serves: 1 cup

1 cup pineapple juice	1 teaspoon grated ginger
¾ cup light brown sugar	1 teaspoon rice wine vinegar
2 tablespoons honey	¼ teaspoon allspice
1 tablespoon soy sauce	
1½ teaspoons chili-garlic sauce	

1. In a suitable saucepan over medium-high heat, Add the pineapple juice, brown sugar, honey, soy sauce, chili-garlic sauce, ginger, rice wine vinegar, and allspice to the saucepan, and bring to a simmer over medium-high heat, stirring often. 2. Reduce the heat to medium-low and let the sauce continue to simmer for an additional 5 to 7 minutes. 3. Remove the sauce from heat, cover, and keep warm if using immediately. If making ahead of time, cool the sauce completely and store in an airtight container in the refrigerator for up to 1 week.

Per Serving: Calories 94; Total fat 10.9g; Sodium 292mg; Total Carbs 21.7g; Fiber 6.4g; Sugars 9g; Protein 1.4g

Maple Herbed Turkey Brine

Prep time: 15 minutes | Cook time: 15 minutes | Serves: 4

4 quarts water	1 cup pure maple syrup
1½ teaspoons coarse sea salt	1 cup chopped carrots
12 peppercorns	1 cup chopped celery hearts
12 cloves, whole	1 cup chopped yellow onions
6 allspice berries, whole	2 rosemary sprigs
6 star anise, whole	2 sage sprigs
6 bay leaves	2 thyme sprigs

1. Add the water, salt, peppercorns, cloves, allspice, star anise, and bay leaves to the stockpot, bring to a simmer over medium heat. 2. Add the maple syrup and then remove the pan from the heat. Let the brine cool, and then refrigerate the pot of brine until it is completely cool. 3. Add the carrots, celery, onions, rosemary, sage, and thyme to the brine. 4. Mix the turkey and brine in a large pot. 5. Place a weight, on the turkey to keep it fully submerged. 6. Refrigerate the marinating turkey for at least 4 hours, or ideally overnight, before cooking according to the recipe instructions.

Per Serving: Calories 24; Total fat 1.9g; Sodium 382mg; Total Carbs 2g; Fiber 0.2g; Sugars 0.2g; Protein 0.1g

Aromatic Pork Marinade

Prep time: 15 minutes | Cook time: 15 minutes | Serves: 8

2 quarts apple cider	3 star anise, whole
12 garlic cloves, peeled and halved	1 tablespoon fennel seeds, whole
3 shallots, trimmed and sliced	1 tablespoon coriander seeds, whole
2 lemons, sliced	1 tablespoon allspice berries, whole
1 jalapeño pepper, sliced	
3 thyme sprigs, rinsed	
3 rosemary sprigs, rinsed	

1. In a suitable stockpot over medium heat, Add the cider, garlic, shallots, lemons, pepper, thyme, rosemary, anise, fennel, coriander, and allspice to the stockpot, bring the prepared marinade to a simmer over medium heat and cook for 5 minutes. 2. Mix to mix the ingredients, remove the prepared marinade from the heat, and cool it completely in the refrigerator before using. 3. To use, mix the pork and marinade in a suitable food-safe plastic bag. 4. Seal it. 5. Refrigerate the marinating pork for 24 hours for best results. Massage the prepared marinade into the pork and flip the bag occasionally. 6. Remove the pork from the prepared marinade and cook it according to the recipe's instructions.

Per Serving: Calories 194; Total fat 10.9g; Sodium 292mg; Total Carbs 21.7g; Fiber 6.4g; Sugars 9g; Protein 6.4g

Asian–Style Marinade

Prep time: 15 minutes | Cook time: 15 minutes | Serves: 8

1 cup cilantro leaves, chopped	3 tablespoons canola oil
3 garlic cloves, minced	3 tablespoons soy sauce
2 limes, sliced	3 tablespoons fish sauce
1 jalapeño pepper, trimmed, seeded, and diced	1 tablespoon toasted sesame oil
¼ cup packed dark brown sugar	1 teaspoon ground coriander
	1 teaspoon black pepper

1. Add the cilantro, garlic, limes, jalapeño, sugar, canola oil, soy sauce, fish sauce, sesame oil, coriander, and black pepper to the stockpot, bring to a simmer over medium heat and cook for 5 minutes. 2. Mix the ingredients, remove the prepared marinade from the heat, and cool it completely in the refrigerator before using. 3. To use, mix the meat and marinade in a suitable food-safe plastic bag. 4. Remove as much air as possible from the bag and seal it. Refrigerate to marinate your meat for 24 hours for best results. Massage the prepared marinade into the meat and flip the bag occasionally. 5. Remove the meat from the prepared marinade and cook it according to the recipe's instructions.

Per Serving: Calories 73; Total fat 3.1g; Sodium 687mg; Total Carbs 69.2g; Fiber 9.6g; Sugars 3.4g; Protein 1.8g

Flavorful Jerk Spice Rub

Prep time: 15 minutes | Cook time: 0 | Serves: 12

2 tablespoons dark brown sugar	1 teaspoon ground cayenne pepper
2 tablespoons ground allspice	1 teaspoon ground cloves
1 tablespoon garlic powder	1 teaspoon ground nutmeg
1 tablespoon onion powder	1 teaspoon freshly ground black pepper
1 tablespoon ground cinnamon	
1 tablespoon fine sea salt	

1. Mix the sugar, allspice, garlic powder, onion powder, cinnamon, salt, cayenne, cloves, nutmeg, and black pepper in a bowl. 2. If the ingredients are fresh, the spice rub can be stored in an airtight container for up to one year.

Per Serving: Calories 28; Total fat 1.7g; Sodium 771mg; Total Carbs 22.1g; Fiber 4.5g; Sugars 3.9g; Protein 7.1g

Chinese-Style Beef Rub

Prep time: 15 minutes | Cook time: 15 minutes | Serves: 12

10 allspice berries, whole	1 tablespoon peppercorns
5 star anise, whole	3 tablespoons paprika
3 tablespoons fennel seeds, whole	1 tablespoon fine sea salt
3 tablespoons coriander seeds, whole	1 teaspoon ground cayenne pepper
	1 tablespoon dark brown sugar

1. Add the allspice, star anise, fennel, coriander, and peppercorns in the skillet. Cook them for 5 minutes over medium heat, tossing the spices frequently to toast them evenly, until light brown and fragrant. Be careful not to burn the spices. 2. Transfer them to a mortar or clean spice grinder and let them cool slightly. 3. Grind or pulse the cooled spices to a fine consistency. Transfer the powder to a bowl and let it cool completely. 4. Add the paprika, salt, cayenne, and sugar, stirring until evenly mixed. 5. Use immediately, or if the ingredients are fresh, store in an airtight container or resealable plastic bag for up to 12 months.

Per Serving: Calories 3; Total fat 0.1g; Sodium 582mg; Total Carbs 0.6g; Fiber 0.2g; Sugars 0.1g; Protein 0.2g

Blue Cheese Cream Dip

Prep time: 15 minutes | Cook time: 0 | Serves: 4-6

1 cup sour cream, whipped	of 1 lemon Flaked sea salt
½ cup buttermilk	Freshly ground black pepper
½ cup mayonnaise, whipped	8 ounces blue cheese, crumbled into fine pieces
Grated zest of 1 lemon, plus juice	

1. Mix the sour cream, buttermilk, mayonnaise, lemon zest, and lemon juice in a bowl. Taste and season them with black pepper and salt. 2. Fold them in the blue cheese. 3. Taste again and add more black pepper and salt, as needed. 4. Cover and let it refrigerate until serving.

Per Serving: Calories 77; Total fat 8.9g; Sodium 292mg; Total Carbs 1g; Fiber 0.3g; Sugars 0.3g; Protein 0.2g

Zesty Lime Guacamole

Prep time: 15 minutes | Cook time: 0 | Serves: 4-6

3 avocados, halved, pitted, and diced	3 tablespoons cilantro leaves, chopped
1 Roma tomato, cored, quartered, and chopped	Grated zest of 1 lime juice of 1 lime
½ cup chopped red onion	Flaked sea salt
1 jalapeño pepper, trimmed, seeded, and chopped	Freshly ground black pepper

1. Combine and mash the avocados, tomato, onion, jalapeño, cilantro, lime zest, and lime juice in a bowl until your desired consistency is reached. 2. Taste and season with black pepper and salt.

Per Serving: Calories 94; Total fat 10.9g; Sodium 292mg; Total Carbs 21.7g; Fiber 6.4g; Sugars 9g; Protein 6.4g

Lime Watermelon Salsa

Prep time: 15 minutes | Cook time: 0 | Serves: 8

½ seedless watermelon, peeled and diced	3 tablespoons cilantro leaves, chopped
½ cucumber, peeled, seeded, and diced	Grated zest of 1 lime juice of 1 lime
½ cup red onion, diced	Flaked sea salt
1 jalapeño pepper, trimmed, seeded, and chopped	Freshly ground black pepper

1. Gently fold together the watermelon, cucumber, onion, jalapeño (optional), cilantro, lime zest, and lime juice in a bowl. 2. Taste and season them with black pepper and salt. Cover the bowl and let it refrigerate until well-chilled. 3. Serve cold.

Per Serving: Calories 44; Total fat 0.9g; Sodium 352mg; Total Carbs 1.7g; Fiber 0.4g; Sugars 0.9g; Protein 0.4g

Ruby Port Orange Cranberry Sauce

Prep time: 15 minutes | Cook time: 60 minutes | Serves: 12

1 cup ruby port	5 star anise, whole
1 pound or frozen cranberries	5 cloves, whole
½ cup packed dark brown sugar	1 cinnamon stick, whole
Grated zest of 1 orange, plus juice of 1 orange	Flaked sea salt

1. If you would like to reduce the alcohol content slightly, preheat a suitable saucepan over medium heat, then pour in the port and let it cook for 1 minute. 2. Add the cranberries, sugar, orange zest, orange juice, star anise, cloves, cinnamon stick, and a pinch of salt. (If you skipped step 1, add the port now.) 3. Cook the prepared mixture to a boil. Reduce the heat to maintain a simmer and cook for 1 hour, or until your desired consistency is reached. 4. Remove and discard the whole spices.

Per Serving: Calories 94; Total fat 10.9g; Sodium 292mg; Total Carbs 21.7g; Fiber 6.4g; Sugars 9g; Protein 1.4g

Chapter 7 Rubs, Marinades, and More

Conclusion

TRAEGER GRILL & SMOKER is a unique and versatile cooking appliance. It is a perfect way to outdoor grilling food. You can use your favorite wood pellets such as Alder, Hickory, Oak, Apple, Maple, Cherry, Mesquite, Pecan, etc. It is a multi-functional cooking appliance. Using different wood pellets, you can grill, bake, roast, smoke, braise, and barbeque your meals. It is pretty simple to clean and maintain. You will get step-by-step instructions about this appliance in my cookbook. I added delicious and healthy recipes for your grill. It is safe to use. I hope you like my cookbook. Thank you for choosing us!

Appendix 1 Measurement Conversion Chart

VOLUME EQUIVALENTS (LIQUID)

US STANDARD	US STANDARD (OUNCES)	METRIC (APPROXIMATE)
2 tablespoons	1 fl.oz	30 mL
¼ cup	2 fl.oz	60 mL
½ cup	4 fl.oz	120 mL
1 cup	8 fl.oz	240 mL
1½ cup	12 fl.oz	355 mL
2 cups or 1 pint	16 fl.oz	475 mL
4 cups or 1 quart	32 fl.oz	1 L
1 gallon	128 fl.oz	4 L

VOLUME EQUIVALENTS (DRY)

US STANDARD	METRIC (APPROXIMATE)
⅛ teaspoon	0.5 mL
¼ teaspoon	1 mL
½ teaspoon	2 mL
¾ teaspoon	4 mL
1 teaspoon	5 mL
1 tablespoon	15 mL
¼ cup	59 mL
½ cup	118 mL
¾ cup	177 mL
1 cup	235 mL
2 cups	475 mL
3 cups	700 mL
4 cups	1 L

TEMPERATURES EQUIVALENTS

FAHRENHEIT(F)	CELSIUS(C) (APPROXIMATE)
225 °F	107 °C
250 °F	120 °C
275 °F	135 °C
300 °F	150 °C
325 °F	160 °C
350 °F	180 °C
375 °F	190 °C
400 °F	205 °C
425 °F	220 °C
450 °F	235 °C
475 °F	245 °C
500 °F	260 °C

WEIGHT EQUIVALENTS

US STANDARD	METRIC (APPROXINATE)
1 ounce	28 g
2 ounces	57 g
5 ounces	142 g
10 ounces	284 g
15 ounces	425 g
16 ounces (1 pound)	455 g
1.5pounds	680 g
2pounds	907 g

Appendix 2 Recipes Index

A

Alder-Smoked Garlic Salmon Steaks 39
All-Beef Hot Dogs with Pickled Onions 59
All-Match Spice Rub 87
All-Purpose Wine Marinade 85
Apple-Flavored Pulled Pork Sandwiches 49
Apple-Glazed Pork Tenderloins with Mustard Greens 46
Apricot-Soy Glazed Country Spareribs 52
Aromatic Pork Marinade 88
Aromatic Rosemary-Garlic Seasoning 83
Asian-Style Marinade 88

B

Bacon-Egg Cheeseburgers 60
Bacon-Wrapped Jalapeño Poppers 72
Bacon-Wrapped Onion Meatloaf Bombs 79
Bacon-Wrapped Pork Chops with Bourbon-Onion Sauce 44
Bacon-Wrapped Pork Tenderloin 54
Balsamic Flank Steak with Baby Arugula 62
Barbecue Chicken 30
Barbecue Tri-Tip Sandwiches 63
Barbecued Beef Brisket 69
Barbecued Dill Scallops 33
Basil Shrimp Pops with Coconut Peanut Sauce 34
BBQ Baby Back Ribs 52
BBQ Baby Back Ribs with Onion-Beer Sauce 51
BBQ Beans with Bacon 76
BBQ Beef Brisket 57
BBQ Breakfast Pork Grits 53
BBQ Candied Spareribs 53
BBQ Chuck Roast 68
BBQ Lemon Trout 34
BBQ Pickle Beef Burgers 60
BBQ Pork Belly Bites 43
BBQ Rub 83
Beer Smoked Whole Chicken 16
Beer-Brined Chicken Drumsticks 17
Best Smoked Chicken Marbella 26

Blackened Cajun Shrimp 32
Blackened Tilapia Tacos 41
Bleu Cheese Butter 85
Blt Pasta Bacon Salad 76
Blue Cheese Cream Dip 89
Blueberry Barbecue Sauce 86
Bourbon-Candied Salmon 38
Braised Beef Short Ribs 58
Brown Sugar Spice Rub 83
Brown Sugar-Pineapple Glaze 88
Buffalo Cheese Chicken Balls 18
Butter Grilled Chicken Thighs 15
Butter-Seared Steaks 58
Buttered Salmon 32

C

Cabbage Slaw Salad 75
Cajun Barbecue Rub 84
Cajun Garlic Butter Shrimp Pasta 41
Cajun Honey-Smoked Ham 44
Candied Bacon 72
Caramel Apple Crisp 81
Carrot Hot Dogs with Jalapeño Relish 75
Cedar-Planked Salmon Fillet 38
Cheddar Broccoli-Cauliflower Salad 75
Cheese Beef Stuffed Jalapeños 79
Cheese Chicken Enchilada Pie 20
Cheeseburger Tomato Hand Pies 67
Cheesesteak Meatloaf with Tiger Sauce 66
Cheesy Corn with Chipotle Butter 74
Cheesy Hash Browns Casserole 79
Cheesy Hassel-back Russet Potatoes 73
Cheesy Meat Stuffed Peppers 69
Cheesy Scalloped Potatoes 72
Cheesy Shrimp Asparagus Risotto 37
Chicago-Style Hot Dog Buns 59
Chicken Breast, Wheat Berries & Pecan Salad 17
Chicken Broccoli Stir-Fry with Peanuts 19
Chinese-Style Beef Rub 89
Chipotle-Lime Chicken Skewers 28

Chorizo Huevos Rancheros 48
Cilantro-Balsamic Bacon-Wrapped Brussels Sprouts 72
Cilantro-Balsamic Sriracha Drizzle 86
Cinnamon Chocolate Sauce 81
Cinnamon Pork Tenderloin 43
Cinnamon Smoked Chicken 25
Cinnamon-Honey Sweet Potatoes 78
Cinnamon-Mustard Beef Ribs 58
Citrus Duck with Blue Plums 27
Citrus Pork Tenderloins 45
Classic Chimichurri Sauce 86
Classic Jamaican Jerk Chicken 24
Coffee-Spiced Pork Loin 47
Combat Rib- Eye Steaks with Mushrooms 64
Country Pork Roast with Apple & Sauerkraut 55
Cowboy Beans and Beef 78
Cream Cheese Sausage Balls 53
Creole Chicken with Tomato-Peas Salad 20
Crispy Sweet Potato Chips 75
Crunch Cheeseburgers 59
Crusted Lemongrass Chicken with Pesto 14
Cumin Duck Breasts with Orange Sauce 23

D

Delicious Bacon Brussels Sprouts 79
Delicious Barbecue Chicken 24
Delicious BBQ Sauce 85
Delicious Cream Onion Dip 79
Delicious Hoisin-Ginger Pulled Pork 50
Delicious Holiday Stuffing 80
Delicious Mandarin Glaze 86
Delicious Turkey Tacos 23
Dry Cajun Rub 87
Duck Breast and Greens Salad 24

E

Easy Brine 87
Easy Carne Asada Marinade 84
Easy Smoked Bacon 44
Easy Smoked Beef Burgers 58

Easy Smoked Butternut Squash 80
Easy Smoked Dill Salmon 32
Easy Smoked Pork Tenderloin 43

F
Feta Chicken Salad 16
Flavorful Brisket Marinade 87
Flavorful Chicken Tacos 14
Flavorful Flank Steak with Asparagus 61
Flavorful Garlic-Herb Turkey Legs 15
Flavorful Jerk Spice Rub 88
Flavorful Pineapple–Brown Sugar Sauce 85
Flavorful Smoked Ham 44
Flavorful Smoked Salmon 39
Flavorful T-Bone Steaks 59
French Onion Cheeseburgers 67

G
Garlic Butter Cauliflower Florets 78
Garlic Chicken Lollipops 18
Garlic Filet Mignons 68
Garlic Roast Prime Rib 58
Garlic Rump Roast 68
Garlic Sage-Rubbed Turkey Breast 29
Garlic T-Bones with Avocado Salsa 64
Garlic-Butter Lobster Tails 39
Garlic-Soy London Broil 67
Garlicky Buttermilk-Brined Chicken 23
Ginger-Curried Lamb Chops with Yogurt Sauce 66
Ginger-Soy Mahi-Mahi with Bang Sauce 33
Grilled All-Beef Hot Dogs with Avocado Mayo 59
Grilled Beef Tenderloin Steaks with Mushrooms 64
Grilled Black Forest Ham & Brie Panini 51
Grilled Chantilly Potatoes 80
Grilled Cheese Corn Pudding 80
Grilled Chicken Breasts on Swiss Chard 15
Grilled Crabs with Butter Sauce 35
Grilled Drumsticks & Peaches 17
Grilled Flank Steak with Black Bean Salad 62
Grilled Garlic-Soy Tuna Steaks 41
Grilled Ginger Porterhouse Steaks 64
Grilled Halibut with Pepper Vinaigrette 37
Grilled Lobster Tail 33
Grilled Mayo Salmon 33
Grilled Pork Chops with Cucumber-Cream Sauce 45
Grilled Pork Kabobs 46
Grilled Potatoes with Onion 71
Grilled S'mores Dip 80
Grilled Salmon Fillet 33
Grilled Salmon with Vegetable Salsa 35
Grilled Shrimp Skewers 32
Grilled Strip Steaks with Barbecue Sauce 65
Grilled Swordfish Steaks with Mango Salsa 37
Grilled Tri-Tip Roast 57
Grilled Tuna Steaks 32

H
Hassel-back Sweet Potatoes with Pecans 72
Hearty Smoked Chicken Cacciatore 25
Hearty Teriyaki Marinade 85
Herb Poultry Rub 87
Herb-Garlic Leg of Lamb with Zucchini Salad 65
Herb-Smoked Brick Chicken 27
Herbed Beef Roast with White Wine–Cream Sauce 62
Herbed Butter Lobster Tails 39
Herbed Catfish with Comeback Sauce 40
Herbed Cheese Prosciutto Pork Chop Pockets 45
Herbed Italian Sausage Pizzas 48
Herbed Spicy Tri-Tip 68
Herbed Turkey Burgers 29
Homemade Crab Cakes with Spicy Mayo 38
Homemade Hickory-Smoked Barbecue Sauce 84
Homemade Java Rub 85
Homemade Smoked Beer Chicken 22
Homemade Smoked Guacamole 71
Honey Beer-Brined Chicken Wings 20
Honey Onion Sauce 84
Honey-Lemon Glazed Chicken Thighs 21
Honey-Orange Glazed Spareribs 52
Hot Barbecue Sauce 84
Hot Caramel Chicken Breasts 25

J
Jalapeño Pork Chops with Pickled Pepper Relish 55
Jalapeño- Cucumber Relish 87
Jamaican Jerk Seasoning Paste 86
Jerk-Spiced Baby Back Ribs with Pineapple Salsa 49
Juicy Chicken Avocado Salad 18
Juicy Chicken Skewers with Avocado Salsa 14
Juicy Garlic Tuna Steaks 39
Juicy Lemon-Pepper Tri-Tip Roast 57
Juicy Lime Snapper 40
Juicy Pulled Pork Shoulder 53
Juicy Shrimp Skewers with Avocado-Chili Sauce 36
Juicy Spiced Chicken 21

K
Kidney Beans Chili 71
Kielbasa-Onion Sauerkraut Sandwiches 46
Kofta Pitas with Cucumber-Tomato Salad 61
Korean-Style Barbecued Beef 62

L
Lager-Brined Turkey with Beer Gravy 22
Lamb Loin Chops with Mint Salsa Verde 66
Lemon Buttered Baby Shrimp 35
Lemon Buttered King Crab Legs 33
Lemon Buttered Oysters in the Shell 32
Lemon Buttered Sea Bass 39
Lemon Curried Chicken Breasts 28
Lemon Herb-Roasted Chicken 19
Lemon Pepper-Dill Seafood Rub 83
Lemon Shrimp with Orzo 36
Lemon-Herb Whole Trout 41
Lemony Artichokes 73
Lemony Oysters 35
Lime Chipotle Butter 86
Lime Garlic Baby Back Ribs 54
Lime Tequila-Marinated Chicken with Rice 21
Lime Watermelon Salsa 89
Lime-Butter Shrimp 40

M
Maple Herbed Turkey Brine 88
Maple Mustard Sauce 84
Maple-Bacon Wrapped Chicken Breasts 20
Marmalade-Mustard Glazed Ham with Orange-Dill Sauce 51
Mint Pork Sandwiches 47
Mixed Berries-Watermelon Bowl 76

Moroccan Chicken Kabobs with Yogurt-Mint Sauce 16
Mushroom-Pepperoni Stuffed Pizza 48
Mustard Beef Roast 57
Mustard Rubbed Pork Shoulder 43

N
New York Strip Steaks with Pesto 65

O
Orange BBQ Sauce 88

P
Parmesan Sweet Onion Bake 76
Planked Butter Scallops 40
Plum Chicken Drumsticks 25
Pork and Chorizo Burgers with Cabbage Slaw 47
Pork Rib Garlic Marinade 87
Pork Sliders with Black Bean Salsa 47
Pork Tacos with Pineapple Salsa 45
Pork Tortas with Guacamole 49
Potato-Egg Salad 78
Prime Rib Roast with Hazelnut Pesto 66

Q
Quick Beef Brisket Rub 83

R
Ranch Smoked Quail 14
Roasted Pork Loin with Maple-Cream Sauce 46
Rosemary-Garlic Potato Wedges 73
Ruby Port Orange Cranberry Sauce 89

S
Salmon Cheese Sandwich 33
Salmon Skewers with Thai Curry–Coconut Sauce 35
Savory Barbecued Meat Loaf 61
Savory Cheeseburgers 60
Savory Chicken Romaine Salad 18
Savory Pastrami 68
Savory Plum Sauce 85
Savory Pork Chops with Roasted Plums 44
Savory Seafood Tomato Salad 36
Shrimp- Mussels Paella 34
Simple Smoked Top Beef Roast 57
Simple Wood-Fired Halibut 32
Slow-Cooked Cinnamon Pork Shoulder 50
Smoked Bacon Kebabs 51
Smoked Bacon-Cheddar Potato Skins 74

Smoked Brats Sliders 54
Smoked Butter Asparagus 73
Smoked Cajun Catfish 32
Smoked Cheese Macaroni 71
Smoked Chicken Gumbo with Rice 26
Smoked Chicken Sandwiches 29
Smoked Corn on the Cob 74
Smoked Corned Beef Brisket 58
Smoked Deviled Eggs with Olives 74
Smoked Dijon Turkey Breast 24
Smoked Dijon-Herb Rib Eye Steaks 65
Smoked Garlic Cauliflower Steaks 74
Smoked Garlic Mushroom Tomato Sauce 83
Smoked Garlic Prime Rib 68
Smoked Garlic-Thyme Whole Chicken 26
Smoked Honey Chicken with Grapes 29
Smoked Lemony Whole Trout 34
Smoked Lime Cod Fillets 37
Smoked Mac 'N' Cheese 78
Smoked New York Steaks 58
Smoked Okra 75
Smoked Pineapple-Pork Kebabs 53
Smoked Plum Tomatoes 78
Smoked Pork Chops 43
Smoked Rosemary Duck Breast with Cherry Sauce 27
Smoked Salmon Candy 38
Smoked Spaghetti Squash 74
Smoked Sweet & Sour Coleslaw 73
Smoked Teriyaki Pork Tenderloin 43
Smoked Turkey with Poblano Poppers 19
Smoked Turkey-Veggie Soup with Bulgur Wheat 27
Smoked Whole Cabbage 73
Smoky Buttered Crab Clusters 41
Smoky Scotch Eggs 54
Smoky Sweet Salmon 34
Smoky T-Bone Steak with Blue Cheese Butter 69
Smoky Turkey and Apples 25
Smoky Turkey Tenders with Honey Dip 29
Sourdough-Sausage Stuffed Turkey 28
Spaghetti Squash with Garlic-Wine Butter Sauce 75
Spiced Grilling Chicken 28
Spiced Orange Chicken 24

Spiced Sweet Potato Mustard 86
Spicy Bacon-Wrapped Onion Rings 73
Spicy Beef and Game Rub 87
Spicy Beef Shoulder Clod 69
Spicy Chicken with Barbecue Sauce 22
Spicy Grilled BBQ Shrimp 41
Spicy Grilled Shrimp Skewers 35
Spicy Mayo Sauce 85
Spicy Pulled Chicken Sliders 19
Spinach Lamb Burgers 61
Steak-Tomato Kabobs with Avocado-Cucumber Sauce 63
Strip Steaks with Horseradish-Cream Sauce 63
Sugar Mustard-Glazed Salmon 36
Sugar-Butter Carrots 71
Sweet & Spicy Baby Back Ribs with Apple Sauce 50
Sweet & Spicy BBQ Sauce 84
Sweet & Spicy Cedar Planked Salmon 38
Sweet & Spicy Chicken Wings 17
Sweet & Spicy Pork Rub 83
Sweet Candied Pineapple 80
Sweet Corned Beef with Cabbage 67
Sweet Lemon-Thyme Chicken 26
Sweet Smoked Beans & Pineapple 71
Sweet Smoked Salmon 41
Sweet Smoky Bacon 43

T
Tasty Smoked Onion Bombs 72
Texas Cheeseburgers 60
Texas Smoked Mustard Brisket 57
Tri-Tip Roast with Corn Salsa & Black Beans 63
Turkey Cheeseburgers 23
Turkey Cutlets with Cranberry Relish 21
Typical Pork Nachos 52

V
Vegetable-Cornbread Salad 76
Vinaigrette Glazed Chicken with Green Olive 15

W
Wine-Flavored Oysters 40
Wood-Fired Scallops 33

Z
Zesty Lime Guacamole 89
Zesty Whole Smoked Jerk Chicken 16

Made in the USA
Coppell, TX
29 June 2024